International Civil Society

To Barbara Kräuter and
José Antonio Colás

INTERNATIONAL CIVIL SOCIETY

Social Movements in World Politics

Alejandro Colás

Polity

First published in 2002 by Polity Press in association with Blackwell Publishers Ltd

Editorial office:
Polity Press
65 Bridge Street
Cambridge CB2 1UR, UK

Marketing and production:
Blackwell Publishers Ltd
108 Cowley Road
Oxford OX4 1JF, UK

Published in the USA by
Blackwell Publishers Inc.
350 Main Street
Malden, MA 02148, USA

A catalogue record for this book is available from the British Library.

Library of Congress Cataloging-in-Publication Data

Colás, Alejandro.
    International civil society: social movements in world politics /
Alejandro Colás.
        p. cm.
Includes bibliographical references and index.
    ISBN 0–7456–2555-X (HB : acid-free paper)—ISBN 0–7456–2556–8 (pbk. :
acid-free paper)
1. Civil society. 2. International relations. I. Title.
JC337 .C65 2002
327—dc21   2001001928

Typeset in 10.5pt on 12pt Times
by Kolam Information Services Pvt Ltd, Pondicherry, India
Printed in Great Britain by MPG Books Ltd, Cornwall

This book is printed on acid-free paper.

Contents

Acknowledgements

The contents of this book derive in large part from a doctoral thesis written in the Department of International Relations at the London School of Economics and Political Science under the supervision of Fred Halliday. My first thanks must therefore go to my supervisor for his unfailing encouragement and support through the years, and to all those friends and comrades at the LSE who in various contexts – most notably the 'Modernity and IR' and subsequently 'Historical Materialism and IR' seminars – shaped many of the ideas contained in this study. In an academic climate where the individualist, utilitarian and commodified values of instrumental rationality are increasingly dominant, it is an especial pleasure to acknowledge how much of what follows is the product of genuinely collective and politically motivated intellectual labour. I am also grateful to the UK's Economic and Social Research Council for financial support through a Research Studentship and to the LSE's Department of International Relations for reception of a Montagu Burton Scholarship in 1997.

My colleagues in the International Relations and Politics subject group at the University of Sussex have in innumerable ways encouraged the further development of the arguments presented in this book. I take it as unnecessary to list specific names, and that the text itself (with its accompanying footnotes) will identify those whose ideas have influenced my own, be it through a sympathetic or a critical engagement. This said, and although it is always invidious to single out individuals, I am particularly indebted to Zdeněk Kavan and Benno Teschke for reading the entire draft manuscript and offering their characteristically sharp and probing comments – I have ignored some of these at my own peril. Sections of chapters 1 and 2 appeared previously in 'The promises of international civil society', *Global Society: Interdisciplinary Journal of International Relations*, 11, 3 (1997), pp. 261–77, and I am grateful to the publishers of that journal for permission to reproduce these extracts.

Finally, and most importantly, I wish to thank four people who, without ever demanding to know too much about its content, have made possible the writing of this book: Sofia, for being a good sister; Ishani Salpadoru, for 'sharing the bread'; and my parents, Barbara Kräuter and José Antonio Colás – to whom this book is dedicated – for, among so many other things, instilling in me the values of internationalism.

1

Introduction

Non-State Actors in International Relations

The aim of this study is to argue for the relevance of voluntary, non-state, collective social and political agency in international relations. The term 'civil society' is initially adopted to describe that social domain where modern collective political agency takes shape. From this premise, I go on to argue that the social movements operating within civil society have displayed international characteristics from their inception, thus warranting the introduction of the term 'international civil society' as a category capable of explaining the dynamics and consequences of collective social and political agency at an international level. The socio-historical implications of deploying this concept will be considered throughout the book with reference to a number of specific historical and contemporary conjunctures, ranging from the American Revolution to the current experiments in global governance. The aim of such an exercise is to uncover and recover for the study of international relations the practices of transnational solidarity among social movements and to evaluate the relevance of these practices for our understanding of international society. Or, put differently, to examine the mechanisms responsible for the reproduction of modes of social and political organization across state boundaries. Thus I hope it will soon become apparent that this is not a historical study as such, but a historically informed investigation into the sociological category of international civil society. In short, the central purpose of the chapters that follow is to illustrate how the concept of 'international civil society' can serve, on the one hand, as an analytical tool for the study of international political agency and its impact upon international relations; and, on the other hand, as a normatively charged category, capable of recovering the past history of internationalist political activity and illuminating its future potential.

These broad objectives immediately raise the important question concerning the novelty of the idea of international civil society: in what ways does this category contribute to or depart from existing approaches to International Relations (IR) with similar concerns? This introductory chapter seeks to answer this question explicitly, but the responses provided here will hopefully also be implicit throughout the rest of the study.

The chapter is organized in the following way: a first section considers the problematic of 'transnationalism' as a springboard for a number of IR theories that place non-state actors of civil society at the centre of the international system. Two further sections aim to distinguish my own treatment of the notions of civil society and agency from those prevailing within the discipline, thereby placing the concept of international civil society within the wider debates in IR. One important reason for these differences, I maintain, lies in the Marxist historical-sociological method adopted in this study. The concluding part of the chapter is therefore dedicated to the definition and justification of such an approach.

Non-state actors in International Relations

For over three decades, IR scholars have been contesting the predominance of 'the state' as the central explanatory category within the discipline. In their seminal collection of essays on *Transnational Relations and World Politics*, Robert Keohane and Joseph Nye captured the beginnings of this reaction to state-centric IR theory – represented in the work of John Burton, Mansbach et al., James Rosenau and Edward Morse, among others[1] – when they insisted: 'A good deal of intersocietal intercourse with significant political importance takes place without governmental control.... This volume...focuses on these "transnational relations" – contacts, coalitions, and interactions across state boundaries that are not controlled by the central foreign policy organs of governments.'[2] The relevance of such interactions had, it can be argued, already been identified by classical thinkers of international relations from Kant and Burke through to Marx and Mill. Certainly the notion of transnationalism has been present in twentieth-century IR theory, whether implicitly – as in the writings of Leonard Woolf or David Mitrany – or more explicitly in Raymond Aron's or Arnold Wolfers's discussions of the subject.[3] Yet the transnationalist literature that emerged in the 1970s marked a substantive departure from these previous explorations in at least two respects. First, rather than being a tangential consideration within a broader analytical framework, transnational phenomena represented *the* central theoretical concern for scholars such as Burton, Rosenau or Keohane and Nye. This, of course, did not entail an outright rejection of the study of inter-state relations, but it did assume that transnational relations were worthy of analysis both in their own right and in so far as they significantly affected inter-state relations. As Keohane and Nye summarized it: 'we believe that the simplifications of the state-centric approach divert the attention of scholars and statesmen away from many important current problems and distort the analyses of others. We have suggested a "world politics paradigm" that includes transnational, transgovernmental and interstate interactions in the hope of stimulating new types of theory, research, and approaches to policy.'[4]

Second, and following on from this, despite some important differences in their arguments, the transnationalist literature adopted a similar methodological stance: one thoroughly permeated by the prevalent behaviouralist trend in the social sciences. Briefly stated, such an approach placed great faith in the explanatory potential of data accumulation. The proliferation of transnational interactions, so the argument ran, had increased the complexity of world politics to such an extent that only the systematic collation of data relating to these interactions could bring some semblance of order to our understanding of international relations. This enthusiasm for the possibilities of quantification was, to be sure, tempered by an emphasis on the identification of appropriate 'variables'. As one notable exponent of the transnationalist approach put it: 'Accurate and reliable measurements are of little value unless they measure the proper variable; and, unfortunately, our speculations about changing global structures involve variables that are not readily observed.'[5] Once the 'puzzlement' over variables was solved, however, the ground was cleared for empirical investigation:

we should recall that the conceptual task of disaggregating the relevant global structures so that their component parts are exposed – and thus measurable – is far more difficult than performing the empirical task of

recording observations. Indeed, once these component parts are conceptually identified, it ought not to take much creativity to formulate
operational measures for them that can be applied to their interaction
across time and in the context of comparable cases.[6]

Transnationalism was subjected to a range of forceful criticisms in the
aftermath of its rise to theoretical prominence in the 1970s. Some of
these objections will be addressed in greater detail below. At this
point, however, it is necessary to pause briefly on the role of collective
social and political activity within the transnationalist framework. For
one of the seemingly novel phenomena that spurred on the transnationalist agenda was the organization of social and political movements across national boundaries. Again, the way in which the
different authors associated to this approach dealt with such phenomena varied considerably. None the less it is possible to identify four
basic assumptions which undergirded the transnationalist treatment of
social movements.

The first of these concerned the relatively recent arrival of non-
governmental organizations to the international political arena. With
a few notable exceptions, the classical transnationalist authors rarely
extended their investigation of non-state actors beyond the twentieth
century, claiming that it was the quantitative explosion of non-
governmental organizations during this century that most merited
the attention of IR students. The transnationalist discussions of social
movements tended to link the rise of such actors with the extension
of international organizations and the intensification of global economic relations after World War II. Furthermore, transnational social
and political activity was explicitly portrayed as a 'pluralization' of
actors in world politics encouraged by US ascendancy in the international system. As Keohane and Nye candidly admitted: 'from a
transnational perspective the United States is by far the preponderant
society in the world... [this] has its origins in American patterns of
social organization and the American "style" as well as in the size and
modernity of its economy.'[7]

Second, although most advocates of transnationalism were at pains
to emphasize that they were not heralding the demise of the state, they
did claim that non-state actors could under specific circumstances be
as important, if not more, than the nation-state when explaining
international relations. Hence, transnationalists granted different
forms of collective social and political agency distinct ontological
status in international relations. This in turn led to a third assumption
closely associated to Keohane and Nye's understanding of interdependence, namely that there existed no necessary hierarchy among the

plethora of actors in world politics. State and non-state actors vied for influence in the international system, sometimes in unison, other times in competition. The upshot of such activity, however, was indeterminate in so far as no one expression of power – military, economic, ideological, political – associated with these different agents could be said to predominate over the other. From this perspective the traditional, state-centric approach to international relations, with its emphasis on geopolitics and military might, was being superseded by a much more complex web of powers and interests including transnational organizations such as revolutionary groups, labour movements, or indeed the Ford Foundation and the Catholic Church. The latter deployed mechanisms of international influence and organization, the impact of which simply could not be ascertained through the use of old analytical categories such as 'national interest' or 'foreign intervention'. Instead IR scholars had to accept that the plurality of forces in world politics had created an interdependent world where structures of international interaction were constantly being rearranged:

> We find ourselves in a world that reminds us more of the extensive and curious chessboard in Lewis Carroll's *Through the Looking Glass* than the more conventional versions of that ancient game. The players are not always what they seem, and the terrain of the chessboards may suddenly change from garden to shop to castle. Thus in contemporary world politics not all players on important chessboards are states, and the varying terrains of the chessboards constrain behaviour. Some are more suited to the use of force, others almost unsuited for it. Different chessboards favor different states.[8]

Last, and by no means least important, all theorists of transnationalism acknowledged, with different degrees of qualification, that theirs was a normative project imbued with the liberal-pluralist values prevalent in US academe at the time. The transnationalist emphasis on competition among a multiplicity of actors in world politics, their belief that the outcome of such contests was not predetermined and that therefore global interdependence was creating a world where the centres of power were increasingly diffuse, all echoed the pluralist theories of democracy applied to the domestic setting by writers such as Robert Dahl or David Easton.[9] From this perspective, the existence of multiple transnational actors was in itself a positive feature of world politics in so far as it ostensibly made the monopoly of power less likely. More interestingly perhaps, in a language reminiscent of their 'utopian' and functionalist forebears in IR, many of the transnationalist theorists attached a privileged role to transnational social and political movements in the promotion of international co-operation, inter-cultural understanding and the peaceful resolution of conflict.

This brief overview of the early transnationalist literature will have hopefully provided some sense of how non-state actors, and social and political movements in particular, were originally incorporated into mainstream IR theory during the 1970s. Much of the later investigation into social movements within IR owes a great deal to this pioneering work. Yet, at the same time, the transnationalist literature displayed a number of analytical and normative shortcomings that require closer critical scrutiny.

The first of these relates to the overall descriptive nature of the transnationalist agenda. For all their boldness in announcing a shift from a state-centric toward a 'world politics' paradigm, students of transnationalism remained surprisingly coy about the explanatory power of this new category. As Michael Clarke has astutely observed, 'In itself [transnationalism] certainly does not constitute a theory; it is rather a term which recognizes a phenomenon, or perhaps a trend in world politics, a phenomenon from which other concepts flow.'[10] With very few exceptions, the authors investigating transnationalism seemed content with identifying non-state agents and describing their intercourse with other actors in world politics. The task at hand was not so much to consider how these interactions might help to *explain* world politics, but simply to recognize their existence and register their impact upon inter-state relations. The closest transnationalism came to acquiring explanatory status was in the conclusions to the volume edited by Keohane and Nye. Here, the two editors surveyed the uses which their colleagues' 'findings' could be put to when studying international relations, US foreign policy and international organizations, respectively. Yet, again, the prospect of a paradigm shift giving rise to an improved explanation of international relations failed to go beyond a hesitant and promissory declaration of good intent premised on the descriptive shallowness of state-centrism:

> Transnational actors sometimes prevail over governments. These 'losses' by governments can often be attributed to the rising costs of unilateral governmental action in the face of transnational relations. For a state-centric theory this is represented as the 'environment'. But it is theoretically inadequate to use exogenous variables of the environment to account for outcomes in the interaction of various actors in the world politics. State-centric theories are not very good at explaining such outcomes because they do not describe the patterns of coalitions

between different types of actors described in the essays [of this volume]. We hope that our 'world politics paradigm' will help to redirect attention toward the substances of international politics.[11]

One important reason for the limited explanatory power of transnationalism is that it lacks any theory of agency. For transnationalists, the 'actors' in world politics become so simply by virtue of their pursuit of self-professed goals. There is no attempt in the transnationalist literature to distinguish between different types of agency, nor to situate the latter in an adequate historical and sociological context. Thus, any form of organization that operates on a non-governmental basis across inter-state borders automatically qualifies as a transnational actor. Why such an organization emerged in the first place, or what motives may lie behind its activities, are not relevant issues for the fundamentally *descriptive* approach endorsed by transnationalists. However, if our aim is to *explain* international relations, it seems imperative to identify and distinguish between different modes of transnational collective agency. This is essential not only for the purposes of creating some explanatory hierarchy of agencies, where actions adopted by some organizations become more relevant than others, but also so as to provide a sense of direction to these actions. As I shall try to indicate below, and more extensively in chapter 3, these questions have been the mainstay of sociological theory for almost two centuries. In recent years, they have finally found their way into IR theory, thus providing a long overdue corrective to the explanatory paucity of transnationalism.

The transnationalist failure in adequately explaining collective agency uncovers a third important limitation of this approach, namely the absence of any clear notion of society. Characteristically, the bulk of transnationalist literature assumes that the actors in 'world politics' operate within a neutral and pre-existing international space they interchangeably term the 'international system', 'world society' or 'international society'. Yet, clearly, the historical and structural characteristics of the existing international system are in many important respects unique. Specifically, once modern international society is understood to be a by-product of the advent and development of capitalism, the structural features of this society and the nature of the agents that act within it become associated with particular interests and specific power relations. For example, in the transnationalist account, multinational corporations (MNCs) are simply identified as another private actor in world politics, this time confined to the private sphere of 'economics'. But the kind of agency that informs the workings of an MNC is plainly different to that which motivates, say, an international trade union organization. Furthermore, in so far as both these forms of collective agency are part of 'world politics', they tend to represent opposing interests and generally interact along a hierarchical axis. All this does not mean that both MNCs and international labour organizations are not equally relevant for our understanding of international relations. On the contrary, it is to suggest that, in order fully to appreciate the nature and import of their role in international relations, it is necessary to investigate their historical provenance and the interests that motivate their actions. One way of achieving this is by reference to the structures and agencies engendered by capitalism. But this, unfortunately, is something that eludes transnationalist theories. Because most of the transnationalist literature is oblivious to the broad concerns of sociological theory, it has been unable to develop any analysis of social relations – be they capitalist or otherwise – beyond that of describing the selective interaction among specific transnational actors.

There is a last facet of transnationalism worth criticizing in this context, this time relating to the state. One facile objection often levied against transnationalist theories is that they overemphasize the relevance of non-state actors in detriment to that of the state. Indeed, one notorious critic of transnationalism ascribed its failings to a particular 'American illusion': 'The curious delusion about the imminent demise of the nation-state has affected Americans throughout their history. ... No matter that the assumption of American politicians and "analysts" about the demise of the nation-state has been proved wrong time and again.'[12] Aside from misrepresenting the transnationalist agenda, criticisms of this nature impoverish the debates over transnationalism by reducing the disputes to an either/or outcome: that is, either states are the most important actors in the international system or transnational actors are. Yet, as I shall argue in the rest of the book, a more fruitful and arguably more accurate approach to the question involves concentrating on the interaction, as opposed to the contrast, between state and non-state actors, or more precisely between state and civil society. Theorists of transnationalism rarely announced 'the demise of the nation-state' but rather sought to highlight the role of social forces outside the immediate control of the state. In their more sophisticated expressions (for example, the work of Keohane and Nye) the transnationalist literature aimed to gauge the impact of transnational activity upon the inter-state system, and not to set one class of actors against the other. Unfortunately, such investigations into the dialectic between state and civil society were pitched at the ahistorical, positivist level geared toward calculating the 'sensitivity' or 'vulnerability' of states vis-à-vis the activities of non-state actors.

The approach adopted below, however, seeks to probe the interaction among state and non-state actors from a historical-sociological perspective, emphasizing the mutual construction of these entities through time. Such a focus upon the historical relations among the agents of state and civil society, I argue, manages to transcend the crude dichotomy between state and non-state actors without thereby obscuring their distinct existence and internal dynamic.[13]

Classical transnationalism, then, is flawed on five major counts: it is essentially descriptive; it has no clear notion of agency; it has no comprehensive theory of society; it fails to consider the interrelationship between state and society; and, consequently, it cannot account for the hierarchies and structures in world politics. The sections below will try to illustrate how these shortcomings can be corrected without thereby foregoing some of the important insights into international relations provided by the transnationalist literature. Indeed, the rest of this book can be read as a contribution toward a historical and sociological understanding of transnational relations. In so doing, subsequent chapters will place considerable emphasis on two concepts which in the past decade have been widely discussed among IR theorists: civil society and agency. While the discussion of these two broad categories allows us to go some way in redressing the sociological paucity of classical transnationalism, significant problems still remain with the prevailing understanding of agency and civil society in IR. It is to these questions, and how my own usage of the categories differs from the existing ones, that I now turn.

Civil society and International Relations theory

The idea of 'civil society' has been all-pervasive in the social sciences over the past two decades. Partly a response to the role of collective agency in toppling dictatorial regimes, partly a reflection of the retreat from the language of class or revolution among the left, the portmanteau concept of civil society has been invoked in a wide range of contexts, generally with reference to that arena of our social and political lives that stands outside the control of the state. The limitations of such an approach to civil society will be dealt with at greater length in chapter 2. Here the aim is to outline the ways in which IR theorists have incorporated this category into our discipline, and to identify the analytical and normative shortcomings of such usages.

In essence, 'civil society' has been deployed within IR in three basic ways. First, there are those authors such as Ronnie Lipschutz, M. J. Peterson or Martin Shaw[14] that resort to the concept in order to retrieve much of the classical transnationalist concerns with non-state actors and what they perceive as a new stage in global interdependence, usually presented under the rubric of 'globalization'. These authors generally consider this renewed activity among transnational actors in world politics as a possible source of progressive politics, and in this sense they express a continuity in the tradition of liberal internationalism under a different guise. For both these reasons, I have labelled them the 'new transnationalists'.

A second cluster of authors shares much of the empirical diagnosis of the new transnationalists, acknowledging a qualitative shift in the nature of world politics, but displaying considerable scepticism as to whether such changes bear the promise of new transnational social and political coalitions. Scholars like R. B. J. Walker and, outside our own discipline, Michael Hardt[15] can be seen to represent this view of the overlap between civil society and international relations. Because most of their critical energies are directed against the 'modernist' readings of international civil society, these scholars can be said to defend a post-modernist approach to the issue.

Last, there are those IR theorists that fall under the category of 'neo-Gramscians' or the 'Italian school' who have applied Antonio Gramsci's conception of civil society to the domain of international relations. According to this school, civil society is associated with the capitalist market and the contest between hegemonic and counter-hegemonic forces that arise from this 'private' sphere of social relations. In so far as the neo-Gramscians apply a Marxian understanding of civil society, their analysis of global or international civil society is closest to that employed in this book.

All three contributions to the question of civil society and international relations have enriched our understanding of the phenomena arising out of this juxtaposition. Each approach emphasizes different aspects of civil society (social movements, market relations, its relation with the state) which lend support to the arguments in favour of taking this concept seriously within IR. Yet, despite these significant advances in bringing civil society into the domain of the international, reservations must still be raised as to the way this manoeuvre has been effected. In other words, while being entirely sympathetic to the *ends* pursued when incorporating civil society into our discipline, I would like to raise some objections as to the *means* employed to do so.

The main targets of critique are what I have termed the new transnationalists. The work of Martin Shaw and Ronnie Lipschutz has been at the forefront of the debates on civil society and world politics. Through their contributions to the 1992 special issue of the journal *Millennium* – dedicated to exploring the terrain 'beyond international society' – these authors provided the first sustained discussions of civil society and international relations (or their derivations, global civil society and international civil society). These themes have been followed up with monographs that apply such concepts to specific issues of world politics like the environment or the impact of the media on humanitarian crises.[16]

The first major fault of these approaches lies in their adoption of an ahistorical and socially disembedded understanding of civil society. Much like their transnationalist forerunners, international or global civil society on this account is identified as a space populated by transnational forces such as international non-governmental organizations and pressure groups that float autonomously within this sphere. Thus, for example, Lipschutz considers global civil society to be represented by 'political spaces other than those bounded by the parameters of the nation-state system',[17] while Shaw suggests that a global civil society 'can be seen at work in a variety of developments: the attempts by global ecological movements to make the state system respond to demands for global environmental management, the attempts by pressure groups to ensure that human rights and democracy are judged by a global standard and the demands, fuelled by media coverage, to make respect for human needs and human rights effective principles in international conflicts.'[18] There is, again, little attempt in these writings to situate the purported agents of civil society within a historical and sociological context capable of identifying the origins of such organizations and the interests they seek to further. The currency of the term 'civil society' is therefore devalued by referring rather blandly to any transnational phenomena beyond the strict domain of inter-state politics. Global or international civil society simply replaces the old-fashioned term 'transnational activity' in its descriptive account of world politics.

It should be noted that Martin Shaw somewhat modified his usage of global civil society in a later contribution to *Millennium*. In the 1994 special issue of this journal dedicated to 'Social movements and world politics', Shaw recognized that the crucial interaction between states and civil society yielded a dynamic process where non-state actors simultaneously undermine and reinforce the international system: 'The emergence of global civil society can be seen both as a response to the globalization of state power and a source of pressure for it . . . [it] in fact corresponds to the contradictory process of the globalization of state power, and the messy aggregation of global and national state power which comprises the contemporary interstate system.'[19] Similarly M. J. Peterson's contribution to the debates on international civil society underlined the need states and civil societies have for their mutual survival.[20] Such qualifications went some way toward charging the prevalent interpretation of global or international civil society with some explanatory power. Yet they still remained silent on the origins and development of the forms of collective agency which operated within this space and, more importantly, continued to ignore the hierarchies and interests which conditioned their interactions, both among the non-state actors themselves and in the latter's interactions with the states-system. In short, the new transnationalists failed to draw out the full theoretical and historical implications of using the term 'civil society', preferring instead to employ it as a generic category useful in updating the catalogue of transnational activity in world politics for the 1990s.

A second set of commentators on civil society and international relations have proved to be more mindful of the concept's lineage and the historical and political baggage it has accumulated. Arguing that the term 'civil society' is inextricably tied to modern conceptions of the social and the political, such approaches focus on the limitations inherent in using modernist discourses under post-modern conditions. R. B. J. Walker has defended this view most ardently within our own discipline. In a recent assessment of the different invocations of civil society within IR, Walker recognizes the value of bringing this concept into the discipline, if only because it unearths the aporias buried within modernist 'meta-narratives':

> The current popularity of claims about a global civil society can thus be read as a partial response to the dearth of ways of speaking coherently about forms of politics that transgress the bounds of the sovereign state. As such, it is sometimes quite illuminating. Nevertheless, as an attempt to extend to the global context a concept that is so historically rooted in the historical experiences of states . . . it is a concept that also expresses distinct limits to our ability to reimagine the political under contemporary conditions.[21]

In a similar vein, although coming from a different problematic, Michael Hardt suggests that we replace 'civil society' with 'postcivil society' as a more adequate tool of analysis for societies which have 'recently experienced a passage from a disciplinary society to a society of control'.[22] Here again, the sources of this shift in modes of dominance are explicitly associated with global transformations: 'Mobility, speed and flexibility are the qualities that characterize this separate plane of rule.'[23]

What emerges from these post-modern explorations of global civil society therefore is an uneasy recognition of the relevance for world politics of those social movements operating within civil society, qualified by a strong scepticism toward the modernist foundations of their outlook and action. In other words, scholars like Walker and Hardt appear to concur with the new transnationalists on the relevance of non-state actors in international relations, but argue simultaneously that labelling this phenomenon global or international civil society simply reinforces the historical association of civil society to the bounded politics of the sovereign state.

The post-modern musings on the overlap between civil society and international relations have the merit of clearly identifying the historical roots of this conjunction. Walker's commentary on the global civil society literature corrects the latter's historical myopia not only by hinting at the predecessors to contemporary transnational social movements but, more importantly, by associating the advent of civil society to a distinct historical epoch, namely capitalist modernity. This in turn opens up the possibility of anchoring our analysis of collective social and political agency at the international level upon a specific understanding of society, that is, one characterized by the structures of the capitalist market. Somewhat paradoxically perhaps, the post-modern approaches to global civil society are allied on this point with the neo-Gramscian writings we shall be exploring in a moment, and indeed with the definition of international civil society adopted in the rest of this study (to be expounded further in chapter 2). The real difference between the post-modernist and the modernist treatment of international civil society lies in the contemporary validity accorded to this category. While, for the post-modernists, international civil society and its cognates are at best a relic of the past and at worst modernist constructs which in Walker's words 'simply affirm the limits of their ambition', the view defended in this study (and therefore falling squarely into the modernist camp) is that international civil society is the term that best captures the dynamics of collective agency obtaining internationally today. Far from experiencing a shift toward modes of domination and contestation that transcend capitalist modernity, the present international conjuncture is characterized precisely by the affirmation of modern claims to state sovereignty, democracy, citizenship rights and civil liberties and by the deployment of modern forms of agency through political parties, trade unions and other comparable organizations. As long as these modes of social and political engagement remain the predominant sources of resistance across the world, reference to civil society and its international ramifications would appear to be the most adequate way of exploring the role of collective agency in international relations.

It is this general appreciation of the contemporary international system that has informed the usage of civil society among several Marxist scholars in IR. More specifically, it is those IR theorists who, inspired by Robert W. Cox's pioneering work, have incorporated Gramscian categories such as 'civil society', 'hegemony' and 'historical bloc' into the discipline. In essence, the neo-Gramscian references to civil society extrapolate the Italian communist's usage of the term in the domestic setting on to the international stage. In a variation on the 'domestic analogy' the neo-Gramscians suggest that the associations, institutions and collectivities that Gramsci identified as forming a civil society distinct from the state within bourgeois democracies can also be seen to operate at the international level, thus warranting reference to a global or international civil society. Following Gramsci and Marx, the authors associated with the 'Italian school' identify civil society with the 'private' sphere of the capitalist market, to be distinguished from the 'public' domain of the state. Thus, global civil society is on this account synonymous with the global capitalist market. Such a conceptualization represents a significant improvement on the transnationalist understanding of global civil society in that it moors discussions of the subject on the concrete socio-economic relations that govern our social lives. Moreover, the neo-Gramscian approach highlights the contestation that takes place within civil society by making reference to the hegemonic and counter-hegemonic interests that play themselves out within this sphere. In these two respects, the neo-Gramscian discussions on global civil society address the key criticisms levelled above at the new transnationalists: the lack of a notion of hierarchy and interests within civil society, and the consequent absence of a sociological and historical grounding of the concept.

These strengths are, however, overshadowed by a number of weaknesses in the neo-Gramscian conception of international civil society, not least in its imprecise usage. As we have seen, all the authors associated with this school equate civil society with the capitalist market. Yet on some accounts global or international civil society additionally refers to a set of 'private, informal transnational apparatuses, such as the private international relations councils'[24] that sustain the international ruling-class consensus and foster the ideological consent among subordinate classes necessary for the maintenance of world hegemony. On this reading, global civil society also encompasses the activity of transnational class coalitions identified in Kees van der Pijl's classic study on *The Making of an Atlantic Ruling Class*.[25] Although these shifts in the meaning of global civil society are not necessarily contradictory, they do beg the question of what is specifically useful about this category. If global civil society simply represents the global capitalist market, why not stick to the latter term? If the concept aims to describe the forging of a transnational ruling class, how does reference to civil society clarify the object of study?

A more substantive problem in the neo-Gramscian discussion of global civil society relates to the place of the state in this domain of world politics. Although one of the major contributions of this school to IR is their insistence on the centrality of the historical interaction between states and civil societies when explaining international relations, it is not altogether clear how these two spheres interrelate once they are projected on to the international realm. In a recent critical appraisal of the new Gramscians, Randall D. Germain and Michael Kenny put the point thus:

> In the end, the concept of a 'global' civil society cannot claim a Gramscian lineage except in relation to some kind of 'international' state . . . any specifically *Gramscian* reading of civil society requires a corresponding structure of concrete political authority in order to become genuinely hegemonic in the sense used by Gramsci. It thus requires an account of a global 'political society' along the lines questioned here. Put in another way, we challenge the new Gramscians to show just how far Gramsci's justly famous equation can be refashioned to read: 'international state = global political society + global civil society'.[26]

The challenge presented by Germain and Kelly is posed in rather stark terms: it *is* possible to conceive of a global civil society that operates at the transnational level but comes short of producing a corresponding international state. Indeed, one of the major arguments of this study is that the social movements that form international civil society simultaneously undermine and affirm the legitimacy of the modern states-system. This notwithstanding, Germain and Kelly are right to point out the difficulties inherent in a self-professed 'Gramscian' view of global civil society that fails to adequately define the latter's relationship to the international society of states. For all their suggestive references to the way in which the reproduction of global capitalism and the transnational class alliances that it generates slowly forge a global civil society, the neo-Gramscians remain elusive about the place of the state and the system of states in the unfolding of this sphere of world politics.

This section has sought to offer a brief overview of the different uses the term 'civil society' has been put to within IR. As we have seen, our

discipline has not been immune from the frustrating practice of at-
taching various, often incompatible meanings to the concept and its
derivations, global or international civil society. All three of the approaches outlined above agree on the usefulness of the term 'global
civil society' when describing the transnational interactions in world
politics and, furthermore, appear to include the world capitalist
market within this domain. While the new transnationalists remain
at this descriptive level, the post-modernist and neo-Gramscian theorists probe the explanatory potential of the concept. The former emphasize the inherent ontological limitations in explaining an ostensibly
post-modern world with reference to modernist categories like civil
society. They are primarily interested in discussing global civil society
as part of a broader campaign against the disciplining schemas of
modernist discourse. The neo-Gramscians, on the other hand, seek
to demonstrate the continuing validity of the term civil society, applying the analytical and strategic insights of Antonio Gramsci's writings
on the subject to the contemporary international system. From this
perspective, global civil society is seen as a domain of transnational
class agency capable of engendering hegemonic blocs that sustain
successive historical world orders. Occasionally, this sphere also
appears as an arena of counter-hegemonic contestation, although the
neo-Gramscians tend to pay lip-service to this aspect of global civil
society more than exploring its full implications for the study of
international relations.

The conception of international civil society to be developed in the
rest of this study plainly overlaps with many of the perspectives
outlined above. There are, however, two important departures from
the existing theories of international society worth flagging here.
First, in contrast to the new transnationalists and following the neo-
Gramscians, I seek to ground the idea of international civil society
historically and sociologically by associating its origins and development with the reproduction of global capitalism. International civil
society is therefore treated in this study as a domain of social and
political activity subsumed under the broader dynamics of capitalist
social relations. Unlike the neo-Gramscians, however, I understand
the modern state and, by extension, the international system to be a
necessary component of any definition of international civil society.
As we have seen, one of the defects of the neo-Gramscian understanding of global civil society is that it fails to grant the sovereign state and
inter-state relations any clear role in the development of this sphere of
international relations. The chapters that follow, on the other hand,
aim to emphasize the centrality of the international system of states in
the formation of international civil society. Secondly, my own under-

standing of international civil society focuses very specifically on modern forms of political and social agency as the constitutive element of this international domain. Contrary to both the new transnationalist and neo-Gramscian approaches to the subject, the question of agency – and particularly the collective agency of exploited classes – figures very prominently in the considerations on international civil society that follow. The last section of this introduction will therefore address the issue of agency and how it relates to the perspective on international relations offered in the rest of the book.

Agents and structures in international relations

One of the major arguments arising out of the preceding discussion is that using the term 'international civil society' necessarily assumes a historical and sociological understanding of international relations. In recent years, this basic premise has gained increasing weight in the theoretical debates within IR. Specifically, the sociological problematic of agency and structure has acquired its own currency within the discipline. As was stated at the outset, this study can in some ways be read as a contribution to a historical-sociological investigation of transnational social and political agency. In this respect, it also represents an engagement with the agency-structure literature in IR. The aim of this section, therefore, is to clarify the status of the term 'agency' as it is employed in the rest of this study. In essence, the standpoint adopted here is that collective social and political agency is the expression of class antagonisms arising out of capitalist social relations. I understand class as a phenomenon that emerges out of determinate historical relations of production which engender an antagonism of interests and values between different social groups. This clash of interests explains the rise and development of most modern forms of social and political agency, although, naturally, the existence of class struggle does not in itself guarantee the emergence of such agency.[27] As I hope to indicate below, adopting a Marxist perspective on collective agency offers two advantages over other approaches to the subject: it provides a socio-historical account of agency, and it manages to reconcile the artificial division between structure and agency. Before contrasting this view of agency with those prevailing in recent IR theory, it is necessary to consider briefly the assumptions behind a historical-sociological approach to international relations.

Any sociological understanding of human life must start by explaining the relationship between human agency and social structures. As Philip Abrams put it: 'All varieties of sociology stress the so-called "two-sidedness" of the social world, presenting it as a world of which we are both the creators and the creatures, both makers and prisoners; a world which our actions construct and a world that powerfully constrains us.'[28] What is distinctive about a *historical* sociology is that it seeks to explain this relationship between agency and structure as one forged through time: 'The two-sidedness of society, the fact that social action is both something we choose to do and something we have to do, is inseparably bound up with the further fact that whatever reality society has is an historical reality, a reality in time.'[29] The key insight here is that social structures like, for example, civil society are the product of historical *processes*. Likewise, the possibility of recognizing social *structures* arises from our capacity to identify a specific logic to these processes. The task which a historical-sociological approach sets itself, therefore, is to explain our social world by identifying the historical interaction between structures and processes. Ernest Gellner once used the analogy of a chess game to elucidate what might be distinctive about this method. Suggesting that our social life be seen as a sequence of moves on a chessboard, Gellner argued that a sociological history would seek to 'elicit and specify... the shared set of rules which connect one move with the next'. Thus, for Gellner, 'A sociological account... is analogous to explaining the story to someone, say a child, who is unfamiliar with the rules of chess: the rules must be specified, and it must be explained why some moves are mandatory, others preferable, some forbidden, some allowed but disastrous.'[30] The way of establishing what these 'rules' of social interaction are is through reference to history; we can only understand our social world by identifying the changes and continuities in the structures and processes of social life *through time*.

From a Marxist perspective, the principal agency behind historical processes is class struggle. On this account, in order to explain structural transformations in the course of human history it is necessary to make reference to the conscious and unconscious antagonism of interests and values between, and sometimes among, social classes. This is, of course, an oversimplified statement of the Marxist view of historical change. For one, it obviates the important Marxist debates on the relative weight of the forces and relations of production, respectively, in effecting social change. Gerry Cohen, to take but one example, famously argued that the level of development of the productive forces in a given society takes precedence over class struggle in the explanation of social change.[31] Furthermore, as a summary statement it cannot delve into the complex philosophical considerations regarding the nature and classification of epochal shifts, nor the historical difficulties involved in the identification of class antagonisms. At this stage, however, it seems unnecessary to elaborate on these points. Instead, while acknowledging the contested character of the position, I would like to press on with an illustration of how a class-based understanding of socio-historical change challenges the prevalent notions of agency and structure in International Relations.

For almost six decades since its emergence as an academic discipline, IR has been oblivious to the sociological problematic of agents and structures. IR theorists have certainly employed these terms in the past, for instance in the transnationalist appraisal of non-state 'actors' examined above, or in Kenneth Waltz's notorious defence of the need to develop the 'systemic' level of analysis in international relations. Yet none of these usages engages with the 'two-sidedness of the social world' mentioned earlier: at best, agents and structures are treated in isolation from one another (as in the neo-realist celebration of 'structure'); at worst, they are stripped of any explanatory power (as in the transnationalist notion of 'actor' discussed above). It was in response to this sociological naivety that several IR scholars turned to meta-theoretical considerations of structure and agency from the mid-1980s onwards. Although many of the insights associated with what later became known as the agency–structure debate in IR had arguably been articulated earlier in the work of Robert W. Cox, Ekkehart Krippendorff, John Maclean or Ralph Pettman, it was Alexander Wendt's 1987 *International Organization* article that set the parameters of later discussions.[32] In this piece, Wendt set off from a critique of neo-realist and world-system theory, arguing that both these approaches 'reify system structures in a way which leads to static and even functional explanations of state action'.[33] For Wendt, reducing international relations to either the agency of states (as the neo-realists do) or the structures engendered by the world-capitalist system (as in the case of world-systems theory) impoverishes our understanding of both the character of these entities and their dynamic interaction. A more fruitful approach, according to the author, involves focusing upon the interdependence between agents and structures in international relations and probing the interconnected nature of their identity. Taking his cue from Anthony Giddens's work on 'structuration', Wendt argued that

> The structurationist approach ... tries to avoid what I shall argue are the negative consequences of individualism and structuralism by giving agents and structures equal ontological status. ... This conceptualization

allows us to rethink fundamental properties of (state) agents and system structures. In turn, it permits us to use agents and structures to explain some of the key properties of each as effects of the other, to see agents and structures as 'co-determined' or 'mutually constituted' entities.[34]

The consequences of this methodological shift for IR were twofold. On the one hand, state agents and international structures were presented as dynamic, historical entities that are shaped through time as a result of their mutual interaction. Secondly, and following on from this, neither agents nor structures were given ontological priority when analysing international relations. The research agenda arising out of these premises was summarized as follows: 'The core of this agenda is the use of structural analysis to theorize the conditions of existence of state agents, and the use of historical analysis to explain the genesis and reproduction of social structures.'[35]

Wendt's contribution had the virtue of laying down rigorous terms of debate on an issue that plainly struck a chord among theorists of IR at the time. By challenging the meta-theoretical assumptions of both the neo-realists and their world-system contenders, Wendt opened up a space for a critical sociology of agency and structure; that is, a sociology that renders problematic the very categories employed in the debate. Yet, though Wendt should be praised for his sense of opportunity, the novelty of his argument must be questioned. Indeed, the accusation of 'reinventing the wheel' levelled at his theoretical mentor, Anthony Giddens, can also be applied to Wendt's work, as we shall see in chapter 3.[36] Although Wendt's points on the 'mutually constitutive' nature of agency and structure are well taken (particularly in the context of a theoretically stunted discipline like IR), it is not necessary to take on board Giddens's own theory of structuration in order to arrive at this conclusion.[37] On the contrary, as was suggested above, the basic insights of structuration theory have been the mainstay of much of the twentieth century's historical sociology, and were arguably encapsulated in the first place within Marx's conception of *praxis*.[38] In the words of one Marxist theorist not known for his sympathies to Giddens's work: 'at the level of their most general presuppositions, there is no necessary antagonism between Giddens' structuration theory and historical materialism.'[39]

A Marxist understanding of agency, then, concurs with the more sophisticated discussions of agency and structure in IR, both on the need to emphasize the necessary interaction between agents and structures (or subject and object), and on the requirement to do so historically, i.e. to consider this interaction through time and place. This said, there are plainly a number of significant differences between

Wendt's structurationism and the Marxist approach adopted in this study.

First, whereas Wendt appears to focus almost exclusively on the agencies and structures generated by states – only making cursory references to other social forces toward the end of his paper – the arguments to be developed below identify *classes* as the major force behind the production and reproduction of structures and agents in international relations. Second, for all his criticism of the static and instrumentalist character of existing treatments of agency and structure in IR, Wendt fails to provide any theory of socio-historical change. State-formation and the reproduction of the international system are, for Wendt, explained as dynamic historical processes, yet nowhere in his contribution was there a consideration of how we might identify structural transformation on a world scale, nor which agents might be responsible for such change. A Marxist approach, on the other hand, identifies the rise and expansion of capitalist social relations as the defining feature of the historical epoch we have come to know as modernity. The structures engendered by the global reproduction of capitalism in turn generate modern forms of collective agency organized around antagonistic class interests. Thus, on this account capitalism is seen as the ordering structure of collective class agency responsible for socio-historical change in the international system. Without forgoing the dialectic relationship between structure and agency, such an approach is at least able to chart the transformations in successive world orders and explain the sources of their dynamic.

Toward a historical sociology of international political agency

The aim of this introductory chapter has been to set out the differences between the uses of 'transnationalism', 'civil society' and 'agency' as they are employed in this study and those developed in other theoretical frameworks within IR. It has been argued that the existing discussions within our discipline of issues pertaining to international political agency are unsatisfactory on a number of counts. The early literature on transnational relations in world politics had the virtue of identifying and exploring the relevance in international relations of actors other than the state. Thus, transnational political agency was ascribed to entities such as multinational corporations, religious institutions, pressure groups, trade unions and so forth. Yet, as we saw above, such a literature failed to move beyond the merely descriptive, presenting a canvas of international relations that was broader in its incorporation of previously marginalized non-state actors but that ultimately lacked explanatory depth. Almost a generation later, several IR scholars sought to retrieve the transnationalist concern for non-state actors, this time cloaking the theoretical poverty of their predecessors through references to the more profound concept of 'civil society'. Though generally alert to the conceptual richness of the term 'civil society', those authors employing the category within our field have inexplicably shied away from exploiting its full historical and sociological potential. The same conceptual pitfalls that bedevilled the original transnationalists emerge in the work of theorists of global civil society like Martin Shaw or Ronnie Lipschutz: the absence of a notion of agency; the refusal to consider hierarchical aspects of civil society; the lack of a clear examination of how global civil society might interact with the international system of states. In order to address these issues, an altogether separate debate on agency and structure in international relations has to be resorted to: that dealing with the more meta-theoretical concerns of structuration theory. As mentioned above, though helpful in exploring questions of agency and structure in a more rigorous fashion, Wendt's structurationist approach to agency in international relations paradoxically returns the discipline full circle to an almost exclusive discussion of agency and structure in relation to the behaviour of *states*. Thus, social and political agency mediated through, for example, social movements escapes the purview of Wendt's analysis.

The combined effect of these developments has been that, while questions of collective social and political agency in international relations have arisen in different guises within our discipline, no overall theoretical category capable of explaining international socio-political agency and its impact upon international relations has emerged to date. It is the aim of the rest of this book to develop a notion of 'international civil society' that is capable of meeting such a challenge. Although a full discussion of the meaning of international civil society is the subject of the following chapter, I will now briefly outline the main features of this concept with reference to the preceding discussion.

International civil society refers to a domain of international relations generated by the global reproduction of capitalism where modern social movements pursue their political goals. Modern social movements are characterized by a historically specific form of agency with four basic components: a universalist ideology; an open membership; a secular or 'disenchanted' vision of social and political action; and a reliance on printed media and novel forms of mobilization such as strikes, demonstrations or electoral rallies. Chapter 3 will elaborate on this definition of modern social and political agency. For the moment, however, it may be sufficient simply to point out that such an understanding of collective agency differs from the existing approaches outlined above in two respects. First, contrary to the ahistorical conceptions of collective action in world politics, the idea of international civil society emphasizes the historical specificity of modern political subjectivity. This not only involves tracing the origins of international social movements back to at least the eighteenth century but, more importantly, suggests that we 'moderns' engage in collective social and political activity in radically different ways from those of our 'pre-modern' forebears. Secondly, in contrast to most contemporary understandings of agency and civil society, I consider the latter as an equivalent, in the Marxian sense, of 'bourgeois society'. In other words, international civil society is treated in this study as an arena plagued by the social and political antagonisms inherent to capitalist social relations. On this account, civil society is by no means a necessarily benign sphere of social and political action, but rather a space of contested power relations where clashing interests play themselves out through analogous but unequal modes of collective agency.

Aside from a distinct understanding of collective agency, the idea of international civil society presented in the following chapters also offers a novel interpretation of the impact of such agency upon international relations. International civil society is certainly viewed as a domain inhabited by international social movements that organize and act across national, ethnic or religious boundaries. Thus, much of the historical illustrations of international civil society will focus on internationalism as a principle and a practice of transnational solidarity (whether it be premised on class, religion or ethnicity). As already mentioned above, in this respect the study forms part of a broadly defined transnationalist agenda. Recognizing forms of international politics that fall outside the domain of inter-state relations does not, however, mean rejecting the existence of an international society of states. Indeed, the chapters that follow will continually underline the need for an analysis of the historical *interaction* between states and civil societies in the construction of the international system. In short, from this perspective international civil society represents a domain of international political activity which, though distinct from the system of states, is in constant interaction with the latter.

These, then, are the basic characteristics of international civil society as it will be developed in the rest of the book. The category aims to offer a novel understanding of social and political agency in international relations by reformulating the use of the term 'civil society' within IR. Furthermore, it seeks to demonstrate the explanatory value of such a concept when interpreting the nature of contemporary international relations, both past and present. Last, underlying this conceptual reworking of the term 'international civil society' is the aspiration of retrieving past experiences of international social and political agency among ordinary activists, and illuminating future possibilities for a progressive world politics premised on transnational political solidarity. The next two chapters will consider in greater detail how these objectives can be realized with reference to the notion of civil society and social movements respectively, while chapter 4 will do so in relation to international society. Chapter 2 offers an extended account of the ideological and historical development of the concept 'civil society', and argues further that the numerous international dimensions to the category merit a leap toward the analysis of an *international* civil society. Chapter 3 aims to clarify the conception of international social and political agency adopted in this study through a definition of modern social movements and their international dimensions, and a subsequent discussion of the structural limits to transformative agency in world politics. Chapter 4 considers the manner in which this new category – international civil society – fits into the broader and more orthodox concerns of IR theory such as sovereignty, nationalism or the norms and values of international society. It will be argued there that the traditional notion of international society is inherently incapable of accounting for social forces other than state elites in the explanation of international relations, and that the idea of international civil society can remedy this flaw while simultaneously retaining some of the relevant insights into the nature and workings of international society provided by the authors associated with the 'English school' of IR. In conjunction, these chapters should prepare the ground for a discussion in chapter 5 of the contemporary uses (and abuses) of the term 'civil society' in the ongoing debates over 'globalization'. It will be suggested there that contemporary theorists of global governance, global civil society and cosmopolitan democracy use 'civil society' in a thoroughly ahistorical and uncritically liberal fashion. Consequently, they simultaneously underestimate the historical centrality of civil society in the construction of the international system, and exaggerate its current potential in effecting radical global change.

2

Civil Society

The Challenge of the International

Three components of civil society

Among the concepts of classical political theory used in contemporary political and social discourse, civil society is probably the term which has staged the most dramatic resurgence in the past decades. Since its medieval retrieval via William von Moerbeke's translation of Aristotle's *Politics*, the term has been reformulated by virtually every significant western political philosopher, culminating in Hegel's magisterial reworking of the idea of civil society and its subsequent critique by Marx. After a long absence initiated at the turn of the century (briefly interrupted by Gramsci's work), the concept of civil society has returned with a vengeance, claiming a new-found legitimacy through its association with the overthrow of dictatorial regimes in Latin America, southern Europe, East Asia and most recently eastern and central Europe. The power of collective action in the struggle against the all-encroaching state was reflected in a number of novel formulations of civil society whether sociologically as a 'public sphere', anthropologically as a 'condition of liberty' or as the political space where new social movements operate.[1]

Paradoxically, this close relationship between the restitution of civil society as a concrete historical phenomenon and its employment as a political and sociological category has occasioned the loss of some of the concept's analytical sharpness. The prevailing definition of civil society refers to that sphere of public life beyond the control of the state. This is the sense which politicians, journalists, activists and no few academics ascribe to the term when they speak of 'civil society' standing as a bulwark against 'the state', or when they defend it as the realm of freedom. As the previous chapter indicated, it is also the way in which many IR scholars have adopted the term when examining transnational and international non-state actors.

Clearly, this understanding of civil society has some analytical purchase, demonstrated among other things in the way that it has captured the imagination of such a broad public. Yet, if it is placed under closer historical and sociological scrutiny, the simple identification of civil society with all social activity which escapes the control of the state gives rise to a rather crude dichotomy which impoverishes the concept in at least two respects.

In the first place, when viewed historically, either as a concrete sociological phenomenon or as a theoretical category, civil society appears inextricably linked to the modern state. The analytical distinction between two spheres need not imply their absolute opposition as concrete historical entities. The conceptual power of the term 'civil society' lies precisely in its reference to an arena of social life differentiated from the state while simultaneously revealing its complex *interaction with* the state. Second, by delving into the historical roots of the sociological and ideological differentiation between civil society and the state, we open the door to an explanation of how and why this distinction was effected in the first place. This avoids the static and ahistorical definition of civil society as a constant, everywhere and always defined as a counterpart to the state. One of the basic claims of this book is that civil society needs to be understood as a historically variable social space. Civil society is not a given, but a concrete sociological sphere which is made and unmade by collective human agency, and which is susceptible to the same historical and social forces which operate upon other parts of our social life.

This double manoeuvre – giving civil society a historical and sociological content – recovers the complexity of the category, thereby reinstating its analytical and explanatory power. In what follows, I will attempt to reconstruct the conceptual richness of the term by addressing three general phenomena which help to define it: the imagination of society; the emergence of capitalist social relations; and the birth of modern collective agency. Once the general parameters of this redefinition of civil society are made clear, I shall turn to the basic claim of this chapter, namely that a historical and sociological evaluation of civil society reveals a number of international factors in its genesis and development. This challenge of 'the international' warrants, I suggest, a further conceptual leap toward the realm of 'international civil society'.

The reciprocity of strangers:
civil society and the idea of society

In Europe, the word 'society' was associated with vernacular notions of 'companionship' or 'fellowship' until well into the second half of the seventeenth century.[2] During the course of that century thinkers like Hobbes and Locke began to use the term scientifically, but outside their own writings 'society' was generally deemed to be a word devoid of any theoretical or analytical pretensions. By the eighteenth century, however, the concept had taken on a new dimension as leading theorists of the time such as Ferguson, Montesquieu, Hume, Rousseau or Smith made the origins and nature of 'civil society' the mainstay of their philosophical inquiries. For all the diversity of their positions and methods, one general preoccupation could be said to be common to all these philosophers: to examine the conditions under which human beings (although they usually meant 'men') could escape the state of nature and enter into a contractual form of government based on the rule of law, i.e. a civil society. Thus, an essential component of this novel deployment of 'society' was its contrast with a real or imagined 'state of nature'; the term 'civil society' denoted a new stage in the evolution of government among the human species.

Initially, civil society was synonymous with the state. As was noted above, the Latin translation of *koinonia politike* as *societas civilis* meant that the term retained much of its Aristotelian inflection. It was defined as a political community rooted in the principles of citizenship. In this respect, civil society was seen as a model of government. Yet underlying this predominantly political understanding of civil society was a deeper sociological claim about the nature of human relations. Although couched in a language still distant from that of modern sociology, what thinkers like Hobbes, Locke, Rousseau or Ferguson were initiating in their ruminations on the origins and development of civil society was the actual imagination of a systematic set of relationships between human beings which gradually came to be known as 'society'. As Keith Tester has emphasized, 'civil society is perhaps best identified as a specifically, and also fundamentally, sociological problem ... as an idea by which the seventeenth, eighteenth and early nineteenth-century philosophers tried to explain how society was possible.'[3]

Thomas Hobbes was probably the first among the modern political philosophers to have posed the question of the origins of society in a systematic fashion. Although his earlier works, *Elements of Law* and *Philosophical Rudiments Concerning Government and Society*, already addressed the idea of society, it is in *Leviathan* that Hobbes presents most starkly his theory on the origins and characteristics of this concept. Hobbes did this by introducing two seemingly innocent and commonsensical assumptions about human nature which laid the foundations for future definitions of civil society.

The first of these assumptions was that human beings constitute individual and comparable entities whose actions are governed by laws of motion similar to those of other physical bodies. Hobbes opened *Leviathan* with a discussion of the physiological and psychological traits common to all human beings, suggesting that 'whosoever looketh into himself, and considereth what he doth, when he does *think, opine, reason, hope, fear*, &c, and upon what grounds; he shall thereby read and know what are the thoughts, and Passions of all other men.'[4] Under the consecutive headings of 'Sense', 'Imagination', 'Speech', 'Reason and Science' and 'Passions', Hobbes discovered the motivations which he considered to lie behind all human action, thus underscoring his methodological empiricism and individualism.

From these initial premises, Hobbes went on to present his famous account of 'the Natural Condition of Mankind' where the human disposition toward competition, diffidence and glory gives rise to a 'time of warre, where every man is Enemy to every man . . . and the life of man, solitary, poore, nasty, brutish, and short'.[5] As C. B. Macpherson has underlined, Hobbes's conception of the 'state of nature' was derived from the experience of his own contemporary 'civilized society': ' "Natural" for Hobbes is not the opposite of social or civil.'[6] None the less, it was clearly essential for Hobbes's argument to posit a *distinction* if not an *opposition* between the state of nature and civil society in order to justify his defence of the Leviathan or Commonwealth as the expression of a free covenant between rational men. Hobbes made this explicit in chapter 17 of *Leviathan* where, in response to the hypothetical claim that, like bees and ants, humans could 'live sociably one with the other . . . and yet have no direction', he retorts that 'the agreement of these creatures is Naturall; that of men, is by Covenant only, which is Artificiall.'[7]

Although perhaps not immediately obvious, the two aspects of *Leviathan* highlighted above – its methodological individualism and the distinction between civil society and the state of nature – provide the rudimentary basis for a theory of society. By envisaging an abstract individual endowed with a set of universal physiological and psychological motivations, Hobbes prepared the ground for the future imagination of society as the sum of interactions between individual human beings. In fact, in *Leviathan*, Hobbes puts this imagination to work by describing how civil society or the Commonwealth is born: 'when men agree amongst themselves, to submit to some Man, or assembly of Men, voluntarily, on confidence to be protected by him against all others'.[8]

A second and more controversial implication of Hobbes's discussion of civil society is its normative identification with a higher stage of human development. Despite the ambiguities in his exposition, Hobbes effected a distinction in *Leviathan* between civil society and the state of nature which has since represented a central tenet of most theories of civil society. This distinction rests on the familiar but none the less conclusive argument that our human capacity to reason allows us to escape the natural predicament of other animals and enter into the higher realm of civil society. As we shall see below, this has important consequences for the two other relationships which I claim define civil society: that between nature and production and that between human agency and history. For the moment, however, it may suffice simply to register that without this rational component it is impossible to imagine civil society, let alone realize the ethical life of which it holds promise.

In his impressive conceptual history of civil society, Manfred Riedel suggests that Hobbes was instrumental in the shift from a natural to a historical conception of civil society; from civil society understood as a natural community to civil society as the artificial product of separate individuals joining together in a commonwealth:

> In the systems of the seventeenth century, the individual, the *Individuum*, comes before the social whole. Bourgeois society doesn't have an original ('natural') existence here, but a derivative one; it is a posteriori and not a priori, the result of a process which begins from the single individual. In [*De Cive*] Hobbes formulated the decisive tenet which rescues this generic concept of classical political theory from its own ahistoricity: that the nature of things and that of human beings cannot serve as a potential principle for the unification of civil society (*societas civilis*). *Nature and human history, which constituted a unity in the classical political tradition, now become differentiated.*[9]

The pervasive influence of Hobbes's formulation of civil society as outlined above is exemplified by the work of Locke and Rousseau on the subject matter. To be sure, these three thinkers derived political conclusions from their examination of civil society which were very different, when not plainly at odds with each other. Yet the retention of the abstract individual and the imaginary state of nature as the two building blocks in the definition of civil society betrayed a continuity in the basic theoretical parameters laid out by Hobbes. In this respect, the work of Locke and Rousseau can be interpreted as a further elaboration on a version of civil society which contained deeper socio-logical claims about the nature of modern society.

Locke opens his *Second Treatise on Government* with a discussion of the state of nature. Unlike Hobbes's bleak vision of man's natural condition, Locke suggests that 'the *State of Nature* has a Law of Nature to govern it, which obliges every one: And Reason, which is that Law, teaches Mankind, who will consult it, that being all equal and independent, no one ought to harm another in his Life, Health, Liberty or Possessions.'[10] But this benevolent picture is transformed in the subsequent chapter into a state of war. Contra-dicting his own advice against confusing the state of nature with the state of war, Locke goes on to insist that 'To avoid the State of War...is one great *reason of Mens putting themselves into Society*, and quitting the State of Nature.'[11] Thus, the origin of civil society is boldly situated in the contract made by free and rational individuals seeking to preserve their life, health, liberty and property:

> Wherever therefore any number of men are so united into one Society, as to quit every one his Executive Power of the Law of Nature, and to resign it to the publick, there and there only is a *Political or Civil Society* ... And this *puts Men* out of a State of Nature *into* that of a Commonwealth.[12]

About half a century later, Jean-Jacques Rousseau echoed this con-trast between the state of nature and civil society in order to come to terms with the new form of social relationships which he observed around him. In the *Discourse on the Origin and Foundation of Inequal-ity of Mankind* Rousseau emphasized from the outset that his depic-tion of the state of nature was based not on historical evidence but rather on 'mere conditional and hypothetical reasoning'.[13] In fact, Rousseau happily admitted that his invocation of the state of nature follows in the tradition of other theorists who have derived this category from their own contemporary experiences: 'The philosophers who have inquired into the foundations of society, have all felt the necessity of going back to the state of nature.... Every one of them ... has transferred to the state of nature ideas which were acquired in society; so that, in speaking of the savage, they described the social man.'[14]

According to Rousseau, man's natural condition is so blissful and benign that 'he can have departed from it only through some fatal accident'.[15] Such misfortune, Rousseau contended, was brought about by the institution of private property. I shall explore the significance of this explanation of the fall of natural man for the idea of civil society in a moment. At this stage, however, it is more important to note that the introduction of private property gave 'rise to a horrible state of war' such that property-owning men

> conceived at length the profoundest plan that ever entered the mind of man: ... 'Let us, in a word, instead of turning our forces against ourselves, collect them in a supreme power which may govern us by wise laws, protect and defend all members of the association ... and maintain eternal harmony among us.'[16]

The attributes of this 'supreme power' were of course expounded in *The Social Contract*. There, Rousseau deployed the contrast between natural and civil society most forcefully by suggesting that 'The passage from the state of nature to the civil state produces a very remarkable change in man, by substituting justice for instinct in his conduct, and giving his actions the morality he had formerly lacked.'[17] Thus, just like his English predecessors, Rousseau came to accept that, once the 'fall of natural man' has been accomplished, civil society is identified with the moral advancement of the human species; civil society becomes the realm of justice arrived at through the rational contract among free individuals.

In exploring the idea of civil society as conceived by these three prominent political thinkers, I have attempted to stress the *sociological* insights offered by what are generally deemed to be *political* theories. It has been suggested that the positing of the abstract, rational individual as the foundation of civil society and its contrast with the state of nature opened the way for the modern understanding of society as the systematic interaction between individuals. The observation which Keith Tester reserves for John Locke is in this context also valid for Hobbes and Rousseau:

> At the very threshold of modernity, Locke used the imagination of civil society to explain how society was possible. ... Locke understands civil society to be the association of individuals beyond the family which are ... based on the symmetric reciprocity of strangers. [Civil society]

involves the reciprocity of strangers who equally and individually give up the state of nature in order to enter into a society.[18]

While the methodological tools applied by Hobbes, Locke and Rousseau to their studies of civil society were broadly similar, there is one crucial variable, already alluded to above, which differentiates Hobbes's account from the other two thinkers, namely the role of private property in the forging of a civil society. As was briefly pointed out above, Rousseau was unequivocal about this; the second part of the *Discourse on the Origin of Inequality* opens with the thundering affirmation: 'The first man who, having enclosed a piece of ground, bethought himself of saying "This is mine" and found people simple enough to believe him, was the real founder of civil society.'[19]

Locke, on the other hand, presented a vision of civil society plagued with ambiguities regarding the place of private property in the genesis and later development of civil society. These contradictions were at the root of C. B. Macpherson's celebrated thesis of Locke (among others) as a political theorist of 'possessive individualism'. Essentially, Macpherson identifies two discrepancies in Locke's account: one pertaining to the difference between the state of nature and the state of war; the other referring to the property requirements for membership of civil society. The first of these, briefly mentioned above, involves Locke's inconsistency in separating the state of nature from the state of war in one chapter of the *Second Treatise*, only to conflate them in the following one. In the second instance, Locke is guilty of shifting his definition of property from the more restricted one of 'life, liberty and estate' to that including goods and land. In both cases, Macpherson argues, the contradictions can be explained by situating Locke within the context of a 'possessive market society':

> [Locke] had in his mind at the same time two conceptions of society, which although logically conflicting, were derived from the same ultimate source. One was a notion of society as composed of equal undifferentiated beings. The other was the notion of society as composed of two classes differentiated by their level of rationality – those who were 'industrious and rational' and had property, and those who were not.... Locke would not be conscious of the contradiction between these two conceptions of society, because both of them ... were carried over into his postulates from his comprehension of his own society.[20]

The connection Macpherson makes between theories of civil society and the emergence of a capitalist market society can be buttressed by a wealth of historical evidence. In his study *John Locke and Agrarian*

Capitalism, for example, Neal Wood identifies the exact intersection between Locke's language of 'improvement', 'commonwealth' or 'labour' and the incipient agrarian capitalism characterized by the process of enclosure, the generalization of wage relations and the extension of the legal mechanisms necessary for their reproduction. This, according to Wood, indicates how Locke 'was indisputably a theorist of landed men and property but also of a society beginning to be transformed by agrarian capitalism, bringing with it changes expressed in his thought'.[21]

It was precisely this transformation which encouraged the growing identification of civil society with the distinct analytical and practical category of the 'economic' during the following decades. By the late eighteenth century, the association of civil society with a capitalist market society was accomplished through the emergence of the new science of political economy. In the writings of Adam Ferguson, Adam Smith and, a century later, Karl Marx, civil society became inextricably tied to the division of labour, the mass production of commodities and the extension of private property relations characteristic of modern capitalism.[22] In this respect, it is necessary to explore the origins and development of this new productive system and the attendant rise of the distinct sphere of the 'economic' as a second constitutive element of civil society.

Die Bürgerliche Gesellschaft: civil society as the capitalist market

The debates over the origins and consequent periodization of capitalism mirror similar disputes among the historians of economic ideas regarding the genesis of political economy. Most commentators situate the beginnings of political economy in seventeenth-century England with William Petty's 1662 *Treatise of Taxes and Contributions* as its founding text.[23] Others cite the economic tracts produced in Tudor England and Renaissance Italy as evidence of the earlier origins of modern 'economics'.[24] Despite the important differences which separate the economic thought of these three periods, a number of conceptual and practical innovations introduced at the turn of the fifteenth century marked the beginning of a new approach to wealth and its relationship to society at large.

The first of these features was the intense preoccupation with the accumulation of data relating to all aspects of commercial and productive life. While not an entirely new phenomenon, the scale and scope of these empirical investigations into rents, prices, money flows and, in the case of England, the amount of land enclosed or the number of poor in each parish signalled the emergence of a particular domain of the 'economic'. Price, value and interest had previously been explained with reference to a wider moral philosophy like scholasticism or natural law theory. By the seventeenth century, however, these phenomena were increasingly associated with an independent economic system, the logic of which could be expressed in abstract quantities. The systematic collection of statistics was therefore seen as the key to understanding the fluctuations in prices, population, wealth and so forth.

It is important to highlight, nevertheless, that this range of empirical data was used to sustain political arguments about the state of the nation. In his survey of what he describes as 'Tudor reformers', Neal Wood emphasizes that 'they did not collect such data for its own sake but for the purpose of discovering the causes of the depressing scene they witnessed and as the basis for recommending changes in governmental policy.'[25] The ongoing public debates about what to do with the nation's poor or how to increase the kingdom's wealth – expressed in countless tracts and pamphlets – were clearly part of the wider political struggles among the ruling classes. None the less, it is significant that the language employed in these debates already betrayed a distinction between technical matters pertaining to the domain of the 'economic' and the more subjective 'political' questions. Joyce Oldham Appleby makes this point particularly forcefully in her discussion of the early seventeenth-century economic thinker Thomas Mun. According to Appleby, Mun's pamphlets indicate how 'For the first time economic factors were clearly differentiated from their social and political entanglements. . . . In differentiating essential economic relations from contingent ones, Mun gave expression at the same time to the idea that the system of exchange was autonomous.'[26]

Thus, well over a century before Ferguson and Smith began to make the connection between capitalist market society and civil society, English intellectuals were preparing the way for this marriage by separating out the 'political' from the 'economic' spheres of public life. This differentiation, however, was not merely the child of a scientific revolution occasioned by a paradigmatic shift in the way wealth was conceived and quantified.[27] The pre-classical economists were describing and in some cases endorsing the gradual replacement of old social relations with those characteristic of capitalism: wage labour, separation from the direct means of subsistence, production geared toward the generation of exchange-value. Much of the new economic language of 'profit', 'improvement' or the 'advancement of private persons', for example, was derived from the ongoing process of land enclosure. Similarly, changing attitudes toward usury reflected the growing importance of credit in commerce and industrial or agricultural investment.[28]

In sum, the new discourse of political economy which developed in parts of Europe during the sixteenth and seventeenth centuries was the product of three interrelated transformations. First, a scientific revolution which lent authority to the idea that the systematic collection of empirical data could explain the logic behind fluctuations in prices, wages, population or interest rates. Second, an intense political debate – mainly fought out in England – surrounding the question of poverty and wealth which for the first time linked the fate of a particular state to the operation of an autonomous social sphere known today as 'the economy'. Third, and perhaps most important, the emergence of capitalist relations of production which underpinned these two developments by gradually separating whole populations from their immediate means of subsistence in order to create a society of individual wage-earners dedicated to the mass production of commodities. These were the transformations which engendered the type of society which Ferguson, Smith and, a century later, Marx encountered when analysing civil society. It is now time therefore to examine the relationship between capitalist market society and civil society in the work of these thinkers.

The approach of the Scottish Enlightenment to the idea of civil society is best summarized in the title of Adam Ferguson's *An Essay on the History of Civil Society* (1767). History, civility and society took on very particular meanings in the work of Ferguson, Smith and their contemporaries. In the first place, the idea of our inherent sociability was firmly entrenched in the world-view of the Scottish Enlightenment. Far from intuiting or implicitly recognizing the notion of society as Locke or Hobbes had done, Ferguson and Smith openly endorsed Montesquieu's dictum that 'Man is born in society, and there he remains.' The question therefore lay in explaining how and why societies differed across time and place.

This entailed the adoption of a distinctive philosophy of history. The understanding of history as a progression of humanity through various stages became central to the differentiation between modern civil society and previous forms of society.[29] This modern idea of history – derived from Vico and, again, Montesquieu – suggested that in order to explain the present type of society it was necessary to examine its *evolution*, thus imputing a particular logic or dynamic to history. Ferguson, for example, opens his *History* by drawing a parallel between humans' development and that of other living matter:

Natural productions are generally formed by degrees. Vegetables grow from a tender shoot, and animals from an infant state. The latter being destined to act, extend their operations as their powers increase; they exhibit a progress in what they perform.... This progress in the case of man is continued to a greater extent than in that of any other animal. Not only does the individual advance from infancy to manhood, but the species itself from rudeness to civilization.[30]

Although Ferguson is careful to point out the contingencies attached to historical development, his account of how certain societies progress from a 'rude' to a 'polished' state is ultimately rooted in an evolutionary view of history. In line with other theorists of civil society, Ferguson situates the motor of historical change in property: 'It must appear very evident that progress is a matter of property ... it is in reality the principal distinction of nations in the advanced state of mechanic arts.'[31] Different modes of subsistence – heavily conditioned in Ferguson's view by climatic factors – yield stages of social evolution which are represented in varying notions of property: 'Of the nations who dwell in ... the less cultivated parts of the world some intrust their subsistence chiefly to hunting, fishing, or the natural produce of the soil. They have little attention to property, and scarcely any beginnings of subordination to government.'[32] It is only in that mode of subsistence characterized by private property, the division of labour and the exchange of commodities that people come to inhabit a civil society: 'the prospect of being able to exchange one commodity for another turns, by degrees, the hunter and the warrior into a tradesman and a merchant.'[33] Furthermore, 'By the separation of arts and professions, the sources of wealth are laid open; every species of material is wrought up to the greatest perfection, and every commodity is produced in the greatest abundance.'[34]

There is hopefully no further need to elaborate the point that Ferguson, like his other contemporaries (most notably Adam Smith), came to identify civil society with capitalist market society. Central to this view was the idea that only the division of labour and the extension of commerce could bring about the prosperity and stability which characterized the 'polished' manners, art and polity of civil society. To be sure, Ferguson had some misgivings about the negative social and political consequences of the division of labour. The point remains, however, that the Scottish Enlightenment represented a culmination in the gradual shift from a 'political' to an 'economic' understanding of civil society.

It is therefore unsurprising to find Marx citing Ferguson in volume 1 of *Capital* in support of his claims about the alienation generated by the modern division of labour. Although Marx's contribution to the idea of civil society was for the most part written in response to Hegel, his interpretation of the concept was undoubtedly coloured by the eighteenth-century theorists examined above.[35] After all, Marx's central enterprise was to mount a 'critique of political economy' and this involved accepting the analytical parameters and much of the language of the subject of critique. This becomes readily apparent when considering two basic elements of Marx's understanding of civil society: its association with the sphere of private market relations between individuals, and its historical character as the defining threshold of modernity.

For Marx, civil society is defined above all as the arena of class conflict. Contrary to Hegel's formulation of civil society as a 'system of needs' which finds sociological expression in the formal estates-system, Marx argues that 'The estate of civil society...consists of separate masses which form fleetingly and whose very formation is fortuitous and does *not* amount to an organization.'[36] These 'separate masses' are defined in relation to the productive sphere: '*lack of property* and the *estate of direct* labour, of concrete labour, form not so much an estate of civil society as the ground upon which its circles rest and move.'[37] Hence, Marx is intent on highlighting how social power relations under civil society are defined by the emergence of two antagonistic classes – the bourgeoisie and the proletariat – whose existence hinges not on the political organization of the estates-system but on a particular organization of production. As Jean Cohen has suggested:

> By demonstrating that political estates and corporations contradict precisely the unique features of civil society that Hegel himself recognized – abstract right, private property, reciprocity, and exchange relations of the system of need – Marx shows that socioeconomic distinctions constitute the differentia specifica of stratification of modern civil society.[38]

What is interesting for our purposes, however, is that the 'differentia specifica' of modern civil society which Marx identified bore close resemblance to that investigated by the classical political economists. For Marx, as for Ferguson and Smith, the crucial precondition for the emergence of civil society lay in the separation of a private sphere of production and exchange from the public arena of the political state. Furthermore, this private domain of production was to be characterized by an exploitative division of labour which facilitated the exchange of commodities – including human labour-power – among

formally free and equal individuals. It is perhaps worth quoting Marx
in full on this point:

> Individuals have always proceeded from themselves, but of course,
> from themselves within their given historical conditions and rela-
> tions.... But in the course of historical development, and precisely
> through the fact that within the division of labour social relations
> inevitably take on an independent existence, there appears a cleavage
> in the life of each individual, insofar as it is personal and insofar as it is
> determined by some branch of labour and the conditions pertaining to
> it.... Thus, on the one hand, we have a totality of productive forces...
> which are for the individuals themselves no longer the forces of the
> individuals but of private property.... On the other hand, standing
> against these productive forces, we have the majority of individuals
> from whom these forces have been wrested away and who... have
> become abstract individuals, who are, by this very fact, put into a
> position to enter into relation with one another as *individuals*.[39]

Civil society is therefore associated with the private realm of relations
among individuals: a social space which was slowly wrenched away
from both the affective universe of the family and the formal domain
of the state through the triumph in Europe of capitalist relations of
production: 'Civil society comprises the entire material interaction
among individuals at a particular evolutionary stage of the productive
forces.... Civil society as such only develops with the bourgeoisie.'[40]

The emphasis on the historical nature of this transformation is
another instance of the overlap between Marx's understanding of
civil society and that of the Scottish Enlightenment. For Marx, civil
society represents 'an historical advance which has transformed the
political estates into *social* estates'.[41] The distinction between the state
and civil society which is hereby effected marks the beginning of the
modern epoch. As Marx boldly put it: 'The abstraction of the *state as
such* belongs only to modern times, because the abstraction of private
life belongs only to modern times. The abstraction of the *political state*
is a modern product.'[42] This identification of modernity with the
separation between civil society and the state, therefore, mirrors Ferguson and Smith's association of civil society with the latest stage in
human evolution. The historical force behind this transformation was,
in both cases, the expansion of capitalist market relations and the class
antagonisms they engender.

We have therefore seen how from the mid-eighteenth century onwards civil society became virtually synonymous with a particular
sphere of production and exchange. The modern state was gradually
seen and in some respects actually evolved as an institution separated

from the 'economic' and ostensibly only concerned with the domain of the 'political'. Far from negating the actual interrelationship between these two spheres, what the distinction between civil society and the state permitted was a clearer understanding of the dynamics of modern society. A vital component of this new arrangement was the birth of modern social movements within the ambit of civil society, a development to which I now turn.

The 'second family': civil society and the birth of modern political agency

The preceding sections have focused mainly on the sociological and ideological dimensions of civil society. Yet the idea of civil society has always borne a great deal of normative significance. Part of this relates, as we saw above, to its association with a rational and peaceful form of government, and to its central role within an evolutionary view of history. Most of the normative content of the idea of civil society, however, has been developed during the past two centuries in relation to the political possibilities which arise within this new social sphere, particularly for modern social movements. This section will therefore examine the key role of modern political movements in forging the space of civil society. By looking at the way in which thinkers such as Hegel, Gramsci, Habermas or Cohen and Arato identify civil society as the appropriate locus of modern political agency, I shall attempt to draw attention to the fact that civil society is also a social space marked by collective struggles for political domination and resistance.

Hegel is in many ways a controversial starting point for an analysis of the intersection between social movements and civil society. His own theory of civil society is a highly original amalgam of previous reflections on the theme, drawing on sources as diverse as ancient republicanism and Enlightenment political economy. As Cohen and Arato note: 'It is by now a commonplace that Hegel attempted to unite, in a scheme that was to be both prescriptive and descriptive, a conception of ancient *ethos* with one of the modern freedom of the individual.'[43] The modern, rational state, represented by a universal class of bureaucrats, was to embody this ideal; a prospect which, as John Keane has highlighted, 'constitute[s] a very broad licence indeed for state regulation and dominance of social life'.[44] It is this contradiction between Hegel's positing a realm of civil society lying between the family and the state, and his endorsement of the need for the state to intervene in civil society in order to uphold the universal interest, that has occasioned a scepticism about his relevance to a democratic theory concerned with social movements. While it is true, as Marx's critique pointed out, that Hegel had not registered the emergence of distinct socio-economic classes as bearers of particular political interests, he did incorporate, as we saw above, the idea of estates (*Stände*) as representatives of a particularly modern 'system of needs'. The constituents of civil society – associations, communities, corporations – were given by Hegel a pivotal sociological and normative role in linking the individual to the wider community realized in the state. In this respect, the independent sphere of civil society, though superseded by the universal interest of the rational state, *is* recognized by Hegel as having an important function within the project of an Ethical Life (*Sittlichkeit*). Perhaps a closer examination of the sociological and normative elements of Hegel's theory of civil society will illuminate its relevance for an understanding of civil society as the original site of modern political agency.

Civil society was identified by Hegel as a historically concrete space of social interaction among individuals. This interaction was conditioned by three elements: a 'system of needs' (broadly speaking, 'the economy'); an 'administration of justice' which protects property as the source of individual freedom; and 'the police and the corporation' as regulators of these two preceding spheres. Hegel explained the functioning of these elements in the following way:

> In the *system of needs*, the livelihood and welfare of each individual [*jedes Einzelnen*] are a *possibility* whose actualization is conditioned by the individual's own arbitrary will and particular nature, as well as by the objective system of needs. Through the administration of justice, infringements of property or personality are annulled. But the right *which is actually present in particularity* means not only that contingencies which interfere with this or that end should be cancelled [*aufgehoben*] and that the *undisturbed security* of *persons* and *property* should be guaranteed, but also that the livelihood and welfare of individuals should be *secured* – i.e. that *particular welfare* should be *treated as a right* and duly *actualized* [in the form of the police and the corporation].[45]

Thus, there is a great deal of overlap between Hegel's vision of civil society and that of his predecessors. The concept of a 'system of needs' is taken directly from the Scottish political economists, while Hegel's emphasis on the idea that civil society is inhabited by right-bearing individuals echoes Locke's formulation. Furthermore, Hegel shares with the Enlightenment commentators the notion that civil society is a product of that distinct historical epoch known as modernity. What is singular in Hegel is his recognition of the role played by social organizations in mediating the political relationship between the individual and the state. Hegel ascribes this role to estates which, representing the corporations, associations and communities of civil society, integrate the public and private spheres of social life:

> Viewed as a *mediating* organ, the Estates stand between the government at large on the one hand and the people in their division into particular spheres and individuals [*Individuen*] on the other . . . this position means that they share the mediating function of the organized power of the executive, ensuring on the one hand that the power of the sovereign does not appear as an isolated extreme – and hence simply as an arbitrary power of domination – and on the other that the particular interests of communities, corporations and individuals [*Individuen*] do not become isolated either.[46]

Hegel's invocation of intermediate associations and organizations of civil society must also be seen within the context of his wider normative project. In a sense, the chief purpose of *Elements of the Philosophy of Right* is to present an ethical and political alternative to the growing individual alienation imposed by modern society. Hegel recognizes the achievements of modern morality: its grounding on universal rationality and its respect for individual conscience. Yet, for Hegel, morality can only become meaningful if it operates within a community, if it is given content through the individual's involvement in public life. As Charles Taylor put it: 'Morality shows human moral life . . . as a purification of the will. But it cannot reach its goal of deriving the fullness of human moral duties from reason, nor realize these unless it is completed by a community, in which morality is not simply an "ought", but is realized in public life.'[47] It is at this juncture that the associative elements of civil society take on not only a representative but an ethical role by integrating individuals into the wider community, recognizing the value of their work and educating them in the virtues of civic life. The corporation, for Hegel, 'has the right to assume the role of *second* family for its members'.[48]

It should hopefully be clear by now that the originality of Hegel's formulation of civil society rests on his skilful combination of a sociological and political understanding of the concept. For Hegel, civil society represented both an independent sphere of ethical life and a mediating element within the wider community governed by the rational state. Hegel was unequivocal about the state's primacy over other spheres of society, yet he also insisted on the importance of allowing civil society to retain certain autonomy from the state. For John Keane, 'Ultimately, from his perspective, the relationship between state and society can be determined only by weighing up, from the standpoint of political reason, the advantages and disadvantages of restricting the independence, abstract freedom and competitive pluralism of civil society in favour of universal state prerogatives.'[49]

The antinomies of Hegel's political philosophy and their wider implications need not detain us here. What I hope to have pointed out is that Hegel's theory of civil society contained two important innovations. First, it made independent associations and public opinion a core component of civil society, granting them a role as political and ethical mediators between individuals and the state. Second, for all its invocation of the communal dimensions of human existence, Hegel's concept of civil society acknowledged the centrality of conscious, reflexive individuals in the construction of modern civil society.

These innovations have been taken up by a number of twentieth-century theorists of civil society. Antonio Gramsci, for example, adopted the Hegelian understanding of civil society in his interpretation of the failures of proletarian revolutions in Europe during the aftermath of World War I. He clearly explained the difficulties of revolutionary strategy in western societies with reference to the hegemonic role played by the independent institutions of civil society which complement the coercive rule of the state with sophisticated cultural mechanisms of consent. In order to challenge this hegemony, Gramsci contended, revolutionary forces – embodied in myriad social movements and cultural associations – must occupy the space of civil society created by western capitalist societies. In a different but related fashion, contemporary thinkers such as Jürgen Habermas or Jean Cohen and Andrew Arato place considerable emphasis on the role of social movements in the construction of a democratic public sphere. Similarly, Jeffrey C. Alexander has defended the view of civil society as a third domain between the market and the state: 'as a solidary sphere in which certain kind of universalizing community comes gradually to be defined and to some degree enforced'.[50] From this perspective, civil society is the realm where – in a republican vein – the potential for a properly 'civic' or 'civilized' form of politics emerges; one where 'economically underprivileged actors have a dual membership. They are not just unsuccessful or dominated members of the capitalist economy; they have the ability to make claims for respect and power on the basis of their only partially realized membership in the civil realm.'[51]

In short, broadly coinciding with the rise of modern forms of political agency, civil society has increasingly been associated with the political activism displayed by different social groups. On this account, civil society offers a public arena separated from both the market and the state where individuals and collectivities can, through successful mobilization, realize the full potential of modern liberal citizenship. To be sure, this conception of civil society situates the rise of social movements within the context of capitalist modernity, and often in opposition to the encroachments of the expanding state machinery. Yet the primary impulse behind civil society according to most contemporary theorists is a particularly modern form of political subjectivity.[52] As Cohen and Arato indicate, 'Modern civil society is created through forms of self-constitution and self-mobilization.'[53]

While this study shares this 'republican' view that civil society is intimately related to the rise of modern social movements, it none the less departs from the liberal rendition of the argument whereby civil society is differentiated through 'boundary relationships' from the 'non-civil spheres' of the market, state, religion or the family.[54] While acknowledging the open, indeterminate nature of socio-political struggles within civil society, the view adopted in this book is that such struggles are none the less resolved within the context of capitalist social relations which significantly structure, and therefore constrain, the potentiality of different social movements. In other words, and contrary to the liberal republicanism of Alexander or Cohen and Arato, I do not consider civil society as being beyond the power relations that characterize the state or the market, but rather as a domain where the class antagonisms inherent in the structural power of both state and market play themselves out, chiefly through the medium of social movements. In order to substantiate this claim it may be worth pausing briefly on the particular conception of social movements adopted here.

Chapter 3 will offer a full discussion and definition of modern social movements and collective socio-political agency. For present purposes, a social movement is considered as a sustained and purposeful collective mobilization by a group of people in pursuit of socio-economic and political change. It will be assumed throughout this book that distinctively modern forms of political subjectivity and organization emerged in Europe by the late eighteenth century and that these were subsequently reproduced across the world in the context of capitalist expansion. Accordingly, because of the *capitalist* nature of modern civil society, special emphasis will be placed upon the antagonistic class relations that inform and sustain such modern forms of political subjectivity. It is worth stressing from the outset that such a claim for the class character of modern social movements does *not* mean reducing all social movements to mechanical representations of a single set of class interests. Clearly, there exist a whole range of social movements that have successfully incorporated a diverse class membership, who have claimed to address political issues that cut across class. It does mean, however, analysing the genesis and development of modern social movements with reference to the class relations that uniquely shape capitalism and which therefore condition the nature of such movements. Moreover, as we shall shortly see, it is important to underline that non-capitalist classes often play a significant role in the unfolding of capitalist social relations and the consequent emergence of modern social movements.

Perhaps the best way of illustrating this class understanding of modern political agency is with reference to Jürgen Habermas's path-breaking study of *The Structural Transformation of the Public Sphere*. In that work Habermas emphasized the close connection between the rise of a distinctively modern, bourgeois 'public sphere' and the advent of capitalist civil society. Following the Marxist insistence on the peculiar separation of the political (public) and the economic (private) under capitalism, Habermas argued:

> The public sphere as a functional element in the political realm was given the normative status of an organ for the self-articulation of civil society with a state authority corresponding to its needs. The social precondition for this 'developed' bourgeois public sphere was a market that, tending to be liberalized, made affairs in the sphere of social reproduction as much as possible a matter private people left to themselves and so finally completed the privatization of civil society.... For in proportion to the increasing prevalence of the capitalist mode of production, social relationships assumed the form of exchange relationships. With the expansion and liberation of this sphere of the market, commodity owners gained private autonomy; the positive meaning of the 'private' emerged precisely in reference to the concept of free power of control over property that functioned in capitalist fashion.[55]

From this initial assumption, Habermas went on to examine in considerable detail the different expressions of this new European 'public sphere', including the political press, debating societies, coffee-houses and salons, book clubs and reading circles, the theatre- and concert-going public, and, paradoxically, secret societies and Masonic lodges. The outcome of this reformulation of 'publicity' and 'publicness' in eighteenth-century Europe was, according to the author, the birth of novel forms of political subjectivity premised on three 'institutional criteria' which could be roughly summarized as: equality; rational criticism; and openness.[56]

Inevitably, such bold propositions attracted widespread critical attention concerning, among other issues, historical interpretation, the gendered nature of the bourgeois public sphere and indeed its socio-political exclusiveness.[57] For present purposes, however, it may suffice to engage with two controversial aspects of Habermas's seminal work which are central to the arguments of this book.

The first of these was acknowledged by Habermas himself in the preface to the book, namely the absence of 'plebeian' or 'popular' socio-political activity in his account of the bourgeois public sphere.[58] This is not simply an empirical lacuna which can be either excused on heuristic grounds or corrected by 'bringing the plebeian back in'. It is a more substantial shortcoming in that it overlooks the historical constitution of the bourgeois public sphere through the antagonistic relations between classes emerging from civil society. As Geoff Eley has argued:

> [Civil society] was an arena of contested meanings, in which different and opposing publics manoeuvred for space and from which certain 'publics' (women, subordinate nationalities, popular classes like the urban poor, the working class and the peasantry) may have been excluded altogether. Moreover, this element of contest was not just a matter of coexistence, in which alternative publics participated in a tolerant pluralism of tendencies and groupings. Such competition also occurred in class-divided societies structured by inequality. Consequently questions of domination and subordination – power, in its economic, social, cultural, and political dimensions – were also involved.[59]

Drawing on the work of several historians of eighteenth-century British popular politics, Eley underlines the importance of understanding the practices and institutions of civil society and its attendant public sphere as arising from specific class antagonisms. Thus, for example, the late eighteenth century witnessed the rise in England of what Günter Lottes called a 'plebeian public'[60] or what John Brewer termed 'popular politics' *within* the confines of the bourgeois public sphere: 'While institutionalized politics stagnated, other means of political expression and new sources of political information became available to a public eager to express its (admittedly fairly unsophisticated) political views.'[61] Encouraged by the revolutionary upheavals in America and France – and in many cases arising directly in solidarity with such events – radical democratic organizations like the London Corresponding Society (LCS) or the Society for Constitutional Information (SCI) sprang up across metropolitan England with the express purpose of articulating the socio-economic and political interests of 'Tradesmen, Shopkeepers and Mechanics'.[62]

These manifestations of a growing 'plebeian' public sphere cannot be neatly categorized as working-class organizations, as the very term 'plebeian' or 'popular' suggests. The radical democratic social movements of eighteenth-century Europe arose in the context of societies that were still in the throes of a historical transition to modern forms of exploitation and political rule. In both town and country, 'labouring people' were exploited and subordinated through social relations that combined and complemented modern wage relations with pre-modern forms of appropriation such as rent, live-in labour, use-rights or guild-regulated filial contracts. Consequently, the 'popular' movements of the period straddled the ground between what E. P. Thompson has called 'the "vertical" consciousness of particular trades' and 'the "horizontal" consciousness of class'.[63] Indeed, in his further discussion of Lottes's work on the plebeian public sphere, Geoff Eley highlights how

> In adopting the democratic principle of 'members unlimited', the LCS itself not only committed itself to a program of popular participation but also to a 'confrontation with the traditional plebeian culture' of which it was certainly no uncritical admirer. As Lottes says, 'The Jacobin ideal of the independent, well-informed and disciplined citizen arriving at decisions via the enlightened and free discussion stood in crass contradiction with the forms of communication and political action characteristic of the plebeian culture.' In other words, riot, revelry, and rough music were to be replaced by the political modalities of the pamphlet, committee room, revolution, and petition, supplemented where necessary by the disciplined democracy of an orderly open-air demonstration.[64]

It should be clear from the above, then, that modern social movements arising out of civil society and its accompanying public sphere cannot be understood without reference to the broader class (i.e. exploitative) relations that characterized eighteenth-century Europe. This does not mean ascribing a unitary, homogeneous and necessarily self-conscious class character to all modern social movements, but it is to suggest that historically these novel forms of political subjectivity – these new 'publics', to adopt the preceding language – sprang from the very real class antagonisms generated by the revolutionary spread of capitalist social relations across that continent. Furthermore, it is worth underlining how remarkably analogous patterns of political subjectivity accompanied the reproduction of capitalism in later centuries, both in Europe and beyond. When considering the rise of trade unions, nationalist organizations or revolutionary parties in, say, the Maghreb or Indochina, similar tensions between modern and pre-modern forms of socio-political solidarity and organization arise, with the historical emergence of 'traditional' patrician and plebeian public spheres eventually being replaced by various modern social movements.[65]

The foregoing reflections on the relation between class and modern political subjectivity raise a second aspect of Habermas's account of the public sphere which is pertinent to the concerns of this study, and that is the contrast between the forms of 'publicness' which emerged in parliamentary Britain and those arising in the absolutist continent. Once again, Habermas is not oblivious to these structural differences between the British and 'continental' routes to modernity and readily acknowledges that 'Why conflicts that were thus fought out [in the bourgeois public sphere] by involving the public arose so much earlier in Great Britain than in other countries is a problem not yet resolved.'[66] One compelling answer to this question, which is by no means antithetical to Habermas's own perspective, is that offered by Ellen Wood in her study of 'old regimes and modern states':

> The capitalist system was born in England. Only in England did capitalism emerge, in the early modern period, as an indigenous national economy.... Other capitalist economies thereafter evolved in relation to that already existing one, and under the compulsions of its new systemic logic. Unprecedented pressures of economic competition generated a constant drive to improve the forces of production, in an increasingly international market and a nation-state system where advances in productivity conferred not only economic but geo-political and military advantage.[67]

The implications of adopting this account when explaining the unequal development of modern economic and political forms across Europe will be briefly addressed further below. At this stage the important thing to note is that, strictly speaking, civil society has historically found expression in two predominant forms – one linked to the private sphere of the capitalist market, the other to the struggles against the all-encroaching power of the state. Though by no means incompatible, these two manifestations of civil society do none the less account for the differences between the more open, constitutionalist and ultimately gradualist forms of popular protest that tend to characterize bourgeois democracies and the secretive, revolutionary and therefore more radical modes of contestation that arise out of social formations where the separation between state and civil society is not as pristine (for example, under absolutism or one-party dictatorships).

Following Charles Taylor's earlier distinction between the Lockean, market-based 'stream' and the Montesquian state-centred 'stream' in the understanding of civil society, we could reasonably contrast the reformist, economistic modes of protest that have characterized British civil society since the eighteenth century with the revolutionary, political and generally republican nature of the continental expressions of civil society. While the former were by the early nineteenth century squarely based around *economic* struggles for improved terms and conditions in the workplace, the latter still focused on the systems of privilege and patronage which defined the largely *political* mechanisms of appropriation of the *ancien régime*. Indeed, for Wood these differences in the degree of separation between state and civil society can account for contrasting patterns of working-class politics across the world: 'The most revolutionary movements have tended to be those in which militantly anti-capitalist working class struggles have been grafted on pre-capitalist struggles, especially those involving the state, and where "traditional" real communities have still been strong and collective loyalties of a kind increasingly destroyed by capitalism have still been available to reinforce new class solidarities.'[68]

Although it is important not to naturalize or exaggerate the foregoing differentiation between two forms of civil society – the 'international' does after all, as we shall shortly see, act as a conduit in the interaction between these contrasting forms of protest – such a distinction does at least drive home the point that there is no simple and mechanical correlation between the emergence of capitalism and the birth of modern forms of collective agency examined in this book. Rather, the causal links between these two processes are understood historically as arising through the international mediation between states and societies: the socio-economic and political transformations that accompanied the international expansion of civil society were effected through the combination of domestic class antagonisms and external pressures arising from inter-state competition, both economic and geo-political. Although capitalist social relations and political forms have acted as the dominant agents in this process, they have historically done so in articulation with pre-capitalist socio-political forces. The net result of this uniquely international combination has been the emergence since the eighteenth century of a differentiated but interconnected domain of modern socio-political action I have called international civil society.

The international dimensions of civil society

The preceding brief and necessarily selective survey of the way civil society has operated as a political, historical and sociological category identifies three basic elements of its constitution. In the first place, civil society assumes the possibility of analysing the systematic interaction between individuals in a scientific fashion. In other words, it marks the beginning of a distinctly *modern* view of society. The emergence of this new imagination of society, however, corresponds to the historical development of capitalist social relations. In this respect, civil society is rooted in bourgeois society. Third, the sociological understanding of civil society is given political and ethical content by modern social movements. Arising out of the class antagonism generated by capitalist reproduction are historically specific modes of socio-political mobilization and protest.

The claim I want to develop now is that civil society has from its inception been moulded by a number of international factors which warrant the adoption of the term *international civil society* as a more accurate category of social, political and historical analysis. Viewing civil society from a wider international perspective, it will be suggested, poses a challenge to the prevailing assumption that civil society can be restricted to a particular national setting. It allows us to examine the same phenomena that have traditionally preoccupied theorists of civil society, while at the same time encompassing the international aspects of its genesis.

Essentially, the international dimensions of civil society are threefold. In the first place, civil society must be seen as a constituent of the modern system of states. Whether understood as an autonomous sphere of economic activity or as the embodiment of a distinct type of political community, civil society emerged in conjunction with the modern sovereign state – the key component of the international system. Second, defined as the expression of capitalist market relations, civil society should be seen as an international phenomenon by virtue of its global expansion. In other words, it is fruitful, as the neo-Gramscians discussed in chapter 1 have done, to conceive of the global capitalist economy as the domain of international civil society. Last, when civil society is viewed as a political and ethical space occupied by modern social movements, the international dimensions of its operation become even more evident in that such movements have arguably always been subject to a host of transnational forces, both ideological and institutional. The combination of these three elements produces the following definition of international civil society: *Inter-national civil society is the socio-economic and political space created internationally and within states by the expansion of capitalist relations of production, where modern social movements pursue specific political goals.*

In what follows, I shall elaborate on this definition with reference to the three elements of international civil society. Special attention will be given to the last component, the functioning of international social movements, for it brings into focus the role of internationalism in reproducing international civil society. This is a concept that will figure prominently in many of the historical illustrations that follow, and it is also of considerable relevance to the normative implications of thinking about international civil society. For these two reasons, I shall spend some time identifying the basic features of international-ism as a political principle and practice – although it should be hastily added that international civil society cannot simply be reduced to the activity of international social movements. The concluding section of the chapter will signpost the analytical and normative promises of employing the term 'international civil society', thereby anticipating some of the themes to be developed in the closing chapter of the book.

Civil society and the construction of the system of states

One of the few obvious aspects of any definition of civil society is that it necessarily assumes reference to the modern state. Although, as we saw above, the nature of the interaction between these two cat-egories has varied through time, they have always been presented within the context of a relationship between two distinctive, if not always separable entities. The modern state being the traditional starting point for the analysis of the international system, it is reason-able to expect IR theorists to have paid more attention to the interplay between civil society and the state in the genesis of the modern states-system.

Yet it is only recently that IR theory has come to interrogate the nature of this relationship and its relevance for an understanding of the international system. In addressing the historical origins of the sovereign state, Justin Rosenberg has laid special emphasis on the place of civil society in this process. For Rosenberg, 'the structural specificity of state sovereignty lies in its "abstraction" from civil society – an abstraction which is constitutive of the private sphere of the market'.[69] Hence, the very possibility of thinking about state sovereignty – and, consequently, the modern international system – only arises when the separation between the 'political' and the 'economic' (state and civil society) is effected under capitalism.

This thesis is of course far from uncontroversial.[70] As Rosenberg readily admits, the historical evidence lends greater weight to the more conventional view that it was the rise of absolutism which – by centralizing the state apparatus, creating standing armies and marking a separation between the state's *internal* supremacy and *external* independence – paved the way for the emergence of a system of independent sovereign states. According to this view, civil society understood either as a market or as political community was inconsequential to the constitution of the modern international system. The emergence of the latter was principally the result of the landed nobility responding to the crisis of feudalism in Europe by concentrating political and economic power in a territorially defined absolutist state. In the words of Perry Anderson: 'The class power of the feudal lords was thus directly at stake with the gradual disappearance of serfdom. The result was a *displacement* of politico-legal coercion upwards towards a centralized, militarized summit – the Absolutist state.'[71]

Clearly, the historical origins of the modern international system remains the subject of a complex and unresolved debate which, though inconclusively, will be addressed at greater length in chapter 4. For the purposes of the present discussion, it may be worth pointing out that neither of the two accounts presented above ascribes a role to the social movements within civil society in the configuration of this new international system. Anderson refers to the centrifugal resistance to the absolutist state displayed at different times by varied groups such as the local nobility, merchants or lawyers, often in combination with a rural or urban 'mob'. Yet as was pointed out in the previous section, and indeed as chapter 4 will endeavour to show, the period also witnessed the gradual emergence of social movements employing a distinctly modern formulation of rights, constitutionalism and even democratic governance which reinforced the legitimacy of the territorial state as a political community. In other words, whether seen as a product of capitalism or absolutism, the modern state was given actual historical content not only by the ruling classes and their attendant systems of property and law, but also by a populace which increasingly identified this particular territorial entity as the locus of modern politics. One of the most noteworthy paradoxes of modern social and political movements, therefore, is that they operate at an international level while at the same time recognizing the political salience of the sovereign state. It is in this respect that international civil society becomes simultaneously an arena of domestic *and* international politics.

The chapters that follow will aim to illustrate in greater historical detail how looking at the emergence and reproduction of civil society can help us to understand key concepts in IR theory such as 'sovereignty', 'self-determination' or 'the standard of civilization'. It will be argued there that the notion of 'popular sovereignty' as a purveyor of self-conscious agency of collectivities has been instrumental in forging the modern states-system. At this stage, however, my aim is merely to highlight the part played by the incipient modern social movements in defining the political limits of the modern state, and hence their contribution to the construction of a modern system of states.

The expansion of international civil society

When civil society is identified as an arena dominated by capitalist relations of production, the international ramifications of the concept become even more apparent. This claim can be elaborated on from two vantage points. On the one hand, seen from an orthodox Marxian perspective, international civil society becomes synonymous with the global capitalist market; the organizations and corporations of capitalist production and exchange come to embody the 'economic' space of a borderless civil society which underscores the 'political' system of sovereign states. Thus, the relationship between the two spheres turns into a domestic analogy whereby international civil society stands in the same relation to the international system as civil society does for the state in a national setting. The position adopted here, however, eschews the domestic analogy and seeks to incorporate the dynamics of the international system into a broader definition of international civil society. While maintaining the notion that international civil society is a social and historical space created by the expansion of capitalism, the claim is also that this expansion altered the very nature of capitalist social formations. Thus, talking of international civil society involves recognizing not just the obvious fact that capitalism expanded globally but, furthermore, that it did so in a distorted fashion. The features which had originally defined capitalism in its European birthplace became refracted through the lens of international phenomena such as sovereignty, war, imperialism or revolution, and were articulated with pre-capitalist structures such as households, kinship networks, caste or indeed pre-existing political communities. The usage of international civil society employed here attempts to convey the intricate set of social and political relations which were thrown up by this process. Perhaps the best way of illustrating this point is through some examples.

Any analysis of international capitalism should involve an examination of European (and to a lesser degree Japanese and American) imperialism, for it was through this process that capitalist social relations were extended across the globe. The controversies over the exact nature of imperialism are of course manifold. None the less, at least three key elements are common to all historical forms of capitalist imperialism. First, the imperial state is at some stage involved in the imposition of capitalist social relations, either through war and conquest, or by means of indirect coercion such as unequal trade treaties and credit arrangements. Second, imperialism involves a mode of political subjugation which, far from laying the foundations of civil society via the establishment of a market of free labour, often employs all its coercive powers to extract surplus through mechanisms ranging from outright slavery to different forms of bonded labour. Third, and not least important, this form of capitalist expansion finds legitimacy in notions of racial supremacy, so that the modes of appropriation are heavily conditioned by racial, ethnic or religious hierarchies which justify unequal market relations.

If we take the case of the Maghreb as an example, the nature of French capitalist penetration bore all the hallmarks of imperialism just mentioned. Algeria and, later, Tunisia and Morocco were invaded under the pretext of safeguarding French financial and strategic interests. In all three cases, but particularly in Algeria, invasion was followed by violent 'pacification' and forced expropriation of land which was subsequently occupied by European settlers. The legal administrative structures erected by the invading power effectively divided the population along two categories: that of the local *indigène* and that of the white *colon*. Thus the upshot of this whole process was certainly the introduction of capitalist relations of production in North Africa, that is, the expansion of international civil society. Yet, because imperialism was the primary agent of this development, the forms of capitalist social relations which emerged in the Maghreb were significantly different from those existing in Europe. The interaction between French and North African civil societies must be seen within its appropriate international context: one of imperialist domination articulated around various racial and national hierarchies and enforced through direct state intervention.

Of course, the extension of capitalist social relations has also taken non-imperialist routes. The Meiji Restoration in Japan is typically cited as an example of state-led capitalist transformation, while in many parts of the world, most notably in Latin America, capitalism made inroads either directly through the mechanisms of the global market or through local middle-men, dubbed by some theorists as the 'comprador bourgeoisie'. There is hopefully no need to labour the point further that world capitalism is what Eric Wolf terms a 'differentiated' mode of production where different modes of exploitation are articulated by the overarching framework of capitalist social relations.[72] The relevant conclusion in terms of our argument is that the category 'international civil society' should suggest much more than an alternative formulation of the global capitalist market. It should represent an approach to the expansion of capitalism which incorporates a host of international dimensions (such as nationalism, ethnic and religious stratification, revolutions or imperialism itself) into the Marxian understanding of civil society as a private sphere of capitalist production and exchange.

International civil society as the arena of international political agency

The foregoing discussion on the nature of world capitalism bears direct relevance to the subject matter of this last section in two important respects. First, it is the extension of capitalist social relations which best explains the emergence across the world of the modern social movements that have been the protagonists of international civil society over the past two centuries. Most political expressions of modern civil society – be they liberal pressure groups, women's movements, nationalist parties or socialist organizations – arise out of class relations present only under capitalism. As was noted earlier, this does not mean that capitalism *necessarily* produces these forms of organization, nor that it is the only force responsible for their emergence. It does mean, however, that historically the forms of modern political agency typical of civil society spring from the socio-economic transformations brought about by capitalism.

Second, and not least important, the uneven expansion of world capitalism examined above engenders a variety of social and political forces which, although broadly comparable, exhibit a number of particularities. As was briefly discussed in chapter 1, positing universal forms of social and political agency does not preclude recognizing their diversity. Indeed, returning to the case of North Africa, it was precisely the reproduction of capitalist social relations in the

Maghreb that generated modern social movements with myriad political programmes: reformist liberals; populist nationalists; socialist and communist parties and trade unions; Islamic revivalists. These movements were in one way or another the product of the expansion of international civil society; yet they simultaneously contested the social and political implications of this process, sometimes in unison and most often in competition with each other. In other words, far from generating homogeneous replicas of an archetypal modern social movement, the expansion of international civil society produced very specific manifestations of universal forms of social and political agency.

Taken together, these two considerations provide the backdrop against which we can examine the normative dimension to the idea of international civil society. The expansion of capitalism only opens up the sociological space of international civil society; in the last instance, however, this space is given political content through the international activity of social movements, both within and across states. I shall now turn to the nature of these movements, how they are defined internationally and how they represent the political space of international civil society.

Taking the earlier definition of modern social movements as a starting point, the claim defended here is that such movements have from their inception been conditioned by international factors in at least three important respects. First, as suggested in chapter 1, virtually all social movements are premised on some form of universal political agency. For the socialist, it is the working class which plays this role; for the feminist, it is women who are the political agents of their own emancipation; for the nationalist, it is the imagined community of the nation which carries this burden. In all three cases, there is an explicit assumption that 'women', 'nations' or 'the working class' exist as potential political agents in all parts of the world. To take a random but illustrative example, the People's International League, a cross-European association established in 1847 by the Italian nationalist Giuseppe Mazzini, defined its objectives thus:

> to disseminate the principles of national freedom and progress; to embody and manifest an efficient public opinion in favour of the right of every people to self-government and the maintenance of their own nationality; to promote a good understanding between the peoples of every country.[73]

A cursory glance at the history of social and political movements of the past two centuries would reveal a sizeable number of similar tracts where the potential audience of the message is consciously deemed to be international. There are plainly some significant exceptions to this general rule: many modern social movements – the National Socialist German Workers' Party or the *Vishwa Hindu Parishad* (World Hindu Council), to take but two examples – are built around exclusionary notions of race and religion. Yet even these overtly racist and national-chauvinist movements have been forced to identify international counterparts to their socio-political programmes. Thus, for example, the Nazi regime sought to enlist the support of assorted pan-Arab nationalists during the late 1930s and in the course of World War II, often successfully implanting fascist ideology in that region but thereby also challenging some of the existing racialist doctrine relating to the inferiority of 'semitic races'.[74] As we shall see in chapter 3, all this doesn't necessarily make such movements *international* social movements, but it does highlight how even the most particularist of social movements cannot escape the challenge of 'the international' to their ideology, organization and actions: to that extent they can be seen as part of the sphere of international civil society. In sum, and notwithstanding the aforementioned exceptions, the very consideration that a particular political discourse might be relevant outside the original national or regional context of its genesis suggests that, at an *ideological* level, most modern social movements have been international from the start.

The most solid evidence in favour of the idea that modern social movements constitute an international phenomenon, however, lies in a study of their forms of organization. Clearly, modern movements which espouse universal ideologies also attempt to realize those aspirations in practice. Thus, again, a historical survey of the organizational forms of the relevant modern social movements indicates a clear international, when not overtly internationalist, disposition. Consider the women's movement, for example. Since the mid-nineteenth century, women have organized internationally with the intention of furthering their common interests across the globe. Emerging out of existing international associations like the Anti-Slavery League or the Socialist International, feminist internationalism took shape in the form of organizations such as the International Congress of Women (established in 1888), the International Women's Suffrage Alliance (1904) or the Socialist Women's International (1907).[75] Although the general objectives of the various organizations which formed the international women's movement differed considerably, the single common denominator remained the explicit attempt at transgressing the existing national political boundaries. This aspiration was realized by a number of organizations which, although predominantly European and North American in membership, still managed to attract sympathizers in Turkey, Iran, South Africa and Argentina. Thus, by the time the women's movement re-emerged as a 'new' social movement in the late 1960s, the international women's movement had a rich experience as a representative of international civil society. Similar stories could be told of the liberal, pacifist, socialist and even environmentalist movements which have been the mainstay of civil society across the world.

These various experiences fall under what in the rest of this book will be described as the principle and practice of 'internationalism'. The notion of internationalism arose during the latter part of the nineteenth century in response to the momentous socio-economic and political changes that were transforming the lives of millions across the world. The emerging 'universal interdependence of nations' captured so vividly by Marx and Engels in their 1848 *Communist Manifesto* was simultaneously generating attempts at forging a corresponding 'universal interdependence of peoples'. This aspiration to create bonds of solidarity among groups of different national, religious and ethnic backgrounds was expressed first as a *principle* which celebrated the internationalization of the world as a positive process which could facilitate the pursuit of universal political goals such as peace, democracy, equality or freedom.[76] Additionally, internationalism came to reflect a particular *practice* of social and political organization of people across national, ethnic or religious boundaries. In the specific case of working-class internationalism, this was realized in the form of the International Working Men's Association (IWMA) or First International formed in 1864, and later in the Second and Third Internationals, founded in 1889 and 1919, respectively.[77] Understood in this way, internationalism becomes both cause and consequence of the expansion of international civil society: internationalist solidarities were certainly encouraged by the increasing interpenetration of societies across the world; yet at the same time a heightened consciousness of this process among, for example, the European working class led to pre-emptive initiatives in internationalist activism geared toward undermining the greater mobility and power of capital. The upshot of all this is that the emergence in a particular society of modern social movements typical of civil society cannot be explained with reference to 'domestic' factors alone. Historically, the principle and practice of internationalism have played a crucial role in extending modern modes of social and political action across the world. In this respect, although international civil society should not be reduced to the practices and principles of internationalism, the latter has certainly been instrumental in encouraging the international reproduction of modern forms of social and political agency.

A last element in the international constitution of modern social movements is what, for want of a less overbearing phrase, can only be described as the impact of world-historical conjunctures. Even when there is no direct organizational affiliation, or a deliberate attempt at ideological propagation, social movements can emerge in a given location in response to events occurring elsewhere in the world. Revolutions provide the classic instance of this type of phenomenon. Whether one considers the democratic revolutions of the late eighteenth century, the socialist and radical nationalist revolutions of the twentieth, or even the Iranian revolution of 1978–9, there is plenty of evidence to suggest that the demonstrative example of these events inspired the creation of social movements typical of civil society in parts of the globe where they had previously been absent. Less dramatic perhaps, but still very much relevant, the political success of a given social movement – the civil rights movement in the US or the Latin American self-help *barrio* associations – clearly impact upon the formation of movements elsewhere without there being any formal links between groups. One interesting instance of this was the adoption by Catholics in Northern Ireland of the language and methods of their black counterparts in the southern United States during their own struggle for civil rights in the postwar decades.

In each of these three respects, then, the international emerges as a key component of modern social movements which inhabit civil society. Cast in this light, international civil society represents a political space which has been constructed over the past 300 years by the international activity of modern social movements. By espousing and propagating universal ideologies; by providing examples of how collective action can be politically meaningful across the globe; and, most importantly, by organizing internationally, modern social movements have for decades been extending the boundaries of political action beyond the territorial state. It is in this sense that international civil society becomes the relevant site of world politics. Taken in conjunction with the preceding arguments on the relevance of civil society when explaining the construction of the modern state and the global reproduction of capitalism, a strong case can be made for considering civil society, and the phenomena it gives rise to, as being inherently international. Thinking of civil society as a social and political space that simultaneously transcends and reinforces territorial boundaries opens new normative and analytical horizons which I shall briefly outline in the concluding section of this chapter.

Conclusions: the promises of international civil society

The notion of an international or global civil society gradually emerging in the aftermath of the Cold War and out of the process of 'globalization' has over the past few years captured the imagination of numerous scholars, commentators and activists the world over. The phenomenal growth in the number of international non-governmental organizations (INGOs) and their often spectacular interventions in different parts of the globe have prompted further talk of 'civil society and its transnational networks [embodying] the *universum* which competing nations have never succeeded in creating'.[78] While the arguments outlined in this book are broadly sympathetic to this point of view, there are none the less a number of important differences between the approach adopted here and that offered by the existing theories of international civil society. Considering these differences more closely may help to elucidate the analytical and normative value ascribed in this study to the notion of international civil society.

The first significant contrast refers to the historical origins of international civil society. The assumption underlying most discussions of civil society is that it developed within a national context. Accordingly, the existing literature on international or global civil society concurs with the idea that this is a space of political action which has only recently shown signs of 'becoming global'[79] or which, less optimistically, 'is still more potential than actual'.[80] The evidence offered in this chapter has attempted to suggest otherwise. As has been indicated, even when the term civil society is deployed in a more traditional sense to refer to the capitalist market or to a particularly modern form of political community, there appear a number of international dimensions to its genesis and later development which suggest that the category 'international civil society' is applicable to the dual process of capitalist development and state formation begun in early modern Europe – a long shot from the post-modern world of 'globalization'. When civil society is defined as a space occupied by modern social movements, however, the case for dating the emergence of an international civil society in the late eighteenth century becomes even stronger. An analysis of the expansion of the diverse eighteenth-century public spheres or the various types of nineteenth-century internationalism should persuade any student of international civil society that the forms of political agency associated with this realm long pre-dated contemporary transnationalism or 'post-international' politics. All this does not mean that the new expressions of international political agency – be they INGOs, humanitarian organizations, 'critical' social movements or whatever – should not be considered part of international civil society. Rather, the point is to situate them in their appropriate historical setting; that is, as part of a sphere which has been developing since at least the eighteenth century.

This reappraisal of the historical origins of international civil society, however, has deeper implications than simply setting back the dates of its emergence. It retrieves two key analytical advantages in employing the term which have been overlooked by most commentators. The first of these relates to the question of modernity and the international system. With the exception of Marxists like Justin Rosenberg or Mark Rupert, few if any IR scholars using the term have developed the implications of civil society being associated with a distinct historical epoch (i.e. 'modernity'). As Rosenberg has so eloquently argued, this is crucial in both de-naturalizing the states-system and providing a richer explanation of its emergence. Yet even as nuanced a usage as Rosenberg's fails to identify civil society with the modern forms of political agency discussed above. Furthermore, there is no recognition of the international features of these new modes of political protest and organization. If the argument outlined in this chapter is compelling, then surely the concept of international civil society can serve as a framework in understanding the distinctly modern forms of political agency which have forged the present international system.

Derived from this identification of international civil society with modernity is a second theoretical advantage of the concept, namely its emphasis on the necessary interaction between the state and the social forces of civil society during this epoch. As was pointed out in the preceding chapter, too much of the literature on global or international civil society focuses exclusively on the transnational non-state actors in world politics without paying sufficient attention to their relationship with the state. The notion of international civil society on the other hand allows us to consider this interface without thereby losing sight of societal forces. The aim here is not to play off a societal reading of international relations against a statist one, but rather to investigate the grey areas where these two interpretations meet: in other words, to probe the historical interaction between state and civil society within an international setting. In order to accomplish this, we could do worse than employ the concept of 'international civil society' which takes the language provided by the classical thinkers of civil society and places it within an appropriate international context.

A last discrepancy between the prevalent understanding of international or global civil society and the one adopted here revolves around the type of political promise which the concept holds. Few scholars interested in international civil society would disagree with Ronnie Lipschutz's remarks to the effect that 'global civil society represents an ongoing project of civil society to reconstruct, reimagine, or re-map world politics.'[81] One ambition of this book, after all, is precisely to identify the ways in which the agents of international civil society have extended the boundaries of the political. The key question, therefore, remains what kind of shape will this world politics take?

One type of answer to this question insists on the impossibility of employing the political idiom of modernity under post-modern conditions. As we saw in chapter 1, authors such as R. B. J. Walker – one of the few IR scholars who has seriously engaged with the role of social movements in world politics – have argued that 'An empirical analysis of social movements, and an interpretation of their significance for what world politics might become, does not have to be bound by the prejudices of modernity. On the contrary, these prejudices can only ensure that the fine lines separating us from them can never be transgressed.'[82]

As a philosophical critique of the excesses of modernity, this kind of stance provides ready solace for those 'anti-systemic' academics disenchanted with the failure of modernist political projects. As a recipe for political action, however, it offers little more than vague invocations about the creation of loose 'networks' and spontaneous 'connections' which might bring together the 'silenced' and the 'subaltern' in world politics. When asked to produce empirical evidence of the kind of movement which might inform this alternative world politics, reference is made to the obscurantist Hindu revivalism of the *Swadhyaya* movement in western India.[83] Ultimately, the relevance of this type of political agency for world politics can only be assessed with the passing of time. The contemporary experience, however, suggests that it has been modern social movements which, through strike action, mass demonstrations, party-political activism and international solidarity campaigns, have managed to effect meaningful political change in places as diverse as southern Europe, Latin America, South Africa or East Asia.[84] Surely it is the example of these kinds of struggle – and not mystical Vedic cosmologies – that a progressive world politics should build on.

A second kind of response to the role of international civil society in world politics focuses more exclusively on the actions of INGOs and international pressure groups. From this perspective – mainly connected with the field of development studies – international civil society represents that space occupied by associations which, although working in collaboration with the different tiers of the state and international organizations, are officially independent and ultimately only accountable to their international membership. Furthermore, since they pursue specific political goals across boundaries, they hold the promise of a new type of world politics. As Mark Hoffman has pointed out, INGOs informed by notions of 'international citizenry' may 'provide a basis for forms of intervention which seek to extend the boundaries of political community while undermining systems of exclusion'.[85] In these two respects, the increasingly complex web of INGO activity often receives the label 'international civil society'.

This understanding of international civil society is plainly at odds with some of the theoretical issues raised here – chiefly concerning questions of epochal change and the relationship to the state. Yet there are two further relevant differences regarding the political vistas opened up by INGO activities. The first and most obvious point is that INGOs are fundamentally pressure groups which do not contest the overall legitimacy of a specific regime but merely seek to alter a particular policy – on human rights, environmental law, women's rights and so forth. They therefore eschew campaigning for structural socio-political change. The conception of international civil society adopted here, however, has maintained that many modern social movements have been precisely concerned with effecting such grand-scale transformations at an inter-state level. Thus, international civil society is identified as a political space which includes 'grand narratives' that can still envisage the possibility of global changes in the socio-economic and political structure of a given society. Secondly, and following on from this point, there remains a degree of ambiguity over the accountability of INGOs. As we shall see in chapter 5, the fact that INGOs are 'non-governmental' does not mean that they are 'non-political'; indeed, their activity necessarily impinges upon existing political communities. Yet few INGOs are willing to recognize the full implications of participating in a given political community – one of which involves defining the sources and limits of a group's political accountability. Other modern social movements, however, have accepted the political nature of their activity from the outset, thus making it very clear to whom they are accountable and in whose interests they participate within a given political community. If international civil society is to be considered as a possible site of progressive world politics, it would seem more appropriate to fix such hopes on the agency of social movements which at least enjoy some democratic legitimacy, rather than on organizations that fail to identify the sources of their political accountability.

Taken in conjunction with the foregoing theoretical discussion, these two general observations on the politics of international civil society suggest that this is still an arena dominated by modern forms of political agency. The argument of this chapter has been that understanding international civil society in this light might provide a clearer and more historically informed picture of the way emancipatory social movements can organize internationally in the future. It has also been the intention of this chapter, however, to indicate how the idea of international civil society can serve as a tool for analysing the contribution of collective socio-political agency to the emergence and development of an international society of states, and indeed the structural limits of such contributions. These interrelated issues are the concern of the following two chapters.

3

Agencies and Structures in IR

Analysing International Social Movements

Chapter 1 emphasized the necessary interconnection between the idea of international civil society and the practice of collective social and political agency. Indeed it was further argued in the preceding chapter that among the key characteristics of civil society is a specifically modern form of engaging in collective socio-political action, generally mediated through modern social movements. Yet it was equally acknowledged that such social movement activity occurs within the confines of concrete social structures (like, for example, the states-system) which simultaneously form and are transformed by our individual and collective agency. This constant interaction between agency and structure – what, it will be recalled, Philip Abrams termed 'the two-sidedness' of the social world – has been a mainstay of modern social theory, and is the central concern of the present chapter.

In some respects, it may appear counterproductive to retrieve this notoriously irresolvable 'debate' in the humanities between structural and voluntarist explanations of our social world; between necessity and freedom or 'holism' and 'individualism'. Discussions of agency and structure have all too often given social theorists licence to engage in simplifying polemics or arguments that tend to run in circles. Certainly in the field of IR, the 'agency–structure' debate has been framed in such highly abstract terms that the reasons for engaging with the debate in the first place often get lost in the mist of arguments over ontology and epistemology. It is therefore not my intention in the pages that follow to enter the fray of this particular debate in support of either 'agency' or 'structure', nor to offer a comprehensive alternative to the current formulation of the debate in IR. Rather, the more modest aim of this chapter is to situate the analysis of international social movements within the broad sociological problematic of agency and structure; or, put differently, to examine the role of social movements in bringing about change in the international system. In line with the criticisms levelled at the 'new transnationalists' in chapter 1, and in anticipation of the arguments to be developed in chapter 5 against those who see in international or global civil society the end of state sovereignty, this chapter seeks to identify some of the structural *limitations* to international socio-political agency. For, although students of international social movements have over the past two decades offered detailed and comprehensive accounts of how diverse political activists across the world organize internationally, they rarely seek to flesh out the explanatory potential of studying international social movements. Such primarily descriptive accounts tend to conflate the self-proclaimed aspirations and objectives of international social movements with their *actual* impact, thereby falling into the trap of an excessively subjectivist and therefore one-sided view of the 'two-sidedness' of our international social world. It is in this respect that the problematic of agency and structure becomes a useful framework when analysing international social movements and their interaction with the structures of international politics.

This chapter is divided into four main sections. The first part is dedicated to a definition of social movements and a brief discussion of the historical specificity of modern social movements. A second section will elaborate on the definition of international social movements offered in the previous chapter, identifying what is particular about this form of social action. This broadly descriptive exercise will eventually feed into the core theoretical focus of this chapter, namely the place of international social movements in the explanation of international change. It will be argued there that a crucial precondition in this endeavour is to develop clear notions of structure, agency, causality and change. Thus, this part of the chapter spends some time considering the broader social-scientific use of these concepts and their centrality to the study of IR. Finally, a brief concluding section makes a case for the more explicit incorporation of international socio-political activism in the theoretical debates on agency and structure in IR. Taking the recent work of Justin Rosenberg and Jan Aart Scholte as reference points, it will be suggested that the discipline of IR alternately ignores or exaggerates the role of international social movements in explaining international change. Overall, therefore, this

chapter aims to consider from an international perspective three key
and necessarily interrelated aspects of modern social life: agency,
structure and change.

What is a modern social movement?

A 'social movement' is a notoriously slippery concept to define. In a
quip that was probably not meant to be entirely facetious, Joe Foweraker once commented of Latin American social movement theory that
'A wide variety of disparate social phenomena have suddenly been
certified by the new social movement label. In some accounts it
appears that folk dancers, basket weavers and virtually any form of
social or economic life may qualify. But not everything that moves is a
social movement.'[1] Indeed, though in some special circumstances folk
dancing and basket weaving (or, more frequently, rock concerts and
Friday prayers) may acquire social and political significance *as part* of
a broader social movement, common sense suggests that these cannot
be considered as political movements in the same sense as are, say,
trade unions or peasant guerrillas. What is required therefore is some
explanatory hierarchy when analysing the socio-political impact of
diverse expressions of collective action; or at the very least some
criteria for differentiating forms of social action – such as basket
weaving – that are routinized by custom, tradition or other sets of
norms, and which therefore lack an inherent political purpose, from
modes of collective action – such as that of modern social movements
– which have an explicit socio-political content and directionality.
   One such set of criteria was that proposed by Perry Anderson in his
famous critique of E. P. Thompson's notion of agency. In that intervention, Anderson suggested (in a Weberian vein) that agency is
defined above all by goal-oriented activity and that it is therefore
helpful to separate out what he termed 'private' and 'public' goal-
oriented actions, such as cultivating a plot of land or contracting
marriage, from what might be called 'transformative' modes of agency
geared to the conscious overhaul of existing social structures.[2] The
latter display a directed and purposeful collective confrontation with
specific structures and agents of power which is absent from other
customary or normative (i.e. rule-governed) collective endeavours
such as organizing a birthday party or attending a football match.
Moreover, the implication of this counterposition is that 'transformative' modes of collective agency such as a revolutionary general strike

or an armed insurrection (or, less dramatically, a political party stand-ing for and winning legislative elections) tend to have a greater impact on the existing socio-political structures than private or customary acts such as basket weaving or folk dancing. Thus, both in terms of aspirations and causal effects, Anderson's differentiation indicates that 'transformative' agency can be meaningfully contrasted with other forms of agency.

With these basic distinctions in mind, a social movement can be defined as a sustained and purposeful collective mobilization by an identifiable, self-organized group in confrontation with specific power structures, and in the pursuit of socio-economic and political change. Such a definition hopefully allows us to place social movements squarely in the camp of transformative agency, thus offering an initial justification to the claim that 'not everything that moves is a social movement'. This preliminary definition of social movements, however, immediately throws up at least two further issues which need to be addressed here. The first relates to what exactly counts as 'transforma-tive' agency; the second to the historicity of social movements.

Under the interpretation just offered, any group that mobilizes for (or against) socio-economic and political change can be considered as a social movement. Thus, in principle, entities as diverse as non-governmental organizations (NGOs), religious associations, single-issue campaigns or indeed political parties could potentially qualify as social movements. Yet, notwithstanding the fact that the boundar-ies between social movements and other forms of socio-political asso-ciation or protest are always relatively porous (social movements can, after all, originate within religious associations and, likewise, social movements have often become political parties), there are two dimen-sions to the definition of social movements offered above that exclude some of these expressions of collective agency. First, a social move-ment must have the capacity to *mobilize* its constituency or member-ship and, second, such mobilization must be *sustainable* over a period of time. On this view, an NGO or a single-issue campaign can only properly be considered a social movement once it mobilizes a group of people for a specific socio-political goal over an extended period of time. Only then is it possible to identify the 'transformative' nature of a given social movement and indeed distinguish it from one-off riots, demonstrations, petitions or rallies – all of which certainly form part of the 'repertory' of protest available to social movements, but which by themselves lack the sustained directionality that would make talk of *movement* meaningful. In other words, the 'transformative' agency of social movements requires that collective mobilization be sustained over a sufficient period of time to identify and evaluate the direction and success (or otherwise) of any given attempt at effecting socio-political change. Whether such change is progressive or reactionary, reformist or revolutionary, short-term or enduring, is not at issue here. Rather, what is at stake is the idea of modern social movements necessarily assuming the possibility of steering history into specific directions through self-conscious collective action. *What* the direction is does not matter in this instance; what matters is that there *is* a direction. From this perspective, then, the analytical currency of the term 'social movement' rests upon its capacity to identify and explain not just how collectivities *intervene* in the political system or *engage with* given structures and agents of power (as do, say, pressure groups or lobbyists), but, more substantively, how they also construct pro-grammatic socio-political goals to be achieved over time by a mobil-ized constituency.

The relevance of these laborious distinctions will hopefully become apparent when the centrality of social movements in explaining inter-national change is discussed below. Before doing so, however, it is important to underline a second reason why the above definition is of some consequence in our understanding of social movements, namely that it allows us to explore the historical specificity of modern social movements. For, on the interpretation just offered, social movements can be readily identified across different historical periods. The slave uprisings in the ancient world, the Hussite revolution of late four-teenth-century Bohemia or the Mahdist revolt of nineteenth-century Sudan can all be reasonably interpreted as instances of pre-modern social movements in action. Yet, as has already been intimated (and as chapter 4 will seek to illustrate in greater detail), the 'long' sixteenth century witnessed innovations in the modes of popular protest in Europe which by the late eighteenth century had consolidated into distinctively modern forms of collective socio-political action. Perry Anderson's discussion of 'transformative' agency is, together with other similar studies,[3] quite explicit about the novelty of modern social movements:

> Finally there are those collective projects which have sought to render their initiators authors of their collective mode of existence as a whole, in a conscious programme aimed at creating or remodelling whole social structures. There are isolated premonitions of this phenomenon ... but essentially this kind of agency is very recent indeed. On a major scale, the very notion of it scarcely predates the Enlightenment.[4]

Let us consider in greater depth this claim for the historical particu-larity of modern social movements.

The first thing to say about modern social movements is that their temporal specificity must be treated with some degree of flexibility. This is the case in two interrelated senses. First, like all historical transformations, the transition from pre-modern to modern forms of socio-political collective action is never a clear-cut process. The discussion thus far has suggested that in Europe this transition took place in a highly uneven and protracted fashion over almost 200 years, from the turn of the seventeenth to the late eighteenth century. Furthermore, many features associated with pre-modern forms of collective agency often survive in modern social movements. Preachers and preaching, for example, are characteristically linked to pre-modern forms of political action where charismatic leadership and the oral transmission of political messages are instrumental in collective mobilization. Yet these phenomena are plainly also recognizable in contemporary, modern politics. The crucial difference, however, is that, whereas pre-modern preachers like Joachim of Fiore or Jan Huss were self-appointed prophets whose authority was exclusively premised on their messianic role as intermediaries between God and his earthly flock, modern preacher-politicians such as Martin Luther King Jr are democratically elected into a position of authority and are seen to be accountable not to God or other-worldly forces, but to a constituency seeking concrete, this-worldly results: in this instance, the advancement of civil rights for black Americans.[5] Preachers and preaching, in other words, take on substantively different forms under modern and pre-modern politics.

To take another example, the petition is a medium familiar to both modern and pre-modern forms of protest. Yet, again, a critical distinction obtains between the norms of deference, secrecy and privilege that regulated medieval petitioning in Europe, and the modern expression of petitioning generally characterized by factionalism, publicity and the assumption of equality. In an illuminating study of petitions and public opinion in seventeenth-century England, David Zaret makes the analytical point thus:

> In the 17th century, innovative use of petitions facilitated the 'invention' of public opinion. This development superseded the norms of secrecy and privilege in political communication.... Printing in the English revolution pushed petitioning and other traditional communicative practices in new directions that altered the content as well as the scope of political communication. It appealed to the anonymous body of opinion. A public that was both a nominal object of discourse and a collection of writers, readers, printers and petitioners engaged in political debate.[6]

This recognition of the occasional overlap between modern and pre-modern forms of protest leads to a second paradoxical dimension to the historicity of modern socio-political agency, namely that pre-modern social movements often emerge and develop within very modern contexts. The examples cited above suggest that modes of political agency are significantly conditioned by the socio-economic and political structures of the specific social formation under which they operate, i.e. that they form part of a broader totality of social relations. Thus, for example, the norms that governed medieval petitioning in Europe were plainly enmeshed within the wider juridico-political structures of feudal and (in towns and communes) oligarchic rule of that continent. Yet, here again, history does not unfold neatly into discrete, clearly demarcated stages, but rather develops unevenly, combining and often resurrecting different socio-economic and political structures and processes which generate historically unique social formations. Accordingly, collective agents often find themselves acting with old, pre-modern political tools in a new, modern social world which they are still in the process of recognizing. To quote at some length Hobsbawm's pioneering study on the 'primitive rebels' of the modern world:

> The men and women [who formed the nineteenth- and twentieth-century 'archaic' social movements of southern Europe] differ from the Englishmen in that they have not been born into the world of capitalism, as a Tyneside engineer with four generations of trade unionism at his back has been born into it. They come into it as first-generation immigrants, or what is even more catastrophic, it comes to them from the outside, insidiously by the operation of economic forces which they do not understand and over which they have no control.... They do not as yet grow with or into modern society: they are broken into it, or more rarely – as in the case of the gangster middle class of Sicily – they break into it. Their problem is how to adapt themselves to its life and struggles... as expressed in their archaic social movements.[7]

Hobsbawm's emphasis on 'adaptability' in this passage is especially pertinent to our discussion, since it highlights the fact that 'archaic' social movements struggle against the grain of dominant social structures – like, for example, capitalism – but are in the last instance forced to adapt to the prevailing, 'modern' forms of political protest. Thus, the implication is that 'primitive rebels' tend to emerge at moments of historical upheaval where, as Antonio Gramsci famously put it, 'the old is dying, and the new cannot be born'[8] and that their contradictory existence as pre-modern social movements in modern times is generally resolved through their gradual conversion into fully fledged modern social movements. Even the most seemingly 'archaic' social movements of our time are on closer inspection unequivocally modern. Islamism – in itself a highly diverse expression of contemporary political protest – is for many a favourite example of how medieval, theocratic and generally atavistic politics exert a staying power under modern conditions. Yet, beneath their rhetorical and highly selective invocation of the Muslim holy texts and traditions, Islamist movements from the USA to the Philippines are thoroughly modern movements in their organization, programme, strategy and international relations. In this respect, contemporary Islamist movements can readily be compared to other populist and revolutionary movements across the world.[9]

All these considerations underline the need to exercise considerable historical caution when approaching the distinction between modern and pre-modern forms of collective agency. The qualifications raised above, however, far from undermining the distinction, reinforce the claim made throughout this book that, no matter how contradictory and protracted the process may have been, the period stretching from the mid-seventeenth to the late eighteenth century witnessed the consolidation in Europe of specifically modern forms of socio-political collective action that today characterize international civil society. The nature of these distinctively modern social movements can be summarized with reference to four of their basic characteristics:

1 *Secularism*   Secularism should not be confused here with atheism or even anti-clericalism. Rather, it is used in a broader sense to refer to a way of engaging in political action which emphasizes human subjectivity and moral agency as opposed to divine intervention or other-worldly determinations. In a way, it involves applying Weber's notion of 'disenchantment' to the realm of collective agency,[10] thus contrasting, for example, messianic forms of political protest with those built around specific programmatic demands. The organizational consequence of this is that the hierarchy of modern political movements is determined by the members themselves and not ordained by God or his representatives on earth. Moreover, modern movements secularize their epistemology by replacing theology with ideology or, in Koselleck's formulation, favouring prognosis over prophecy, philosophy of history over the conjectures of cosmology.[11]

2 *Open membership*   Modern political movements tend to have an open membership, the sole requirement being the sharing of political world-view.[12] The notable exceptions to this rule were women[13] and, in many cases, peoples of colour. These are, of course, no minor or accidental exceptions and they reflect the contradictory nature of

some modern social movements. Yet, in so far as the general rule of open membership for adult men marked an obvious contrast to the previously restricted forms of association, it must be maintained as an elementary component of modern collective agency.

3 *Universalism*   Virtually all modern social movements have a universal message, i.e. they are aware of the wider validity of their claims for other people elsewhere in the world. As opposed to pre-modern forms of collective agency, modern political movements rarely base their objectives exclusively on the very particular and concrete issues of their immediate surroundings. Modern social movements thus break with the pre-modern tendency to present corporatist grievances at the parochial level, and in a generally deferential fashion. They are certainly premised on a specific source of political identity (e.g. 'working class', 'women', 'black people') but the general assumption is that anyone, regardless of their territorial, cultural or professional affiliation, is entitled to support the particular cause. Moreover, as has already been noted, a significant number of modern social movements organize around exclusionary notions of race, nationality or religion. Yet even these movements are forced to accept that other 'races', nations or religions are entitled to their particular, exclusive political community. To that extent, such movements simply reinforce the universality of particularity.

4 *Publicity*   Modern political agency is strongly dependent on the use of new printed media: newspapers, journals, manifestos, programmes, pamphlets, petitions, declarations and so forth. Habermas and others have rightly underlined the importance of these media in the rise of a bourgeois 'public sphere' while print-capitalism is of course a crucial element in Benedict Anderson's account of the birth of nationalism. It should also be noted that modern social movements introduced new modes of protest. As Louise and Charles Tilly have pointed out: 'the food riot, the tax rebellion, the invasion of fields, and the other standard ways of voicing eighteenth-century demands give way to the strike, the demonstration, the public meeting, the electoral rally.'[14]

In combination, these four features of modern socio-political agency mark an unequivocal rupture with previous forms of popular protest. These in turn accompanied the wider socio-economic and political changes that inaugurated the modern world. Indeed, on the above definition, the archetypal modern social movement is intimately tied to the advent of industrial capitalism. The labour movement, the first generation of women's movements, pacifist organizations and indeed nationalist parties all display the characteristic features of modern collective agency and they were all arguably the product of the global expansion of industrial capitalism. Moreover, despite recently fashionable claims about the inexorable rise of post-industrial, post-modern, post-Enlightenment social movements, empirical analysis suggests that contemporary social movement activity is in most parts of the world very much organized around the modern, Enlightenment notions of social justice, civil rights, gender and racial equality or national self-determination. The debate over 'new' social movements that dominated this field of study in the 1980s appears today to have run its course with the acknowledgement that, although a new generation of social movements after 1968 sought to break with the organizational forms and ideological content of their predecessors, they were not especially successful in doing so, nor was their challenge so historically unprecedented.[15] In short, on both empirical and theoretical grounds, contemporary modern social movements are associated in this study with modes of collective action that found expression during the nineteenth and twentieth centuries in the context of capitalist social relations. Without reducing the myriad instances of modern social agency to a direct or automatic expression of particular class interests, it should none the less be emphasized that, historically, movements as diverse as first-generation feminism, pacifism or early environmentalism all emerged within the confines of a recognizable class and in response to problems and inequalities uniquely shaped by capitalism. It is this mode of production, with its characteristic social relations and political structures, which to this day constrains the nature and development of modern social movements across the globe.

Yet, if the social movements associated with industrial capitalism are in important ways paradigmatic of modern forms of collective agency, there are also significant exceptions which need to be explained. For there are clearly numerous historical instances of modern social movements emerging from social formations that are not recognizably capitalist. In fact, the working assumption thus far has been that modern socio-political agency arose in Europe from the middle of the seventeenth century onward – long before the advent of industrial capitalism. Uncomfortable questions therefore immediately arise about the temporal connections between modernity and capitalism.

The discussion in chapter 2 about class and the rise of the public sphere indicated how one way of addressing these queries lies in recognizing the historical paradox whereby modern social movements often arise in non-capitalist contexts which are none the less externally conditioned by capitalist social forces: modern social movements may be *of* capitalism but not *in* capitalism. To some extent, this insight pre-empts the discussion below on the international dimensions of modern social agency, but it is important to highlight once again that the historical links between capitalism and modernity cannot be treated mechanically. As was suggested above in relation to the persistence of archaic social movements under modern conditions, the spatio-temporal connections between capitalism and modern social movements should also be seen as heavily mediated by other social processes and structures, including the international system itself.[16]

Consider, for example, the case of Jacobin political clubs. Despite springing up within the pre-capitalist social formation that was absolutist France, this expression of modern social agency was explicitly influenced by the socio-economic and political structures and processes experienced by capitalist Britain. The singular combination of ruling and subordinate classes that supported the scores of Jacobin clubs across France after 1789 was certainly a product of very local class antagonisms, presented in an Enlightenment language that was in many respects unique to that country. Yet it would be wrong to exclude the influence on Jacobin revolutionary thought and practice of the British and American political tracts of the time – admittedly through the mediation of Rousseau, Montesquieu or Voltaire – and indeed their organizational features and methods of mobilization were comparable to the contemporaneous English radical democratic societies. Thus, once the discussion of modernity, social agency and capitalism is placed within an international context, the paradoxical modernity of French Jacobins appears as equally complex but perhaps less perplexing: here was a characteristically modern social movement which emerged from a pre-capitalist social formation with the bourgeois aspiration of transforming absolutist France into a fully fledged capitalist nation in the image of Britain.[17]

A similar story might plausibly be told of the liberal-democratic revolutions of 1989. Here again, social movements such as Poland's Solidarity or the Czech dissident group Charter 77 emerged from patently non-capitalist societies. Yet, on the definition offered above, these organizations must qualify as modern social movements. Once again, however, it would be wrong to interpret the links between capitalism and modern social agency without the mediation of the international system. For, like their Jacobin forebears two centuries earlier, Solidarity and Charter 77 were (among various other opposition movements of the Soviet bloc) inspired and explicitly supported by their international counterparts – in this case the liberal-democratic states and social movements of the capitalist west. The activity of such movements – both in its ideological and organizational expression – was certainly conditioned by very specific local power structures.

Thus, the problematic of 'civil society' was generally presented by the dissident movements of the Soviet bloc in the 'civic' or 'republican' idiom examined in chapter 2: as a domain defined not so much by the positive features of the capitalist market, but rather as a democratic ambit outside the control of the all-encroaching communist state. This notwithstanding, it soon became apparent, and definitively so after 1989, that this 'third space' between the state and market was unsustainable both theoretically and in practice. To that extent we can reasonably include the opposition movements of the Soviet bloc under the category of 'modern social movement', while simultaneously arguing that without the dominance of distinctly capitalist social relations across the globe such movements would not have taken the shape they did.

Modern social movements, then, are sustained and self-organized collective mobilizations in the pursuit of socio-economic and political change, characterized by historically unique modes of protest and organization. These new modes of protest are historically unique in the double sense that they signalled a radical and irreversible break in the form and content of popular collective action, and that they first flourished under a new mode of production: capitalism. Thus, while some expressions of popular mobilization such as preaching or petitioning may be identified in previous periods, they acquired a distinctively modern hue by the end of the 'long' European sixteenth century. Likewise, though modern social movements have often emerged and persisted in non-capitalist societies, their specifically modern character was historically acquired through an interaction with the internationally predominant capitalist social relations. The explanation for this contradictory modernity of some modern social movements, it has been argued, lies in the necessary *international* mediation of modern socio-political agency. The next section of this chapter aims to substantiate this claim by considering the nature and development of international social movements.

Social movements: global, transnational or international?

International factors have shaped the nature of most modern social movements from their inception. It was suggested earlier that modern social movements generally espouse and promote some form of universal ideology; that they are often inspired by and connected to similar movements across the world; and, most importantly, that they therefore tend to create an international organization – with all the attendant representative and administrative institutions – for the purposes of generating and co-ordinating international solidarity to their cause. In all these respects, few modern social movements escape the impact of the international. Presented in this way, such a proposition appears as self-evident and unworthy of further attention. Yet recent studies of social movements in world politics tend to contest the notion of *international* social movements, arguing in contrast that terms like *global* or *transnational* better describe such activity in today's world.[18] It may therefore be worth pausing briefly for a justification of the specifically *international* nature of social movements adopted in this book.

The first point to be made about the definition of international social movements is that, while there may indeed be international dimensions to the genesis and development of most modern social movements, not all social movements are *international* social movements. For our purposes, the key distinguishing feature of a properly international social movement lies first in its capacity to mobilize a specific constituency or membership across state boundaries – usually, though not exclusively, via some international co-ordinating body such as an international secretariat, committee or congress; and, second, in its sociopolitical objectives being conceived as inherently international, i.e. adopting from the outset a programme that seeks to transcend existing national boundaries. Many modern social movements emerge within the context of a specifically local struggle – this is the case, for example, of the *Occitan* movement in France or some Hindu revivalist movements in India.[19] Such movements may develop all kinds of international links (indeed, Hindu nationalism in India relies very heavily on a transnational diasporic network of supporters) yet they rarely meet the second condition mentioned above, namely that their sociopolitical objectives be deemed inherently international. Because their programmes are, almost by definition, focused on local grievances, these forms of collective action may involve 'social movements that organize internationally', but not 'international social movements' as such.

The term 'international social movement', then, is reserved in this study to describe the activity of organizations such as the International Confederation of Free Trade Unions or Friends of the Earth International, which conceive of and co-ordinate socio-political struggles in an explicitly internationalist fashion from the very outset; for those social movements that self-consciously organize to wage specifically international socio-political struggles. This can certainly include organizations with particularist objectives, such as nationalist movements, since the latter have historically built on the solidarity of comparable movements, endorsed the rights of other peoples to 'self-determination', and accordingly often established complex international organizations to support such objectives. In other words, as has been stated thus far, and as the conclusion to this book will further indicate, there is no a priori impediment to nationalist organizations forming part of a broader international social movement (such as the Socialist International), nor, once their aspirations are realized in the form of a sovereign state, their still being an important component of international civil society.[20] Once again, the claim here is simply that the universality of the international can readily find expression in the particularity of specific societies and political communities.

Social scientists from across a range of disciplines have increasingly recognized the importance of such international dimensions to our social world and have consequently turned their attention to what they term 'transnational' or 'global' social relations. Sociologists and political scientists in particular appear to have broken the conceptual shackles of national or territorially bounded analyses, and it is now almost a professional requirement to recognize the impact of 'global' forces when explaining the dynamics of any specific polity or society. Students of social movements have in important ways been at the forefront of this gradual shift, as indicated by two recent contributions to this field of study.

Sidney Tarrow's work is perhaps the most representative instance of this shift. In the second edition to his now seminal introduction to the study of social movements, *Power in Movement*, Tarrow introduced a new chapter dedicated to 'transnational contention', arguing that 'There is a growing potential for contentious politics beyond the borders of national states as the world enters the twenty-first century.'[21] Though he is suitably cautious about the novelty and scale of such transnational contention, Tarrow gives credence to the notion that new forms of globalized socio-economic, political and communicative interaction are opening up specifically transnational opportunities for contentious politics. Yet at the same time Tarrow is at pains to stress that transnational contentious politics neither undermines nor circumvents the power or the existence of the sovereign state. On the contrary, for Tarrow, 'These movements may identify themselves ideologically – and financially – with their transnational collaborators; but unless we focus empirically on what happens within national political struggles, we miss the true significance of transnational contention.'[22] There is therefore an uneasy tension in Tarrow's discussion between an apparent insistence on the novelty of specifically *transnational* social movement activity and the continuing structural constraints imposed on such activity by the sovereign state.

A similar ambivalence as to the concrete explanatory value of transnationalism is evident in the work of Jackie Smith and her colleagues gathered in an edited volume on *Transnational Social Movements.*[23] Even allowing for the diversity of perspectives inherent in a collection of essays, the core substantive claim of this volume as summarized by its editors is that 'Increasing global interdependence, coupled with the emergence of institutions that move decisions of relevance further from local populations, forces social movements and other actors to target political arenas beyond those of single states.'[24] Drawing explicitly from the transnationalist IR theory of the 1970s, Smith et al. argue that, although political processes are increasingly globally interdependent, they are still articulated through the structures of 'domestic' politics. Thus, like Sydney Tarrow, Smith and her fellow political sociologists appear to be stretching the term 'transnational' simply to avoid the perceived state-centric notion of the 'international', even though their substantive analyses suggest that transnational social movements are significantly conditioned by state sovereignty.

All these considerations suggest that the opposition between the 'transnational' or 'global' on the one hand and the 'international' on the other is in most respects unnecessarily contrived. While international relations obviously cannot be reduced to relations among states alone, very few actors in world politics operate without the mediation of the state. As was suggested in chapter 1, it seems more fruitful to define the 'international' more broadly so that it can encompass relations both *between* and *across* states, thereby focusing our attention on the arguably more interesting question of the constant interplay between state and non-state actors in the unfolding of international relations. Thus, as Thomas Risse-Kappen has usefully suggested, 'To set the debate in terms of "state-centred" versus a "society-dominated" view of world politics misses the mark.... Confusing the impact of transnational relations on world politics with a "society-dominated" view of international relations leads one to overlook the more interesting question of how inter-state and transnational relations interact.'[25] In terms of our present discussion, what this means is that the state, in all its expressions, should be conceived as a significant component of international social movement activity. This is the case in two related senses.

At a purely empirical level, international social movements are often associated with states through what we may loosely term 'patronage relations'. Many international social movements have been supported, when not overtly created, by states. International trade union and party-political organizations are perhaps the clearest example of this interconnection. The Third International or the present Socialist International both serve as instances of international social movement activity that is simultaneously transnational (in that it mobilizes non-state agents across state boundaries) and inter-state (in so far as those non-state agents are represented in the institutions of several states). To be more specific: the Third International was throughout its history both the international expression of self-organized communist movements across the world and a component of the Soviet Union's inter-state relations. Likewise, the present Socialist International has often acted simultaneously as a non-state actor in world politics (in its support of democratic transitions in southern Europe, for example) and as an agent of inter-state relations (in its capacity as co-ordinating body of centre-left governments across the world).[26] Other examples of international social movements sponsored by states (especially revolutionary states) could no doubt be cited. In fact, scholars concerned with the study of international non-governmental organizations (INGOs) have playfully broken this broad category of actors into GONGOs (government-organized NGOs), DONGOs (donor-organized NGOs), BONGOs (business-organized NGOs), QUANGOs (quasi non-governmental organizations) and even GRINGOs (government-run/initiated NGOs).[27] Chapter 5 will discuss the international role of such organizations in greater detail; the point at this stage is simply to register that a sizeable number of international social movements have historically been associated with the interests and organs of sovereign states.

There is, however, a more substantive way in which the actions of international social movements and states intersect. For, no matter how forceful and systematic the challenge of international social movements to state sovereignty may be, the structures of the international system still oblige these movements to pursue their socio-political goals through the different organs of the sovereign state. As we shall see in chapter 5, even the burgeoning institutions of so-called 'global governance' are not significantly subverting the sovereign state as the primary locus of socio-political power. However limited in scope, non-state collective action geared toward the transformation of international relations must, at different stages in the pursuit of its objectives, engage with the socio-political agents of the state. Thus, to take two related examples, in their quest for new international regimes on ozone depletion and women's rights, international environmentalist and feminist movements have been forced to accommodate differing national legislation in the formulation of their goals, and thus to engage directly with the relevant departments of particular states. Naturally, this does not undermine the international character of these social movements, but it does alert us to the continuing relevance of state sovereignty in the analysis of international social movement activity. Indeed, it underscores the point made throughout this book that the international social movements which inhabit international civil society reinforce the legitimacy of the sovereign state through their recognition of local particularities in the expression of global problems as much as they weaken it by organizing across state boundaries when addressing such problems.

In both these respects – the tight historical connections between states and international social movements, and the fact that the latter reinforce as much as they undermine state sovereignty – it seems more accurate to speak of *international* as opposed to *transnational* or *global* social movements. There are, to be sure, both global and transnational dimensions to most international social movements. But for the purposes of explanation and analysis it is essential to fix our sights on the interface between international social movements and the international system of states. In this regard, it seems appropriate to insist further that the term 'international' can be usefully deployed to mean social relations *both* between *and* across states.

International social movements, then, involve the voluntary mobilization of a group across national or state boundaries in the pursuit of social and political change on a self-consciously international scale. Although there have historically been distinctly international dimensions to the rise of most modern social movements, it has been suggested that only social movements which from the beginning set out to organize across territorial boundaries with an explicitly internationalist programme can properly be called 'international social movements'. Such movements have been a constant feature of world politics since the late eighteenth century, with the international network of 'patriotic' clubs, inspired by the Jacobin example, as perhaps the first prototype of international social movement.[28] Since then, socio-political movements with diverse international agendas have sought to further their cause by mobilizing across and within sovereign states. Broadly speaking, it is possible to identify three 'generations' of international social movements.

The first corresponds to what might be termed 'classical internationalism'. The path-breaking work of F. S. L. Lyons exhaustively documented how the spread of industrial capitalism across Europe and beyond during the nineteenth century was accompanied by the rise of numerous self-consciously internationalist organizations.[29] As the socio-economic and political interdependence between nations deepened, as the international social and cultural patterns became increasingly homogenized, and as long-distance communication and travel facilitated the transnational co-ordination of political campaigns, groups that might previously have confined their activism to the national level sought – indeed were sometimes forced – to organize internationally. Thus, as we saw in chapter 2, all the major ideological tendencies of the period – pacifists, feminists, socialists, anarchists, nationalists – established explicitly internationalist organizations with their corresponding organs of international communication, co-ordination and representation. Additionally, the internationalist principles underlying these organizations found expression in a rich and varied body of internationalist thought – again, ranging from the liberal internationalism of Richard Cobden, Woodrow Wilson or Norman Angell to the utopian-socialist and anarchist internationalism of Flora Tristan or Emma Goldman. Finally, it should be pointed out that, though the experience of classical internationalism was initially rooted in Europe, it soon expanded, or was independently reproduced, outside of that continent. The nineteenth and early twentieth centuries witnessed the emergence of what one scholar has termed 'macro-nationalisms' such as pan-Islamism, pan-Africanism or pan-Americanism represented in organizations such as the Society of Muslim Brethren, the *Alianza Popular Revolucionaria Americana* (APRA) or the Universal Negro Improvement Association (UNIA), respectively.[30] Despite basing their internationalist solidarity upon particularist ethnic, religious or national identities, such movements can be deemed 'international' in so far as they explicitly invoked the transcendence of existing state boundaries in the organization and realization of their political objectives.

A second generation of international social movements can be said to have sprung up in the context of the struggles for Third World liberation and, in the advanced capitalist countries, over issues ranging from ethnic, sexual and religious equality to environmental degradation and nuclear armaments. The former became increasingly associated with some leading Third World states and inter-state organizations, such as the Afro-Asian People's Solidarity Organization (AAPSO) emerging out of the 1955 Bandung Conference, while the latter fostered transnational networks of activists – for example, the European Nuclear Disarmament campaign (END) and Greenpeace. Though in some instances these two expressions of post-war internationalism coalesced into a single political struggle (for instance, in the anti-Vietnam War protests), by and large they represented the widening gulf between the 'post-materialist' concerns of protest groups in the 'Northern' advanced capitalist countries and those very 'materialist' programmes of social movements from the undeveloped 'South'. Notwithstanding these important differences, this second wave of international social movements could plausibly be categorized as movements for 'recognition' in all its socio-political dimensions.

Finally, the past decade has witnessed the rise of transnational networks, alliances and coalitions of diverse socio-political groups chiefly dedicated to the contestation of 'globalization' in its various guises. Thus, the recent anti-World Trade Organization and 'anti-capitalism' protests in Europe and North America have been 'disorganized' by groups such as the People's Global Action against 'Free' Trade and the WTO (PGA) or Reclaim the Streets which aim to combine the nineteenth- and twentieth-century anarchist tradition of direct action with the elements of contemporary 'deep ecology' with its attack on technology, international trade and industrial society more generally.[31] Somewhat paradoxically, a major distinguishing feature of these new global activist 'networks' is said to be their use of the Internet and electronic mail as a means of communication, thereby claiming the status of spontaneist, non-hierarchical and non-bureaucratized movements. Additionally, these movements are characterized by a 'disinterest towards the idea of seizing political power. It appears that the traditional goal of taking political power and gaining control over the state apparatus has given way to a desire for immediate control over the conditions of existence and to claims to independence from the system.'[32] In all these respects, we could, following Lucy Ford and Marc Williams's terminology, class these recent expressions of transnational collective action as 'rejectionist' global movements.[33]

Like all taxonomies, this breakdown of international social movements into distinct 'generations' should be treated cautiously. Clearly there exists an overlap both between and within the different 'generations' of international social movements: 'classical' and Third World internationalisms are in some quarters as alive today as they were a century ago, while there is plainly some continuity in the principles and practices of, say, liberal and feminist internationalism. Moreover, there are doubtless other ways of classifying these movements. Overall, however, this typology could be said to reflect accurately both the continuities between classical internationalism and the contemporary experiments in transnational activism, on the one hand, and the changes in the geographical reach, political influence and organizational patterns of, say, Amnesty International and the nineteenth-century Anti-Slavery League, on the other. Whatever the classificatory permutations, the important thing is to conceive of these successive phases in international social movement activity as being simultaneously cause and effect of the expansion of international civil society. International social movements may have arisen in response to the transformations effected by global capitalism; but they have also extended the reach of modern socio-political agency by proselytizing their ideas globally, often in non-capitalist contexts. To the extent that international social movements have given actual historical content to the notion of international civil society as a distinct sphere of socio-political collective action in world politics, they merit the close attention of students of international relations. They also deserve our attention, however, for a deeper analytical reason, and that is their central role in explaining *change* in international relations, the issue to which I now turn.

International social movements and international change

The preceding sections have identified the ways in which international social movements represent a distinctive feature of modern international relations. Their constitutive character has been described and their historical relation to modern forms of socio-political agency established. But beyond this descriptive recognition, what does the study of international social movements tell us about the nature of modern international relations? Put differently, how can the latter help to explain the dynamics of the modern international system? Posing these questions is important, for, as was suggested at the start of this chapter, international social movements do not just mould the world according to their own choosing, but encounter all types of constraints to their actions in the form of social structures. Indeed, the core assumption of this book is that the agents of international civil society are implicated in almost equal measure with both the reproduction and transformation of the social structures that make up the international system. The next chapter will consider in greater detail how these agents have contributed to the historical *reproduction* of such structures. The remainder of this chapter, however, will focus exclusively on the *transformative* dimensions to international civil society: on the role of international social movements in explaining international change.[34] Moreover, because the principal concern of the present chapter is that of the relation between agency and structure, special attention will be given to the notion of *structural* change in the international system. As will hopefully become apparent, this should not foreclose the study of other forms of international change, nor need it imply the necessary relation between international social movements and structural change. On the contrary, much of what follows is aimed at highlighting how the transformative agency of international social movements is best understood with reference to the structural constraints they encounter.

In essence, the argument developed below is that international social movements bring about change in international relations when they challenge the structural basis of state sovereignty. For when the constitutive relations of state sovereignty are radically transformed, the structures that sustain the modern international system are also necessarily affected. Thus, for example, the Bolshevik Revolution can be said to represent a significant rupture in the history of the international system because it signalled the rise of a form of sovereignty premised upon radically different state–society relations from those prevailing internationally. In so far as the agents of the Bolshevik Revolution were in important ways part of a broader international movement – in this case the international working-class movement – we can posit a powerful causal relation between this instance of international socio-political agency and what later transpired to be a significant conjunctural challenge to the structures of the international system. In short, international social movements should be seen as mediators of international change, standing in a dialectical relation to the international system of states: they shape and are shaped by state sovereignty, but contribute to historical changes in international relations when they subvert the constitutive basis of that very sovereignty.

These claims by themselves raise complex and certainly unresolved issues including, among others: historical causation, epochal change, internal relations, explanatory hierarchies and unobservable structures; in sum, the perennial agent–structure problem in social science. As was stated at the outset, I do not pretend (for reasons of both space and competence) to offer a comprehensive account of the debates surrounding this problematic of social theory, nor indeed is it my intention to offer an alternative rendition of this problematic. The aim, rather, is to place the foregoing discussion on international social movements in the context of the structure–agent debate, so as to illustrate the explanatory potential of this phenomenon. In doing so, however, the argument implicitly cautions against an excessively 'voluntarist' reading of international social movement activity and its impact on international relations. Like most other social theorists, I start from the premise that our social world is reproduced through human activity, i.e. that there are no social structures outside of human reality. However, unlike much contemporary IR theory concerned with agents and structures, I consider this proposition to be a mere starting point when addressing the far more vexing issue of how exactly agency and structures combine to produce and reproduce our social world. In approaching this question, the notions of agency and structure must be accompanied by a consideration of 'change' and 'causality'. Having dealt with the idea of 'agency' at length earlier in the chapter, the following paragraphs will therefore consider in greater detail the possible uses of 'structure', 'cause' and 'change'.

Because in the real world all of these concepts find concrete expression in multiple forms, our first task is to abstract out those particular agents, structures, changes and causes that are relevant to the discussion: to set out a 'problematic'.[35] Without some degree of abstraction and a reasonable selectivity on what it is that needs to be studied, it is impossible to analyse let alone explain the infinite combination of processes and relations that characterize social life. Hence, the earlier sections of this chapter emphasized that this book is concerned above all with *transformative* agency mediated through modern social movements: customary or normative (as in rule-governed) agency are patently present in our social world, but they are not the main concern of this study. To that extent, one guiding problematic of this study is explaining the role of international social movements in effecting change in the structures of international relations. This being the case, it is not just with any form of social pattern or order that we are concerned here, but with *deep* or *underlying* social structures; not with 'change' and 'causes' *per se*, but with *structural* change and *underlying* causes. Moreover, the focus below will be on specifically *international* structures, changes and causes. Though there are clearly connections between international and other more local manifestations of structure and change, it is necessary, once again, to abstract out a specific domain of inquiry – in this case 'the international' – so as to provide some kind of theoretical explanation. Before doing so, however, it is equally important to flesh out these various distinctions in the forms of structure, change and causation.[36]

Structure, change and causation: an excursus

All social life is to some extent patterned in ways that allow observers to identify regular connections between distinct social phenomena. Sometimes such patterns arise through the unintended consequences of human action; in other instances they are consciously created through the establishment of rules, norms and regulations. Either

way, such connections often lead social scientists to speak of 'structure' and to hazard generalizations about the world based on the
perceived regularity of these connections. One notorious pattern in
international relations, for example, is the historical absence of war
between liberal-democratic states. This enduring connection between
liberal states and international peace has in turn led to the generalization that liberal-democratic states do not fight each other – the 'democratic peace' thesis.[37] Similarly, international society has established
institutional norms in the form of, say, diplomatic immunity or the
veto power of the five permanent members of the United Nations
Security Council. These patterns, rules and generalizations clearly
give a shape and coherence to different aspects of international relations – they form what Hedley Bull and his followers have called an
international 'order'. To that extent we could plausibly speak of
diplomacy or the UN as 'structures' of international politics.

Yet, on closer inspection, this understanding of 'structure' yields
very little by way of explanation, chiefly because it is incapable of
identifying let alone accounting for unobservable structures. Put differently, observable and enduring connections do not by themselves
amount to a structure; or at least not in the sense used here of a deep
or underlying structure. To use a familiar analogy: explaining the
dynamics of international politics through the 'structures' of international society such as international law, international organizations
or diplomacy is akin to explaining how an electric light is turned on
and off by means of a switch on the wall – these causal connections
may tell us *how* but not *why* such a sequence results in particular
outcomes.[38] Such classically empiricist accounts establish the existence
of a pattern exclusively on the basis of an observable connection over
time between given entities. They do not, however, seek out the
underlying structural properties that make it possible for the notion
of the 'international' to exist at all, or for electricity to be transmitted
in the first place. The type of structures discussed here, on the other
hand, are not simply those arising out of enduring connections, but
rather from 'deep' or 'underlying' social structures. The latter are
'structures' because they are constituted by *internal* or *necessary* relations between their component parts; they are 'deep' because without
them other relevant entities could not exist.[39] As we shall shortly see,
this need not imply that 'external' or 'contingent' relations are unim-
portant in explaining social life, but simply that they must be distinguished from 'structural' relations.

The two key *underlying structures* that arguably reproduce the
modern international system are the capitalist mode of production
and state sovereignty. These entities are internally related in ways that

produce an overarching system – or a social totality – we have come to identify as the modern international system. On the one hand, modern sovereignty is historically characterized by the separation between the 'political' and the 'economic' (or between state and civil society; between public and private spheres). It follows from this that an internal or necessary relation exists between capitalism and the modern form of sovereignty: the modern state requires the existence of a differentiated sphere of civil society (the capitalist market), while the latter presumes the existence of a distinct public, political domain – historically, the territorially discrete national state. On the other hand, this internal relation between capitalism and the modern state generates a further necessary relation: that between state sovereignty and the international system. For an international system of states cannot, by definition, exist without the principle and practice of state sovereignty, and, likewise, the latter would be redundant without the plurality of sovereign states that make up the international system. Far from representing a tautology, this last proposition – as the next chapter will illustrate – is central in understanding the historical specificity of modern sovereignty and the consequent structural singularity of the modern international system.[40] Any consideration of the transformative agency of international social movements should therefore acknowledge the constraints imposed by these two structures of the international system. This notwithstanding, two cautionary provisos must immediately be registered: first, that these structures emerge in the course of a protracted and unevenly spread historical process, i.e. they are not emplaced uniformly at a particular historical juncture; second, these structures, we shall now see, undergo internal transformations which are relevant to the nature of their 'internal' relations.

Although social structures are characterized by their continuity in time and space, they are clearly not immutable. In other words, *social change* cannot be understood in isolation from social structure, and vice versa. Despite being a longstanding axiom of classical social theory, this straightforward assumption has in recent years been repackaged with some degree of wilful amnesia under the brand of 'structuration' theory. Indeed, it is hard to identify a single contemporary IR scholar dealing with the agency–structure problematic who doesn't ritually endorse the supposedly path-breaking 'discovery' that our social world is characterized by a 'duality of structure'.[41] Reinventions of the wheel aside, this rediscovery of the 'two-sidedness' of our social world is, as was suggested earlier, just a starting point; an initial premise from which to embark on the much harder task of identifying and explaining structural change. There are in this regard two considerations which must immediately be borne in mind.

First, as in the case of 'agency' and 'structure', 'social change' comes in many guises. Indeed, it is precisely because in reality, as Heraclitus famously noted, everything is in a state of flux that distinctions in the forms of change are called for. One way to proceed involves mirroring the above distinction between internal and external relations by differentiating structural and conjunctural forms of change. Whereas the latter refers to changes that do not upset the necessary relations which constitute a structure, the former pertains to transformations which by their very nature undermine the structural basis of particular relations. Thus, for example, the USA's awakening from its isolationist slumber in the course of World War II must qualify as a significant change in the dynamics of the international system; yet it did not undermine the structural relation between capitalism and sovereignty, but rather obviously encouraged it. In contrast, the consolidation of agrarian capitalism in England during the seventeenth century arguably marked the beginning of the structural transition from medieval 'geo-politics' to the modern system of states. To posit a differentiation between conjunctural and structural transformations in the international system, therefore, is not to ignore or dismiss the agents and impact of local, contingent and often piecemeal change. It is, however, to insist that the existence of very real social structures requires that social theorists set up the corresponding explanatory hierarchies where some forms of change are recognized as being more powerful than others in bringing about structural change to the international system.

Second, the fact that social structures are reproduced through human agency does not preclude that such structures exist independently of our volition, nor does it imply that all instances of human agency are equally important in the reproduction of such structures. Social structures can arise as the unintended consequence of human agency. In Roy Bhaskar's much-quoted rendition: 'people do not marry to reproduce the nuclear family, or work to reproduce the capitalist economy. But it is nevertheless the unintended consequence (and inexorable result) of, as it is also a necessary condition for, their activity.'[42] Similarly, though I may resist it vehemently, in typing at a computer manufactured in Malaysia and sipping at some Nicaraguan coffee while I do so, I am contributing to the reproduction of global capitalism. But, by the same token, refusing to use a 'global capitalist' word processor or cutting down on caffeine consumption would plainly not herald the demise of world capitalism. Andrew Sayer puts this point more scientifically with reference to the position of individuals in social structures:

One of the most pervasive illusions of everyday thinking derives from the attribution of properties of the position ... to the individual occupying it. Whatever effects result, it is assumed that particular people must be responsible; there is little appreciation that the structure of social relations, together with their associated resources, constraints or rules, may determine what happens, even though these structures only exist where people reproduce them.[43]

In international relations, a common instance of this voluntarist illusion occurs when excessive expectations are placed on a particular individual or set of individuals transforming relations between states by, for example, appointing women to senior diplomatic positions, or incorporating people with working-class backgrounds to executive power. While these individuals may come to office with the best intentions of effecting change, they will no doubt encounter structural constraints to their position. It is therefore unlikely that they will by themselves generate structural change, simply because the structural quality of social relations, as Sayer rightly suggests, is based on the properties of a specific position, not on the character of the people that occupy it.[44]

This realization is especially important when acknowledging that once again, while social structures may be reproduced by human agents, not all human agents are equally implicated in the reproduction of such structures. Clearly, the structural position of individuals determines the causal power of their actions, so that (to continue with the above example), though both our actions contribute to the reproduction of global capitalism, a decision by the chief executive of Toshiba to invest in Malaysia is obviously far more consequential in this regard than my purchasing a Malaysian computer. Our unequal structural position within global capitalist social relations requires that the power of our agency be correspondingly differentiated in the field of IR. Similarly, the dual structures of the international system generate obvious hierarchies of power: it comes as no surprise, therefore, that – so long as these structures are not significantly challenged – those international agents (state or non-state alike) positioned at the centre of global capitalist production have historically been the most successful in exercising their sovereign power over other agents in the international system (again, be they state or non-state actors).

These considerations on internal relations and change lead to the final key component of the agency–structure problem: that of *causality*. In particular, because all social change, structural or otherwise, happens in time and place (i.e. is characterized by a sequence of events, or a process), it is the study of *historical* causality that offers a privileged site for explaining change. Historians, like other social scientists, have also grappled with the underlying structural causes of historical change. In line with the arguments presented above, historians who accept the existence of social structures are obliged to posit what E. H. Carr called an explanatory 'hierarchy of causes':

> the historian, in virtue of his urge to understand the past, is simultaneously compelled, like the scientist, to simplify the multiplicity of his answers, to subordinate one answer to another, and to introduce some order and unity into the chaos of happenings and the chaos of specific causes . . . the historian must work through the simplification, as well as through the multiplication, of causes. History, like science, advances through this dual and apparently contradictory process.[45]

For Carr, as for any social theorist that takes the 'duality of structure' seriously, causal hierarchies are not about 'determinism', 'inevitability' or 'hollowing out' the subject from history, but rather about identifying those social structures that explain why human action (collective or otherwise) produces significant historical change in one context but not in another. It is precisely because of the infinitely diverse manifestation of human agency, and its concomitant expression in such intricate sequences of events through time and place, that social theory must once again draw on abstraction when explaining social change. In other words, the existence of multiple causes of events is taken for granted; the question is: are some events (or agents) more important than others in explaining change?

For most historians, the answer has to be affirmative – few would want to claim that history is just 'one damn thing after another'. Nor would most historians settle for a purely empiricist explanation along the lines of 'The outbreak of World War II was caused by the German invasion of Poland in September 1939.' Clearly, then, theoretical criteria must be developed to justify foregrounding some events and privileging some causes over others when accounting for social change.[46] It has thus far been suggested that one way of setting out such criteria is through the identification of underlying social structures that condition human agency. An explanatory account of sociohistorical change, it has been argued, involves recognizing the complex interplay between the goal-oriented actions of individuals and collectivities, and the unobservable social structures that generate and are generated by such activity. This in turn calls for a causal analysis premised not only on the chronological sequence of events, but also on the synchronic relations between different structures and agents – for example, between the uneven and combined development of

Russian capitalism and the absolutist nature of tsarist rule. On this account, the student of socio-historical change can usefully construct a hierarchy of causes premised on, say, immediate (diachronic) and underlying (synchronic) causes when explaining a particular process of change. While this hierarchy need not be static or mechanical, it does, however, require acknowledging the primacy of some causes over others in the process of explanation.

Such an analysis, it should be swiftly added, does not rule out either empirical investigation or the role of contingency in explaining historical change. The existence or otherwise of social structures needs to be continually ascertained in the explanation of concrete historical processes. Likewise, positing the structural property of causal relations does not amount to reducing causes to a mechanical or automatic correspondence between 'cause' and 'effect'. On the contrary, it is – again – precisely because history is experienced by human beings in such diverse ways, and because it often unfolds in such unpredictable directions, that we must draw on explanatory structures that allow us to make sense of this variegated experience and unforeseeable contingency.[47]

We have therefore seen that making a claim for the role of international social movements in effecting international change involves adopting very specific views on the nature of structure, change and causality. On the analysis presented above, deep structures are constituted by internal relations which require not just the presence of enduring connections between entities, but the *necessary* interdependence between them. Thus, it was suggested, the two central structures of the international system are capitalism and state sovereignty in that they are mutually interdependent: one cannot exist without the other. The reality of underlying structures in turn leads to the further distinction between, on the one hand, structural and conjunctural change and, on the other, underlying and immediate causes. These different expressions of change and causality naturally coexist in the concrete social world, but they need to be abstracted out in this form for the purposes of explanation. Thus, the claim being made is not that conjunctural change is inconsequential in human history, nor that immediate causes are 'surface expressions' in the sense that they are the inevitable outcome of deeper underlying causes. Indeed, as we shall now see, the history of the modern international system hinges more on conjunctural changes external to the dual structures of the system, rather than internal, structural transformations. The point, rather, is to identify the differentiated position of these various forms of agency, structure, change and causality in the broader totality of social relations so as to adequately explain change in international relations. With these considerations in mind it is now finally possible to demonstrate how international social movements contribute to the transformation of the international system.

International social movements as mediators of international change

On the definitions offered above, international social movements are collective agents which confront, and often seek to transform, the dual structures of the international system. As such, it is helpful to consider international social movements as mediators of international change in two interrelated senses. On the one hand, international social movements have served as conduits in the reproduction of these structures after they make their first world-historical appearance, so to speak. Hence, as we shall see in the following chapter, international social movements have – often as an unintended consequence of their actions – contributed to the emergence, extension and consolidation of state sovereignty, nationalism, or the capitalist 'standard of civilization' as constitutive components of the modern international system. On the other hand, however – and this of course has been the concern of the present chapter – international social movements have also been instrumental in challenging both the 'internal' and 'external' sovereignty of particular states, thereby undermining the very structural basis of the international system. Though this goal has to date proved elusive, the very challenge to these structures, it will be argued, has produced important conjunctural changes in the international system.

It is perhaps modern revolutions that provide the best example of how this interaction between agency, structure and change plays itself out in the international system. In his recent study on *Revolution and World Politics*, Fred Halliday has noted that

> it is social movements ... that pose the challenge to states, in both internal and external dimensions: social movements defy the authority of states from within, they overrun or aspire to overrun the frontiers between states. The social movements that make revolutions are ... ones that are formed in an international context: they respond to change produced within their society by international factors, and at the same time they espouse ideologies that go beyond the frontiers of states.[48]

Narrowing the focus to twentieth-century revolutions, it is clear that the full array of historical tools examined earlier must be deployed when explaining the unfolding of, say, the Bolshevik, Vietnamese and Nicaraguan revolutions. In all these cases, domestic and international factors, immediate and structural causes, and assorted – often incompatible – collective agents combined in intricate fashion to produce revolutionary conjunctures. Yet underlying these complex revolutionary processes there has always been some form of transnational solidarity mediated through international social movements. Be it the Second and, after 1919, the Third International, or, in the case of Nicaragua, the international counterparts of the different organizations that made up the FSLN, the practical and ideological support of international social movements has been central to the success of these revolutions. The specific degree of causality between, say, the Comintern's influence on the Indochinese Communist Party and the successive revolutionary wars in that region after 1945 is, of course, a matter of concrete historical analysis. But, to the extent that the revolutionary agents of these various upheavals almost invariably formed part of a broader international social movement, we can reasonably posit the existence of an international civil society as an *underlying cause* of revolutionary change. In other words, revolutionary conjunctures arguably reveal in the starkest light the role of international social movements in mediating the twin structures of the international system (capitalism and sovereignty). Put differently, if the global expansion of capitalism and the accompanying aspiration to state sovereignty represent the dual structures which set the historical terrain for revolutionary change, it is international social movements that act as conduits of the collective agency which realize such change.

International social movements, then, should be seen as one of the key causal forces in the explanation of modern revolutions. Yet, while this dimension of 'the international' has been at the core of structural transformation within particular states and regions, the question still remains as to the structural impact of such movements upon the international system. It was suggested earlier in the chapter that structural change in the international system obtains when the internal relations between the constitutive components of this system are radically subverted. Since the modern international system is characterized by the dual structures of capitalism and sovereignty, it follows that structural change in the system will arise when the necessary relation between capitalism and sovereignty is undermined. This is exactly what most modern revolutions have set out to do.

If we take the three examples just cited, each of the revolutions attempted in different ways to develop alternative state–society relations to those previously dominant; that is, to generate a different form of sovereignty from that prevailing internationally. In all three cases, this alternative was premised on the severe curtailment, or outright abolition, of capitalist social relations in ways that radically altered the expressions of political rule through, for example, the fusion of a single ruling party with the state apparatus, the concomitant 'corporatization' of previously autonomous movements such as women's, peasant or cultural organizations, or the militarization of state office.[49] This necessarily had an impact on international relations as revolutionary states sought to 'export' their revolution by means of direct and indirect political, economic and military support for revolutionary organizations across the world. Needless to say, this internationalist commitment by revolutionary states was subject to all kinds of vagaries and abuses, to the extent that, for example, 'proletarian internationalism' under Stalin became a thinly veiled instrument of the Soviet state's international *Machtpolitik*. Equally, however, it would be hard to explain the Soviet Union or Cuba's engagement in Africa during the 1970s without taking the notion of 'proletarian internationalism' as a serious expression of those two states' intent in exporting their alternative form of state–society relations. In short, therefore, revolutions that undermine or abolish capitalist social relations domestically not only change the internal nature of a particular state's sovereignty, but also threaten the very basis of the international system by subverting the separation between 'politics' and 'economics' or 'state' and 'civil society' as the prevailing basis of state sovereignty.

The benefit of hindsight allows us to see that this revolutionary challenge had collapsed by 1989. Yet for the better part of the twentieth century it was the protracted upheavals against capitalism and its attendant forms of political rule that defined the dynamics of the international system. Indeed, the Cold War – the conflict that shaped international relations for much of the short twentieth century – should be understood as the historical expression of this antagonism between the dominant capitalist form of sovereignty born during the long sixteenth century, and a broadly conceived communist alternative that arose from the Bolshevik Revolution. It must of course be recognized that revolutionary states adopted many of the institutional trappings of bourgeois sovereignty, from membership of international organizations to the general acceptance of diplomatic protocol. Yet, as David Armstrong's interesting study has demonstrated, this gradual insertion into international society was characterized as much by resistance as by accommodation, revealing again the underlying challenge of revolutionary states to the predominant norms of international intercourse.[50] Likewise, the fact that revolutionary states often replicated the expressions of capitalist state sovereignty through, for example, the merciless control of international boundaries, or the chauvinist celebration of national particularism, or by engaging in military competition (occasionally outright war) with each other need not vindicate the realist argument regarding the transhistorical systemic anarchy of international relations. For it was arguably the very historically specific processes of revolutionary state-formation and their accompanying external counter-revolutionary pressures that explain why self-proclaimed socialist states adopt the survival strategies of their bourgeois counterparts. In other words, it is perfectly possible to acknowledge the reproduction of the logic of power politics among revolutionary states while simultaneously identifying the historically particular features of such contest for power.[51]

These brief and necessarily sketchy illustrations will have hopefully indicated how the study of international social movements can help to explain international change. Clearly, these movements are not necessarily involved in all instances of international change, nor have they historically been successful in effecting international *structural* change. But it should be clear from the above discussion that, without incorporating the role of international social movements in the explanation of international change, it is very hard to identify the historical *causes* of change – both structural and conjunctural. Similarly, accounts of international change that fail to give due attention to the structural constraints faced by international social movements will tend to conflate agents, causes and changes in ways that devalue the explanatory potential of studying such movements. In order to escape these respective 'structuralist' and 'voluntarist' pitfalls, it has been suggested that we analyse international social movements as transformative agents which engage with the dual international structures of capitalism and sovereignty, thereby *mediating* international change. Those international social movements that challenge the structures of the international system, it was argued, undermine the internal relations of the system in ways that produce significant conjunctural shifts in the international distribution of power. In the case of twentieth-century revolutions, the radical transformation of state–society complexes across the globe generated one of the key changes in the history of modern international relations, namely the rise of a Cold War between two antagonistic blocs of states. By way of conclusion, the final section of this chapter will briefly consider how IR theorists have dealt with questions of agency, structure and change in the international system, thereby highlighting the advantages of the approach adopted here.

Conclusions: international social movements matter

As was noted at the outset of this chapter, the agency–structure problematic has in the past decade been the focus of much meta-theorizing in IR. The work of Alexander Wendt in particular has encouraged a number of interventions into the nature of structure and agency in the international system. Most of this literature has been concerned with diverse epistemological and ontological dimensions to the study of IR – many aspects of which, it should be said, have long been addressed in other social sciences. In this regard there is little a specifically IR perspective on agency and structure can add to the existing debates in social theory more broadly. Unfortunately, it is the one arena of the contemporary social world where this discipline *can* make a contribution – the study of international social movements – that is largely ignored by IR discussions on agency and structure. As was suggested in chapter 1, the writings of Wendt and his critics – following the Waltzian quest for theoretical 'parsimony' – deliberately eschew muddying their explanatory frameworks with 'non-state' actors, and rather choose to focus on the state as the principal agent of international relations. The arguments in this chapter will have hopefully presented compelling reasons for contesting this state-centric approach to the study of international politics. For, it has been suggested, it is especially worthwhile taking the international social movements seriously in the explanation of international change. Yet, even among those scholars concerned with historical transformation in the international system, there is an ambiguous engagement with international social movements as agents of international change. By way of illustrating how the conception of international social movements as *mediators* of change defended here departs from existing accounts, this concluding section to the chapter briefly considers two influential perspectives on international change which tend either to exaggerate or to downplay the role of social movements in explaining international change.

Among the more striking examples of the first type of work is Jan Aart Scholte's study on the *International Relations of Social Change*. In that volume Scholte insists on the necessity of adopting a 'structurationist' approach to social change, where 'Transformation occurs through an interrelation of order and action; not through one or the other; not through one plus the other; but one through the other in a unity that may be called structuration.'[52] The danger of using 'structuration' as an endpoint rather than as a presupposition in the investigation of agencies and structures, however, becomes readily apparent in Scholte's eclectic call for a 'world-historical-sociological synthesis' which 'examine[s] social change in terms of a fivefold interplay of political, economic, cultural, psychological and ecological forces'.[53] Because on this account 'people are internationally interdependent through everything from disease to the arts',[54] it is never entirely clear whether some agents are more important than others in explaining international social change. In other words, though Scholte clearly recognizes that international social movements are not all-powerful and do not always attain their stated objectives, he stops short of engaging in the difficult task of establishing causal hierarchies which might grant the actions of some social movements greater explanatory power than those of others. The inevitable consequence of this indeterminacy is a descriptive and voluntarist rendition of international transformation where virtually all forms of international collective agency appear as responsible for change: 'transnational corporations, international non-governmental organizations and intergovernmental agencies... all these institutions can be positively involved in the transformation process as actors in their own right.'[55]

Yet, as the preceding pages have endeavoured to show, if the role of international social movements in explaining international change is to be taken seriously, it is imperative that an appropriate explanatory framework be developed where different forms of agency and structure are granted varying degrees of causal power in bringing about such change. In other words, it is essential that the place of international social movements in effecting change be situated within a broader totality of hierarchical social relations. Approaches to international transformation which, in the name of 'multi-causality' and the 'duality of structure', avoid pinpointing the specific sources of (and limits to) change lead very quickly to sterile compilations of sundry social forces which might plausibly be held responsible for international transformation. In the end, such random listings of potential agents of international change return us full circle to the descriptive and atheoretical accounts of change of the 'classic' transnationalists criticized in chapter 1.

A proper explanation for the role of social movements in bringing about international change, then, requires a sharper focus on the specific nature of the social relations that structure modern collective socio-political agency. And this is arguably one of the central achievements of Justin Rosenberg's influential account of the rise and expansion of a historically unprecedented *Empire of Civil Society*. As we saw in chapter 2, in that text Rosenberg charts the rise of modern sovereignty 'as a form of political rule peculiar to capitalism' in order to suggest further that the 'structural connections (between capitalist relations of production and the sovereign form of the state) underpin a distinctive form of modern international power – and indeed explain how it is that we can have a global states-system at all.'[56] In other words, Rosenberg offers a powerful explanation for the structural transformation in the relations between political communities which took place in Europe over the course of the 'long' sixteenth century – the birth of the states-system – and which to this day governs world politics.

The appeal of Rosenberg's explanation lies in its structural understanding of international change – in this case, the rise of the modern states-system – as a historical *process* which unfolds through the transformation of specific social relations. To that extent, Rosenberg's work perfectly exemplifies how a 'structurationist' approach can readily accommodate the specification of those structural forces responsible for change – in this instance, capitalist social relations and their accompanying political form of state sovereignty. Yet, elegant and rigorous as such structural explanations might at first appear, they also carry the risk of screening out the role of political contestation in the unfolding of such structural transformations. For, as intimated hitherto, and as the following chapter will further illustrate, the structural transformation of the 'international' system was effected not only through the birth of new social relations of appropriation and their attendant political institutions, but also through the often violent antagonisms generated by these new forms of socio-political relations. Thus, Hazel Smith has rightly criticized Rosenberg for a

> lack of discussion of Marx's understanding of capitalist social relations as being formed in relation to antagonistic social relations of class power. Omitted from Rosenberg's work is any discussion of key Marxian concepts such as exploitation, alienation, class as a category, communism, indeed all those concepts which would allow Rosenberg to add a value focus on his understanding of historical materialism.[57]

There is, in fairness, some consideration of such antagonisms toward the end of *The Empire of Civil Society*, in the context of the discussion of 'primitive accumulation'; there are, furthermore, isolated illustrations (e.g. the 1984–5 miners' strike in Britain) of how capitalism stacks the discrete political power of the state against the working class. But the overall point Smith makes is well taken: a resistance to the Marxian language of class struggle, exploitation, alienation and, most important for our purposes, revolution paradoxically renders Rosenberg's account of international change somewhat static. By focusing so much of his attention on the structural features of the modern international system, Rosenberg tends to underplay – if not omit – the dynamics of class antagonism mediated through collective socio-political agency which arguably underpin such social structures. The result of such silences is, in the case of *The Empire of Civil Society*, a powerful elucidation of the *sequence* of international structural change, but a weaker rendition of the *causes* behind such change. Thus, for example, though it is clear from Rosenberg's account that it is the advent of capitalist social relations which explains the historical emergence of modern sovereignty, it is not altogether clear why this particular form of rule was reproduced, say, in the African continent during the period of decolonization. Surely there is more to an explanation of African decolonization than the encroachment in that continent of capitalist social relations? The answer offered in this book is that there is indeed more: the global reproduction of capitalist social relations – the international expansion of civil society – paves the way for modern socio-political agency which, in the case of Africa as elsewhere in the colonized world, gave state sovereignty a specific political content and legitimacy at that time. In other words, the structural *causes* of international change (decolonization in the present example) are deemed to reside not only in the reproductive dynamics of the international capitalist market (the 'empire of civil society'), but also in the antagonistic collective agency thrown up by such dynamics within the domain of international civil society.

The analysis of international social movements, then, matters to the study of IR principally because it can help to explain international socio-economic and political change. As this chapter has sought to demonstrate, international social movements represent a particular form of collective agency, which both generates and is therefore constrained by the structures of the international system. The best way of capturing this complex and often contradictory role of international social movements in the processes of international transformation, it was suggested, is to consider the latter as *mediators* of international change. Thus the collective agency of international social movements should be treated neither as self-evidently significant in the explanation of change, nor simply as a tangential consequence of broader structural transformations. Instead, international social movements can helpfully be understood as mediating agents of international change in so far as they simultaneously challenge the dual structures of the modern international system, and incorporate new collective agents into the broader structural relations of this system.

While this chapter has focused quite narrowly and (for heuristic purposes, quite artificially) on the structural constraints to such international agency, the next chapter will widen the scope of international collective agency and consider the role of international civil society at large in the dynamic reproduction of international society. It will hopefully become even clearer there how the various international dimensions of civil society – and the social movements that inhabit it in particular – play a crucial role in explaining the rise and expansion of the modern international society of states.

4

International Society from Below

The Role of Civil Society in International Relations

For the past two decades IR theory has undergone an intense process of critical self-reflection. As the theoretical insights and preoccupations of other branches of the social sciences and the humanities have entered the discipline, the meta-theoretical presuppositions inherent to mainstream IR have been subjected to closer scrutiny by approaches such as feminism, historical materialism and post-modernism. Consequently, the received wisdom as to how one should go about analysing 'the international' has been contested, and, in its stead, a variety of perspectives on the study of international relations now compete for theoretical dominance. This methodological revolution in IR theory has certainly affected the parameters of what should be included within the domain of the international, so that questions relating to culture, gender, the environment or capitalism are now deemed to be central to our discipline. Yet, paradoxically, it has also given new lease to many of the key concepts and concerns of orthodox IR theory such as sovereignty, international society, nationalism and the system of states. Rather than entirely replacing these categories, much of contemporary IR theory has sought to investigate their origin and changing nature, thus subjecting the conventional use of these concepts to an *immanent* critique.

It is the aim of this chapter to engage in precisely this kind of critique by investigating the notion of international society and its attendant categories – sovereignty, nationalism, the system of states

and the 'standard of civilization' – from the vantage point of international civil society. The argument will be that many of the features
associated with the idea of international society emerged from the
interaction with international civil society. More specifically, I seek to
demonstrate in the course of this chapter how civil society has played an
instrumental role in the reproduction of the modern states-system, thus
offering an alternative historical account 'from below' of the rise and
consolidation of modern international society. In line with the claims
made in the previous chapter regarding the role of international social
movements in reproducing the structures of international society, it will
be suggested here that modern social movements have from the very
beginning shaped the forms and content of modern state sovereignty
and its accompanying institutions, norms and values. The point, therefore, is not to reject the concept of international society *tout court*, but
to uncover the social and historical content accumulated from its
interaction with an expanding international civil society.

In order to develop the argument, I have chosen to focus upon the
writings of the so-called 'English school' of International Relations.
This is for two reasons. First, and most obviously, because it is the
authors associated with this school that developed the notion of
'international society' most thoroughly, and who investigated with
greatest historical sensitivity concepts such as sovereignty, nationalism
or the expansion of the western 'standard of civilization' – all of which
are closely linked to the arguments of this book. Second, because the
normative value attached to the concept of international society is
crucial in understanding its interaction with international civil society.
Throughout this book, great emphasis is placed on the fact that the
construction of the modern international system owes just as much to
international civil society underpinning the institutions of international society, as to international society legitimizing the social
movements associated with the expansion of international civil society. As I hope to elucidate below, the choice of international *society* in
opposition to international *system* as the preferred term for a discussion of the theoretical purchase of international civil society reflects
the acceptance that the international is a domain permeated by a set of
identifiable norms and values. That these norms and values were
imposed across the world by the expanding capitalist powers does
not cancel out their continued relevance in the explanation of contemporary world politics. In the same way that Marx accepted the categories of classical political economy when unpacking the fetishism of
the commodity, critical IR theory must engage with the concepts of
classical international theory like 'international society' when demys-
tifying the workings of the contemporary international system.

Given the controversial nature in IR theory of the term 'international society', the first section of this chapter investigates the meaning of the concept, thereby bringing into the discussion three issues relevant to the interface between international society and international civil society: sovereign statehood, the western 'standard of civilization' and the 'revolt against the west' through anti-colonial nationalism. These three areas of concern for the English school will then serve as headings for a sustained criticism of this approach to international relations. It will be argued that the 'international society' perspective fails to account for the forces of international civil society in each of the domains just mentioned, and is consequently unable to consider the relevance of collective social and political activity in the expansion, consolidation and transformation of international society. The chapter will close with a general discussion of the way in which the study of the expansion of international civil society can further our understanding of international relations.

'International society': a malleable concept

The term 'international society' was given its contemporary meaning in the essays produced by the British Committee on the Theory of International Politics from the late 1950s onward. Since then, the concept has been the focus of much scholarly attention in IR, spawning an important literature which is often presented under the guise of the 'English school' of IR. There has been considerable debate regarding the existence of an English school and, indeed, whether the term 'international society' should be exclusively associated with the authors connected to this 'school'.[1] The position taken here will be the conventional one, namely that the members of the British Committee did share a common set of assumptions about the nature of international society and its centrality in world politics, and that these assumptions have been carried through into a number of contemporary studies investigating the relationship between international society and aspects of world politics such as nationalism, revolutions, decolonization and human rights. Furthermore, the authors registered with the English school are distinguished by their historicist understanding of the present international system and the importance they attach to normative values in explaining the emergence and consolidation of this system. In this respect, the 'international society' approach to IR has, through different generations, displayed both an internal consistency in terms of method, problematic and guiding assumptions, and an external identity, built around the emphasis on the idea of international society, which distinguishes it from other theoretical perspectives in IR. At the risk of some simplification, the broad outlines of this approach to IR can be summarized through the identification of four components of international society.

The first and arguably the constitutive element of international society is state sovereignty. Put most succinctly by Hedley Bull, 'An international society . . . presupposes an international system.'[2] Virtually all the writers following the 'international society' approach set out from the basic premise that international society is above all a society of sovereign states. This is certainly explicit in the recent contributions to the study of international society from Alan James,[3] Robert H. Jackson,[4] James Mayall[5] and David Armstrong,[6] but it was also evident from the outset in the proceedings of the British Committee. The collection of essays on international theory published under the title of *Diplomatic Investigations*, for example, all endorsed the realist assumption that what was under investigation in International Relations was a system of states with no overarching authority, and the practices and institutions such as diplomacy or international law which accompanied this anarchical system. In contrast to American realism, however, the 'international society' approach has always emphasized the distinctly modern nature of the present international system. Martin Wight's historical comparison of systems of states was perhaps the clearest expression of this. In his essays on 'The origins of our states-system', Wight is unequivocal: 'The simplest speculation about the origins of the Western states-system . . . is bound up with the question as to when modern history began.'[7] The answer, for Wight, was 1648: it was the Peace of Westphalia which consolidated the norms of intercourse among European states that prevailed in the next three centuries:

> In retrospect, Westphalia was believed to mark the transition from religious to secular politics, from 'Christendom' to 'Europe', the exclusion from international politics of the Holy See, the effective end of the Holy Roman Empire by the virtual recognition of the sovereignty of its members.[8]

Later investigations into international society, most notably Adam Watson's *The Evolution of International Society*,[9] follow Wight in accepting that what distinguishes contemporary international society from other systems of states is the secularized interaction among sovereign political communities sealed with the Peace of Westphalia. In short, one of the basic features of international society, according to the authors which have developed this term in IR, is the emergence during the long sixteenth century of the specifically modern entity which forms this society: the sovereign state. An investigation of how contemporary international society operates, the English school maintained, requires a historical understanding of the rise and evolution of this kind of political entity.

The broad consensus over the basic unit in the study of international relations allowed the proponents of the 'international society' approach to open up a second research agenda, namely the world-wide expansion of this society of states. Presented in the seminal volume on *The Expansion of International Society*, the basic concern here was to provide a historical account of how the norms, values and institutions of European international society were extended across the globe, eventually to produce what Bull termed a 'universal international society'. In line with the English school's acceptance of European international society as a novel historical phenomenon, the contributors to this volume sought to explain how regional international systems outside Europe were incorporated into a wider global international society: 'We are concerned to see how, by the flood-tide of European dominance over the world and its subsequent ebb, the one [regional systems] became transformed into the other [a universal international society].'[10] The criteria employed to determine the nature and pace of this transformation were highly legalistic: non-European powers joined the club of international society by signing up to international treaties, by engaging in diplomatic relations with other states and by attending international conferences.[11] In a more sophisticated treatment of the process, Bull's student Gerrit W. Gong defined this combination of benchmarks as a 'European standard of "civilization"'.[12] When enumerating the features of such a standard, Gong not only included the external requirements regarding sovereignty, international law or diplomacy, but also referred to domestic arrangements such as a 'civilized' state guaranteeing basic rights to life, liberty and property, or its abolishing internationally unacceptable practices such as polygamy, slavery or suttee.[13] As the author himself stresses,

> by definition, it was expected that members of the same society of 'civilized' states would share sufficiently in fundamental, underlying assumptions about the world; in customary, historically proven institutions; and in ordinary, everyday life-styles, so as to feel part of a common society and a shared civilization.[14]

This linkage between domestic and international standards of 'civilization' when defining membership of international society resonates, as we shall shortly see, with Robert H. Jackson's discussion of positive and negative sovereignty in contemporary international society. For the moment, however, it is important to note that, as Fred Halliday suggests, the expansion of international society was a process buttressed by the increasing homogenization of the internal socio-economic and political make-up of states.[15] In so far as the nineteenth-century diplomatic practices, legal documents and international conferences reflect the universalization of international society, they do so as one dimension of a wider process of economic, social and political unification across the globe, governed by the logic of capitalist accumulation. Despite eschewing a materialist explanation of how the 'standard of civilization' might have become the expression of an international society of states, Gong at least points to the interaction between state and society in the extension of this phenomenon, thereby making explicit what in the contributions to *The Expansion of International Society* is only implied. In this respect, he enriches our understanding of international society by recognizing, if not explaining, the vital societal forces underscoring the diffusion of the norms, values and institutions which compose this society of states.

It is a mark of the English school's intellectual honesty and its sensitivity to historical change that most of the recent contributions to this theoretical approach have been concerned with the challenges to the idea of international society in the post-war period. One of the school's masters, Hedley Bull, himself led the way by considering the implications for international society of the Third World's 'revolt against the west'.[16] In his last piece on the subject, Bull recognized that international society had largely been a product of European imperial domination, and that 'as Asian, African and other non-Western peoples have assumed a more prominent place in international society it has become clear that in matters of values the distance between them and Western societies is greater than . . . it was assumed to be.'[17] The consequences of this for the concept of international society, however, were never clearly spelt out by Bull. It was left to his successors – Armstrong, Jackson and Mayall – to examine further the impact upon international society of decolonization and the revolutionary struggles of the post-war period. Although all three authors set out from very similar definitions of international society, their conclusions regarding the influence of revolutions, decolonization and nationalism vary considerably. In his own discussion of the 'revolt against the west', for example, Armstrong identifies the existence of four different approaches to international society after World War II. Two of these – the reformist and revolutionary perspectives – were adopted and defended either by Third World states which, like India or Ghana, sought to transform institutions of international society such as the United Nations into the principal agents of anti-colonialism, anti-racism and a more equitable international economic order, or by those states, such as Iran or Cuba, which entirely rejected existing international society as being a product of western imperialism. The upshot of this, for Armstrong, was a profound disagreement over the rules and norms of international society after 1960: 'although all four groups upheld the idea of sovereign equality, there was far less agreement amongst them in relation to other norms of international society.'[18]

In a different take on the same theme, Robert H. Jackson made a distinction between an 'old sovereignty game' and a 'new sovereignty game'. Whereas the former was a product of the Westphalian system where 'states historically were empirical realities before they were legal personalities', the latter reflected a decolonized world where 'rulers can acquire independence solely by virtue of being successors to colonial governments'.[19] For Jackson, the anti-colonial struggles of the post-war period had substantially altered the central premise of international society by creating a new conception of sovereignty: one in which ex-colonial 'quasi-states' benefited from a negative sovereignty acquired through international recognition but which was not complemented by a positive sovereignty guaranteeing a liberal democratic order domestically. Despite identifying the transition from one understanding of sovereignty to another in international society, Jackson seemed to accept that the 'new sovereignty game' would not upset the norms and institutions of the society of states, as in the last instance it upheld the principle of non-intervention. Since 'Nonintervention is the foundation stone of international society',[20] it followed that quasi-states built on the concept of negative sovereignty would in the future continue to be participants in the society of states.

That the emergence of some 100 new states in the aftermath of decolonization did not substantially alter the nature of international society was a central argument in James Mayall's study of nationalism and international society. Like Armstrong and Jackson, Mayall set off from the assumption that the anti-colonial struggles for national self-determination challenged the Eurocentric understanding of international society which had predominated over the past three centuries. Yet, unlike his two colleagues, Mayall contended that the revolt was not necessarily against 'the west' but rather against the idea of dynastic sovereignty. It was the advent of popular sovereignty, chiefly propagated through the principles of the French Revolution, that allowed the idea of national self-determination to modify the rules and institutions of European international society. In the conclusions to his study, Mayall recognized the importance of Third World nationalism in constructing the multilateral institutions of the post-war years, and in extending the scope of international law to areas such as colonialism and international economic inequality. Yet, ultimately, the revolts inspired by notions of popular sovereignty were also obliged to accommodate existing patterns of international relations. This tension between challenge and accommodation produced a situation where 'the primacy of the national idea amongst contemporary political principles has modified the traditional conception of an international society but has not replaced it.'[21]

This brief survey of the English school's approach to the term 'international society' will hopefully have revealed the core elements of the concept. We have seen that, for the authors associated with this school, international society refers to a set of diplomatic practices, legal precepts and institutional arrangements which bind sovereign states into a shared understanding of how international relations should be conducted. These norms, values and institutions are buttressed by a common standard of civilization which was not substantially contested until the middle of the twentieth century. Since then, international society has adapted to these challenges by extending its membership and modifying some of its guiding principles. Despite its historical evolution, so its advocates argue, the concept retains both descriptive validity and analytical purchase: it helps students of international relations to explain the behaviour of states and it does so in ways which are at once more sophisticated and more accurate than those offered by alternative theories.

The rest of this chapter aims radically to contest this understanding of international relations. It will be argued that the 'international society' approach offers a historical and analytical account of the modern international system that reifies the discourse and practices of ruling classes, and which consequently fails to credit the essential role of popular political action in the development of this system. In essence, the claim being made is that the English school's conception of international society is fundamentally state-centric and therefore inherently incapable of theorizing the role of collective political agency in world politics.

One of the basic reasons behind this disregard for questions of collective agency lies in the superficial usage of the term 'society' by the English school. In order to accommodate social movements within a theory of international society, it is imperative to have some notion of how and why modern collective social and political activity emerged in the first place. Chapter 3 indicated how social theory has generally recognized that social and political movements are central to our understanding of the term 'society', while chapter 1 argued that theories of civil society, both classical and contemporary, reflect this longstand-

ing preoccupation with the link between self-conscious collective action
and the constitution of society as we know it today. Yet, like the 'moral
and political paucity' of IR once decried by Martin Wight, our discipline has also suffered from a general sociological shallowness. Until
very recently, and with a few notable exceptions, IR theory had very
little to say about how inter-state relations might be connected to wider
social structures and processes. Class conflict, gender inequality, racial
hierarchies, the workings of the capitalist market and the bureaucratic
extension of the state, to take but a few examples, seem to have been
excluded from the domain of the international. This sociological naïv-
ety is especially damaging when IR theorists employ the loaded term
'society' without recognizing its complex and contested genealogy.

A classic example of this conceptual poverty is, of course, the
English school's use of the term 'society' simply to denote a loose
association of states; a collection of political entities which share some
basic behavioural characteristics. Without exploring the historical and
sociological evolution of the idea of 'society', however, it is impossible
seriously to consider the role of social movements in the construction
of the international system. Employing the term 'international civil
society' can, I suggest, begin to redress the English school's narrow
conception of international society and provide a richer account of the
origins and development of the modern international system.

The sections that follow will therefore attempt to show how, by
considering the interplay between states and social movements, we can
arrive at a historically and sociologically deeper understanding of
international society. From this perspective, the practices and institutions of international society are seen not as natural outgrowths of
an autonomous system of states, but rather as the product of the
historically specific interactions between states and societies. The essential components of international society – sovereignty, the standard
of civilization, national self-determination – are explained with reference to the concrete social and political struggles between and within
states and civil societies, and not as the result of the mysterious expansion of international codes of conduct through negotiation and consensus among ruling classes.

State sovereignty: the popular contribution

A striking feature of recent IR literature on sovereignty is the absence
of sustained discussions of the notion of popular sovereignty. With the

notable exceptions of James Mayall's juxtaposition of nationalism and popular sovereignty, and Daniel Deudney's heterodox retrieval of the 'Philadelphian system',[22] few contemporary IR theories consider the principle and practice of popular sovereignty in the construction of the international system. Yet, as this chapter has suggested thus far, an adequate understanding of the nature and development of state sovereignty requires that we pay attention not only to the transformations in the practices and institutions of the ruling classes, but also to the changing forms of resistance and agitation among what, for want of a better term, we shall refer to generically as 'ordinary people'.[23] Again, the point here is not to replace the traditional elite-centred account of modern sovereignty with an equally facile 'populist' narrative focused exclusively on 'ordinary people'. Rather the claim is that the advent of modern state sovereignty was ultimately the historical product of a clash of interests between – and often among – ruling and subordinate classes, and that, consequently, explaining sovereignty requires that we investigate the antagonistic relations between rulers and subjects in late medieval and early modern Europe.[24] The paragraphs that follow will further elaborate this claim with reference to some historical examples from Europe and North America, both before and after the advent of the modern epoch.[25] Before doing so, however, it is necessary to clarify and qualify the invocation of 'popular sovereignty' and 'civil society' within this context, since the period we shall initially be referring to – that between the crisis of feudalism in the fourteenth century and the consolidation of the modern European states-system in the seventeenth century – is plagued by historical contradictions and complexities.

First, it should be stated from the outset that, strictly speaking, many of the concepts and institutions associated with the modern state pre-dated the advent of civil society. As we shall shortly see, numerous scholars within and outside the field of IR have convincingly charted the pre-modern origins of modern sovereignty by exploring the processes of political centralization and territorial monopolization begun by thirteenth-century European kingdoms, principalities, duchies, catellanies and other jurisdictions.[26] Because civil society – in the various guises presented in chapter 2 – only emerged as a discrete social sphere during the course of the seventeenth century, it cannot properly be said to have *given rise* to modern sovereignty. What will be argued below, however, is that civil society, and in particular the social movements that acted within this domain, were instrumental in *shaping* and indeed consolidating the modern form of state sovereignty. The generalization of modern state sovereignty in the course of the 'long' sixteenth century, it will be suggested, was paralleled and reinforced by the gradual appearance of modern social movements during this same period. On this account, the uneven and extended process that characterized the emergence by the seventeenth century of modern state sovereignty was mirrored by an analogous transition from medieval to modern formulations of popular sovereignty. The terminal crisis of feudal rule in western Europe that ushered in a modern order of sovereign states was accompanied and spurred on by a simultaneous shift in the modes of popular protest away from generally local, corporate and deferential forms of collective action and toward increasingly secularized, class-based and international expressions.

Second, and partly resulting from the above, it is important not to conflate the term 'civil society' as it is employed in this study with 'popular sovereignty'. The idea of popular sovereignty has medieval origins which once again pre-date the concept and sphere of civil society, and, while the agents of civil society usually endorse popular sovereignty as a source of political legitimacy, claims for popular sovereignty need not be rooted in civil society. Similarly, as with the concept of civil society, the notion of popular sovereignty should not be confused with that of democracy. Struggles for democracy have certainly been premised on the idea of popular sovereignty, but not all formulations of this principle are inherently democratic. This is true both conceptually and historically. The early modern theorists of popular sovereignty invoked the concept in the battle against dynastic absolutism, but their vision of enfranchisement never extended beyond that of propertied men. In contrasting the early expressions of popular sovereignty in France and England, Ellen Meiksins Wood points out:

> This conceptual device, with roots in the Middle Ages, had no necessarily democratic implications, since the 'people' could be very narrowly defined. It had long been available to aristocratic opponents of royal pretension and had been forged as a weapon against absolutism elsewhere. Bodin's conception of absolute and indivisible sovereignty, for example, was constructed in just such claims of popular sovereignty, enunciated by Huguenot pamphleteers to justify resistance during the Religious Wars.[27]

Likewise, contemporary history offers plenty of instances where popular sovereignty has sustained undemocratic regimes. Yet the interesting point about popular sovereignty in this context is not so much its connection or otherwise to democracy, but the fact that, despite its medieval origins, it has been at the root of the transformations in the modes of popular protest which I have identified as being characteristic of modern civil society – in other words, that the notion and practice of popular sovereignty was appropriated by such modern social movements in the pursuit of their goals. This in turn altered the terms of the political relationship between state and society in such a way as to affect the nature and practice of sovereignty. In the words of Reinhard Bendix:

> Until the revolutions of the seventeenth and eighteenth centuries, European rulers assumed that the general population would quietly allow itself to be ruled. Popular uprisings were regarded as violating the divine order and were suppressed by force.... If some questioned this practice, it was without much effect.... But with the Reformation, the persuasiveness of the ruler's old appeal to divine sanction was irreparably weakened. And since the French revolution, the right to rule has come to depend increasingly on the mandate of the people.[28]

There is, to be sure, an uncomfortably Whiggish resonance in Bendix's account of the shift from absolutist to popular mandates in the west. Although this does not cancel the overall validity of his argument, one should be wary of an excessively linear conception of this movement, and certainly of somehow associating this development with a theory of modernization. The third clarification to be made, therefore, is that the transition from dynastic to popular conceptions of sovereignty was the subject of bloody social and political upheavals; or, in Koselleck's more elegant formulation, the product of 'critique and crisis'.[29] Far from representing a natural, evolutionary process, the acceptance that ordinary people might have a say in government was the outcome of a protracted struggle from the seventeenth century onwards which yielded very uneven results across Europe. Arno Mayer's documentation of the 'persistence of the Old Regime' into the twentieth century serves as a timely reminder of just how variegated historical change can be.[30] These caveats now registered, my primary aim at this stage has simply been to recognize the ascent of popular sovereignty and its attendant forms of mobilization in Europe during the course of the 'long' sixteenth century, and to relate these changes in the terms of political engagement to the consolidation of state sovereignty since then as a norm of international society. I hope the foregoing discussion will have clarified that this does not involve conflating the related but distinct notions of civil society, popular sovereignty and democracy, nor subscribing to an evolutionary understanding of historical change. It is merely an attempt to recover for IR theory and, more specifically, for our comprehension of international society the centrality of the principle and the practice of popular sovereignty – a move that runs counter to the English school's account of sovereign statehood.

The prevailing explanation among theorists of international society for the emergence of state sovereignty focuses upon the transition from an overlapping patchwork of fragmented political communities which characterized medieval Christendom to the secularized states-system that sprang up in Europe from the fifteenth century onward. As was mentioned above, Martin Wight, the English school theorist with greatest historical acumen, placed the chronological limits of this transition somewhere between the Council of Constance (1414–18) and the Peace of Westphalia (1648): 'In the fifteenth century the old constitution of the Respublica Christiana finally breaks down.... The papacy is transformed from an ecumenical theocracy into an Italian great power. The assertion of sovereignty by secular powers, growing since the thirteenth century, becomes normal.... At Westphalia the states-system does not come into existence: it comes of age.'[31] This has since become the standard interpretation among scholars adopting the 'international society' approach and has indeed acquired wider currency in recent IR scholarship on the historical specificity of the modern states-system.[32] On this account, the parcellized, heteronomous and personalized forms of rule that characterized feudal Europe were in the course of the late medieval and early modern period transformed into the anarchical system of discrete, exclusively territorial and therefore 'sovereign' states which still govern contemporary world politics. At a purely descriptive level, such an account is perfectly cogent – even the most sophisticated neo-realist arguments for the continuity between pre-modern and modern international politics are obliged to recognize the substantive difference between medieval and modern forms of rule and the consequent historicity of the term 'sovereignty'.[33] The real challenge, however, lies in *explaining* this transition from medieval to modern state forms. Signalling the historical changes in European politics and society which accompanied the Renaissance, the Reformation and the wars of religion certainly sharpens our awareness as to the historicity of state sovereignty; but it explains very little about how the transition from a continent dominated by feudal jurisdictions to one characterized by sovereign states was actually accomplished. The famous principle of *cuius regio, eius religio*, for example, was plainly a manifestation of the growing capacity among local princes and other dignitaries in establishing exclusive military and juridico-political supremacy over specific territories; but in itself it hardly serves as a category capable of explaining the sources and nature of this transformation. In order to provide a satisfactory explanation of the origins and development of modern state sovereignty, it is necessary to consider the socio-historical roots of phenomena like the Reformation and the wars of religion, a task left largely unaddressed by the members of the English school.

A telling admission in Martin Wight's essay on systems of states which goes some way in explaining this kind of omission is his distinction between 'internal' and 'external' sovereignty: 'Historians of political thought... have traced the development of internal sovereignty. ... We are more concerned with the development of external sovereignty, the claim to be politically and juridically independent of any superior.'[34] The uncontested acceptance of this separation between sovereignty 'inside' and 'outside' the state suggests that Wight saw no necessary link between these two spheres: 'external' sovereignty (mutual recognition, regular communication, international law and so forth) could be taken for granted as the central preoccupation for IR students without regard to the social and historical conditions which allowed for the distinction to be made in the first place. The problem with such an approach is that it gives rise to a descriptive and circular account of state sovereignty ('external' sovereignty is defined with reference to a state's capacity to engage in legal-diplomatic relations with other independent states, yet the latter is conditional upon states being externally sovereign), while the crucial interaction between 'external' and 'internal' forms of sovereignty is left unexplored. The net result of these manoeuvres is an understanding of modern state sovereignty that necessarily obviates the contribution of rebellions, revolutions, uprisings and other forms of popular protest in the development of this phenomenon. The historical record, however, suggests that popular contestation among ordinary people has been instrumental in defining the shape and limits of modern state sovereignty. While an exhaustive account of how popular collective action has shaped state sovereignty is plainly beyond the scope and expertise of this study, I shall none the less endeavour to illustrate this claim with historical examples from three 'moments' in modern European and North American history where ordinary people raised the banner of popular sovereignty in an attempt to appropriate for themselves the practices and institutions of state sovereignty. These are respectively: the early modern period of revolutionary civil wars; the late eighteenth-century 'age of democratic revolutions'; and the nineteenth- and twentieth-century experience of working-class agitation.

The English Civil War provides one of the earliest instances of a self-organized populace affecting both the discourse and practice of sovereignty. Although by no means exclusively pitched in terms of a contest between patrician and plebeian interests, the social and political upheavals experienced across England during the 1640s and 1650s generated a number of popular movements which, by challenging the authority of the ruling class, were to have a longstanding influence upon the nature of the English and, later, British state in the decades to come. Foremost among these organizations were the so-called Levellers, a heterogeneous group of individuals represented by pamphleteers such as John Lilburne, William Walwyn or Richard Overton, who campaigned for the extension of the male franchise and the radical reform of the institutions of political representation in England. The Levellers organized as a party, drawing their membership from the rank and file of the New Model Army, and radicalized parishes and the 'middling sorts' around London. Their main vehicle of mobilization, however, was petitions which in some cases accumulated over 40,000 signatures. One of the most celebrated Leveller documents was the *Agreement of the People*, a first version of which was released in 1647 in the context of the famous Putney debates over England's constitutional future. In opposition to the moderate schemes of 'mixed government' presented by Cromwell's second-in-command, Commissary-General Henry Ireton, the Levellers' *Agreement* aimed to form the basis of a constitution

> That would embody the fundamental principle that just power was derived from the consent of the people, which meant ending the veto of the king and Lords, since they did not represent the people, and subordinating them to the Commons, which did, or should, represent the people. But the Commons would be supreme only in matters delegated to it by the people. . . . Therefore the *Agreement* bridled not only the king and the Lords but also the Commons in the interest of sovereignty of the people.[35]

The Leveller movement was short-lived and regionally circumscribed. Furthermore, as noted earlier, the Leveller conception of 'the people' was strongly limited. This should not, however, blind us to the impact this kind of collective action had upon early modern notions of popular sovereignty. As one prominent student of the period has suggested,

> the Levellers soon came more and more to abandon the ground of the past and a restorationist perspective. Instead, they based their position increasingly on abstract reason, on what was due to man as a rational being. . . . Even religious apologies for radicalism derived from God's law were subordinated to these overwhelmingly secular themes. The latter furnished them with their strongest justification for founding all government on consent as expressed through democratic institutions.[36]

Moreover, the Levellers were in several important respects part of a broader pattern of struggles for popular sovereignty across Europe. In France, the mid-seventeenth-century uprisings against the absolutist state, collectively known as the 'Fronde', included movements such as the republican *Ormée*, which drew on the Leveller experience, and particularly on the *Agreement of the People*, to support the call for popular sovereignty.[37] Although it is important not to conflate the very specific and often contradictory expressions of popular discontent in early modern Europe, it would likewise be a parochial oversight not to recognize the similarities in the language and aspirations of groups as diverse as the French *Ormistes*, the English Levellers or even the Castilian *comuneros* a century earlier.

The link between early modern struggles for popular sovereignty and the process of state-formation in Europe is by no means definitive. As we saw above, the social movements defending the right to popular sovereignty operated within the existing territorial boundaries already imposed by the ruling classes. In so far as these movements had an impact on the contours and nature of the emerging sovereign state, it was expressed in a reactive fashion. Early modern resistance movements shaped the modern state form not by constructing it *ex nihilo*, but rather by grating against existing state structures when these impinged upon the interests of specific sectors of the population. By the eighteenth century, however, revolutionary movements emerged along both shores of the Atlantic and gave a new impulse to the aspiration of popular sovereignty. It is in this 'Age of Democratic Revolutions' that the connections between the agitation within civil societies and the construction of state sovereignty become most apparent.

In the cities of colonial America, new forms of political engagement had been developing since the beginning of the eighteenth century. The growing integration of the New England seaports into the world market, coupled with the inflationary consequences of war with France, accentuated the impact of wage and price fluctuations upon the 'middling' and 'lower' ranks of the colonial population.[38] The response to this economic hardship was hardly new: as in the past, different forms of direct action ensured that those responsible for unpopular policies felt the heat of discontent. The novelty lay in the mechanisms and language of agitation. Whereas fifty years earlier popular protest may have been expressed through spontaneous responses to the infringements on the 'moral economy', the first decades of the eighteenth century witnessed the rise of factional politics organized around specific interests and disseminated through printed media such as pamphlets, newsletters and petitions. The deferential politics geared toward maintaining a semblance of cohesion within the body politic gradually gave way to the overt recognition that contradictory political viewpoints could be expressions of socio-economic divisions within a community. The very notion of forming a 'party' to defend particular interests would have been anathema to the seventeenth-century public accustomed to the medieval emphasis on the pursuit of a collective harmony of interests. Yet by the early 1700s the political life of cities like Boston, Philadelphia and New York was transformed by the rise of political clubs and caucuses which for the first time deliberately organized and mobilized the poorer sectors of society in defence of their own interests. It is worth stressing again that, together with the timeless and well-tested methods of violent co-option and the prospect of free liquor, the medium privileged in this endeavour was that of the printed word:

> in the eight years from 1714 to 1721, economic dislocation brought forth a rush of pamphlets. Printed at the expense of political factions and often distributed free, they made direct appeals to the people, both those who enjoyed the vote and others who participated in the larger arena of street politics.... It was testimony to the power behind the written word that even those who yearned for a highly restricted mode of politics were compelled to set their views in print for all to read. For unless they did, their opponents might sweep the field.[39]

It was the consolidation of this kind of modern political agency which by the last quarter of the century produced the revolutionary ferment that led to independence for the American colonies. Naturally, the American War of Independence was not simply the result of accumulated plebeian agitation. Like the other democratic revolutions, crises emerged principally out of the contradictions among different sectors of the ruling class. Yet the popular input into these crises should not be underestimated. Through their participation in militias, political clubs or town assemblies, the ordinary people of the American colonies had by the late eighteenth century begun to take conscious control over their own lives. The patriotic struggles against English despotism thus became inextricably bound to the broader struggles for the social and economic transformation of colonial society. In this respect, the realization of American independence was in part the assertion of popular sovereignty. For all the limitations of the revolution – and there were certainly many for the women, the peoples of colour and the unpropertied of the colonies – the creation of a new state was achieved through the mobilization of the populace into modern social movements. As Gary B. Nash has put it:

Although no social revolution occurred in America in the 1770s, the American revolution could not have unfolded when and in the manner it did without the self-conscious action of urban labouring people... who became convinced that they must create power where none had existed before or else watch their position deteriorate....Thus, the history of the Revolution is in part the history of popular collective action and the puncturing of the gentry's claim that their rule was legitimized by custom, law and divine will.[40]

Across the Atlantic, similar experiments in popular politics contributed to a period of revolutionary transformation in Europe. The notion of popular sovereignty was given concrete historical expression as the events in France during 1789–92 inspired similar upheavals across the continent and beyond. Again, far from being the exclusive consequence of an unstoppable surge in popular agitation, the French Revolution and its ramifications emerged out of specific crises within the absolutist state which were exploited by enlightened sectors of the ruling class. As in the American case, revolutionary change did not necessarily engender a more democratic or egalitarian society. Yet the participation of previously disenfranchised sectors of the population in the construction of new state forms certainly had a momentous impact on the character of state sovereignty during following centuries. For one, the French Revolution generalized and radicalized the practices of state sovereignty which had been developing in Europe since the sixteenth century: small standing armies gave way to the *levée en masse*; the corporate rights of estates and cities were abolished and codified into universal citizenship rights; the process of fiscal centralization encouraged by Colbert and Louis XIV was finally completed under the Republic; the baroque ideological symbols sustaining royal absolutism were transformed into a nationalist iconography. All these familiar characteristics of the contemporary state bear the imprint of the transformations effected by the French Revolution in the name of 'the people'. Even more pertinent to the substance of the argument being presented, however, was the consolidation of factional politics during the course of the French Revolution. As Lynn Hunt has suggested, during the Revolution 'the very nature of "the political" expanded and changed shape. The structure of the polity changed under the impact of increasing political participation and popular mobilization; political language, political ritual, and political organization all took on new forms and meanings.'[41] By the late eighteenth century, the debating societies and discussion circles which had proliferated under absolutist France were transformed into political clubs such as the Parisian *Société de la Révolution*, otherwise known as the

'Jacobins'. For generations to come, the Jacobin political club remained one of the most important models of popular mobilization. Socialist and communist parties certainly drew on Jacobin principles, as did many of the nationalist movements which emerged in Europe during the nineteenth century. In this respect, again, the social movements associated with the French Revolution can be seen as the practical incarnation of the idea of popular sovereignty.

The history of nineteenth- and twentieth-century working-class and nationalist movements clearly underlines the role of civil society in the construction of state sovereignty. The relevance of nationalist organizations in this domain should be obvious: most of today's states are the product of national liberation struggles generally sponsored by mass nationalist movements. Socialism, on the other hand, appears as a weaker candidate for a force behind state sovereignty. Proletarian *internationalism* was from the outset one of the guiding principles of working-class movements across the world. The global expansion of capitalism was, according to socialists, breaking down ancestral ties of locality, ethnicity or creed and replacing them with the universal conflict among bourgeois and proletarians. As such, socialists organized internationally, making class, and not nationality, religion or colour, the mainspring of their political solidarity. The avowed cosmopolitanism of working-class organizations, however, did not preclude their commitment to democracy and equality at the national level. As Marx himself once put it: 'It is perfectly self-evident that in order to be at all capable of struggle the working class must organise itself *as a class* at home and that the domestic sphere must be the immediate arena of its struggle.'[42] Since then, working-class movements have been among the staunchest advocates of national unity and have arguably been the most important force behind processes of state-building.[43] One need only consider the socialist contributions to the extension of the franchise, the development of the welfare state or, in the case of many Third World states, the anti-imperialist struggles in order to acknowledge the centrality of modern social agency in the explanation of state sovereignty.

The examples of popular sovereignty briefly outlined above should provide some sense of the limitations inherent to a view of sovereignty which excludes any consideration of modern social movements. The idea of international society is premised on the notion of state sovereignty; the latter, in turn, must be explained as the outcome of historical changes – still under way today – unleashed by modernity. This much can be conceded to the advocates of the 'international society' approach to international relations. The problems arise when a definition of modernity and an explanation of the historical and sociological sources of state sovereignty are requested from the theorists of the English school. Here, the clearest answer comes in the shape of Martin Wight's idealist philosophy of history which ascribes the origins of modern international society to the Protestant Reformation. However, if the preceding discussion carries any weight, a richer and ultimately more accurate rendition of the rise of state sovereignty must consider the interaction between state and civil society since the seventeenth century. It must address the changing nature of popular contestation and agitation – some of it inspired by the Protestant Reformation, to be sure – and examine the consequences of such modes of political agency for our understanding of sovereignty. Once this is accomplished, I have argued, the principles and practice of popular sovereignty take on a deeper significance for international relations as they help us to identify the agency of change in the struggles between ruling and subaltern classes. In this respect, the history of international society becomes the history of its interaction with the forces of international civil society.

The standard of civilization as the expansion of capitalism

For the thinkers of the English school, a central feature of international society is the adoption of common norms and values in the interaction among sovereign states. A *society* of states is distinguished from a *system* of states, among other things, through the existence of a shared understanding of what rules and institutions should guide international intercourse. From this perspective, international society becomes a reality through the behaviour of states and statesmen in their dealings with each other. As we saw above, Gerrit W. Gong gave specific historical meaning to these interpretative norms in his study on the standard of civilization. According to Gong, the end of the nineteenth century witnessed the codification of this standard through international law, diplomacy and the spread of international institutions. Such was the triumph of the standard of civilization that by the turn of the century a general consensus on the norms, rules and values of international relations had fashioned a 'universal' international society.

The notion of a standard of civilization provides a useful tool with which to chart the expansion of international society. It clearly identifies the process by which the ruling classes across the world came to accept an international code of conduct, and there is no a priori reason to reject the view that these elites actually attached a meaning to such practices. Yet, however historically enriching such an account of international society may be, it still remains a fundamentally descriptive exercise. There is precious little in the English school's investigations on the standard of civilization to explain why this standard was accepted in the first place. Astonishingly, there is no sustained discussion in Gong's work, nor that of his fellow contributors to the volume on the *Expansion of International Society*, of capitalism and its international diffusion. An examination of the origins and development of the idea of 'civilization', however, reveals that it was contemporaneous with, and indeed germane to, the extension of capitalist social relations in Europe and beyond. It is in this sense that the expansion of international society must be studied in conjunction with the extension of capitalism.

The word 'civilization' was invented in the second half of the eighteenth century as a derivation of the terms 'civility' and 'civilize', recovered in Latin for the modern period by Erasmus in the context of a pedagogical treatise, *De civilitate morum puerilium*.[44] The new word appeared in French and English, in 1756 and 1772 respectively, as a means of distinguishing a 'polished' and 'civil' society from a 'barbarian' or 'savage' existence. The second chapter of this book has already highlighted the connections made in Ferguson's *History of Civil Society* between the idea of civilization and the institutions of commerce, specialized labour, private property and commodity exchange. Together with notions of rationality, politeness and refined manners, these components of capitalist market society defined the essence of 'civilization' as it became understood after the eighteenth century. Indeed, the Scottish Enlightenment – one of the privileged sites for the theorization of 'civilization' – reveals in the starkest light the association between the extension of capitalism and the development of this concept. In a recent study 'On the Scottish origin of "civilization"', George C. Caffenztis argues that

the development of 'civilization' is genetically intertwined with that of the British financial system, with the subjugation of Scotland to the British crown, and the eighteenth-century social struggles in and out of Scotland. Thus, 'civilization' originally referred to three different but interconnected processes: the rationalization of intercapitalist relations (civilization *qua* reason); the disenfranchisement of the English workers from their 'traditional' rights and liberties (civilization *qua* repression); and the destruction of communal relations in the Scottish Highlands, resulting in the integration of Scottish society into the orbit of Britain's imperial economy (civilization *qua* progress from Barbarism).[45]

Of these three expressions of civilization it is the latter which is most pertinent to our discussion. For one, it undermines the identification of civilization with something inherently or exclusively 'western'.[46] Far from being an exclusively geographical or cultural category, the modern idea of civilization originally referred to a socio-historical phenomenon tied to the birth and expansion of capitalism – what Marx termed the process of 'primitive accumulation'.[47] To be sure, it acquired a culturally specific meaning as European imperialism extended across the globe, imposing its own laws and values on other societies; but these laws and values were not so much 'western' as *capitalist*. The 'civilizing mission' visited upon non-European peoples during the nineteenth century was in many ways the extension of the very processes that had been tried and tested with the Scottish Highlanders and other European populations in the previous centuries. This constitutes the second significant reason for paying attention to the early processes and representations of 'civilization', namely that the features of the standard of civilization invoked by the English school actually refer back to the eighteenth-century experiments in 'civilization' *within* Europe.[48] With minor modifications, the standard of civilization which guided the expansion of international society at the end of the nineteenth century was the very one which inspired the eighteenth-century Scottish Enlightenment in its quest for extending capitalist market relations across Britain. It should therefore follow that an investigation into the standard of civilization as a vehicle for the expansion of international society must be studied as part and parcel of a broader process of capitalist expansion.

The spread of capitalist social relations across the globe was of course effected in a number of different ways. Direct and indirect imperialism, colonialism, unequal treaties and capitulations all served as vehicles in the construction of a world capitalist market. One consequence of this differentiated articulation of global capitalism was that the legal framework imposed on pre-capitalist societies was equally versatile. Many early modern trade colonies, for example, operated as commercial outposts with no intention of altering indigenous law. The widespread acceptance of consular jurisdiction (i.e. the privilege accorded to foreign merchants to live according to their own laws within the parameters of their settlement), coupled with the imperatives of commercial activity, made any European encroachment on autochthonous law unproductive. As Jörg Fisch has pointed out, in those situations where they represented a minority of the population, 'Europeans usually tried to adopt procedures used by the extra-European side rather than to impose their own legal forms and figures. The reason was obvious. If they attempted to bind their counterparts with obligations that were meaningless to them, there was little chance of their being kept.'[49]

Once European powers began to construct territorial empires, however, the question of jurisdiction became more acute. In the case of the Maghreb, for example, the standard of civilization was imposed either through outright annexation (as in the Algerian case after 1848) or through the establishment of 'protectorates' (Tunisia 1882, Morocco 1912). Differences in administrative structure were replicated in the sphere of law: the French authorities left much of the pre-colonial framework intact in the two protectorates, but in Algeria substantial changes were imposed. Similarly, the Moroccan sultan and the Tunisian bey remained nominally sovereign and their subjects bound by shariah law, Berber customary law and the special *dhimmi* status for the religious minorities. In Algeria, however, Islamic law was gradually confined to personal status through the *sénatus-consulte* of 1865 which separated French citizens (including most Algerian Jews and Christians) from the mass of the Muslim population.

One arena where legal transformation proved to be uniform across the Maghreb concerned property law. Here, all three countries experienced the gradual abolition of pre-colonial systems of land tenure – private shareholdings (*mulk*), religious endowments (*habous*), communal lands (*arsh*) – and their incorporation into modern European property law. Thus, by the second decade of the twentieth century, a standard of civilization had certainly penetrated North Africa through the vehicle of imperial conquest: the anarchic and unproductive pre-colonial regimes – so the European imperialists saw it – had been 'civilized' through their incorporation into the European sphere of commercial and property law.

Although capitalist imperialism clearly played an instrumental role in the expansion of international society, it remains notably absent in the English school's investigations into this phenomenon. Curiously, the volume edited by Bull and Watson prefers to focus on those parts of the world – the Ottoman empire, China, Japan – where capitalist imperialism made no significant inroads. Yet, despite never being formally colonized or subjected to European rule (Hong Kong, Macao, Formosa and France's North African acquisitions are of course exceptions), these states were only accepted into international society as they underwent a process of capitalist transformation 'from above'. Both the Ottoman empire and Japan introduced socio-economic reforms during the second half of the nineteenth century with the explicit aim of countering European encroachments. Their gradual integration into international society was therefore accomplished not only through the adoption of 'civilized' mechanisms of international

intercourse, but also by way of radical changes in the domestic political and socio-economic arrangements of these states. To this extent,
the expansion of international society can be seen as the 'internalization' of international norms and values and the 'homogenization'
of domestic structures in accordance with those prevailing internationally.[50]

In Japan, for example, the Meiji Restoration of 1868 transformed
the feudal regime dominated by the Tokugawa shogunate into a
modern capitalist state within the space of three decades. Much of the
impetus behind this extraordinary change in Japan's socio-economic
and political make-up was the result of internal contradictions within
the country's social structure. Peasant revolts against the com-
modification of agricultural production, coupled with an undermining
of overlord (*daimyo*) and warrior (*samurai*) status in favour of the
merchant (*chonin*) class, gave rise to a feudal-merchant coalition which
eventually overthrew the Bakufu, or central Tokugawa government.
These internal crises, however, were spurred on by the external challenge of European imperialism. Indeed, the anti-Tokugawa forces
rallied around the slogan, 'Revere the Emperor, expel the barbarians';
the latter in this case referring to the European merchants who had
been granted licence by the Bakufu to trade in Japan. Paradoxically,
the 'expulsion of the barbarians' did not entail the rejection of western
ideas. Quite the contrary: the protagonists of the Meiji Restoration
(*samurai, chonin* and some of the *daimyo* households) had maintained
extensive contacts with foreigners and in many cases adopted western
technological, economic and military innovations. In the words of
E. Herbert Norman, '[The Restoration] was carried out under the bril-
liant leadership of *samurai*-bureaucrats who, in the teeth of opposition
directed against them even by members of their own class, wisely
pursued the path of internal reconstruction ... in preference to the
path of foreign conquest.'[51]

Over the space of the forty-odd years which delimit the Meiji
Restoration (1868–1912), Japan experienced the radical overhaul of
the feudal legal-political structures that had prevailed for almost three
centuries, and their replacement by a modern capitalist framework. A
series of laws in the early 1870s legalized the sale of land and enforced
a taxation system which facilitated the expropriation of peasants from
their holdings. This in turn produced a sizeable reserve army of labour
which fuelled the beginnings of state-sponsored heavy industry. Organizing and legitimizing these infrastructural transformations was
the rationalized bureaucracy run by ex-*samurai* imbued with the orga-
nicist ideology of Herbert Spencer, and the attendant constitutional
representative bodies like the Diet. Finally, as in other parts of the

world, the turn of the century also witnessed the gradual emergence in Japan of political parties and trade unions which both contested and reinforced the legitimacy of the new regime.

The Meiji Restoration therefore represented the internalization of western standards of civilization precisely as a means of resisting their imposition from without. As such, it remains one of the clearest instances of the overlap between capitalist transformation and the expansion of international society. The Japanese adoption of the 'standard of civilization' cannot be gauged merely with reference to the practices of international relations, but must also consider the internal socio-economic and political adjustments made in the face of imperialist challenges.

A similar story could be told of the Ottoman empire's reformist experiments in the face of European expansionism. As in the case of Tokugawa Japan, the Ottoman empire had been subject to increasing commercial penetration by European traders since the sixteenth century. It was not until the second half of the eighteenth century, however, that European dominance in this sphere was codified in the form of 'capitulations' which granted foreign vessels freedom of navigation in Ottoman waters. The Treaty of Küçük Kaynarca (1774) first secured these rights for Russians, but similar treaties soon followed with Austria (1784), Britain (1799), France (1802) and Prussia (1806).[52]

To be sure, these capitulations were imposed in the aftermath of military defeat; yet their content betrays the economic motivation behind European encroachment. During the following decades, both trade and investment from the west increased exponentially, while the Sublime Porte became increasingly indebted to European creditors. By the turn of the century, the most significant regions of the Ottoman empire had been integrated within the capitalist world economy through trade, investment and debt. Interestingly, this process was accompanied by the development of institutions of external relations. As Rešat Kasaba has noted:

> Concomitant with the new treaties that were being signed with European states, the Ottoman government set up its first permanent embassies in London, Paris, Vienna and Berlin....In addition to the embassies, a consular network was set up, covering North and South America, parts of Africa and Asia, as well as Europe. Also, starting from the early nineteenth century, this global network was supported at home by a strengthened Translation Office...which in effect became the seed of the Foreign Ministry. During the nineteenth century this office would become the most developed component of the Ottoman

state apparatus, second only to the Interior Ministry in budgetary allocation.[53]

The nineteenth-century construction of Ottoman institutions for external relations plainly resulted from pressures exerted by foreign, mainly European powers. As in the case of Japan, however, this challenge also elicited responses in the sphere of domestic politics. From 1839 through to 1876, the Ottoman state underwent a process of social, political and administrative reform which historians have dubbed the *Tanzimat* (reordering) period. The *Tanzimat* reforms introduced substantial changes in the military organization, the fiscal system and the political institutions of the empire. Most important for our purposes, however, were the changes which affected the status of religious minorities (*millets*) and the land tenancy laws. An imperial edict of 1856, known as the *Hatt-i Hümayun*, stipulated the legal equality of all religious communities of the empire, thereby securing the status of Christian communities as commercial intermediaries of European capital. Two years later, a Land Code legalized the private ownership of land, while in 1867 this right was extended to foreigners. Both these sets of reforms were implemented as a direct result of European pressure and petitioning. They were also a perfectly logical response to the domestic socio-economic and political requirements of the empire. For all their admiration for western values and institutions, the bureaucrats which instigated the *Tanzimat* were operating at the interface of the domestic and the international: the reforms were as much a result of European penetration as they were a failure on the part of the existing Ottoman authorities to rise to this challenge. As Çaglar Keyder has noted, 'In the Ottoman Empire the secular bureaucracy accepted and justified their adhesion to European models and principles in the name of progressive reformism. They welcomed the institutionalisation of economic integration into Western capitalism as a victory over the retrograde tenets of the old Ottoman statecraft.'[54] The incorporation of the Ottoman empire into international society was therefore accomplished in tandem with its insertion into the world market. In this respect, one can discern a similar pattern of response to that of Japan. The outcome was certainly different in both countries: while Japan managed to pursue an autonomous route of capitalist development, the Ottoman empire experienced a dependent integration into the world capitalist market. Yet there was a crucial common denominator in both cases, namely the need to engage in radical political, social and economic transformation at the domestic level in order to be accepted into the international society of states. On the surface of it, the expansion of international society was measured by the adoption of civilized norms of international intercourse; underlying this process, however, were the more surreptitious forces of capitalist accumulation and exchange, imposing the universal logic of value creation and appropriation.

The point of this excursus into the nature of Japanese and Ottoman entrance into international society is not to ignore the relevance of norms, values and institutions in this process but rather to explain their adoption with reference to the broader experience of capitalist expansion. It is a reflection of the English school's one-dimensional approach to the expansion of international society that the contributions in the Bull and Watson volume dedicated to Japan and the Ottoman empire make no mention of capitalism, and only a passing reference to the momentous socio-economic upheavals brought about by the Meiji Restoration and the *Tanzimat*. The authors of these chapters seem oblivious to the fact that the first treaties between the western powers and these two states were commercial treaties. More seriously, their exclusive focus on the external indices of membership of international society obscures the internal reforms along capitalist lines which accompanied this privilege. In short, through their highly legalistic and statist interpretation of the expansion of international society, English school authors such as Gong, Naff and Suganami[55] fail to consider the fundamental transformations operated at the societal level in order to meet the capitalist standard of civilization. The argument presented above, on the contrary, has suggested that separating the 'high politics' of diplomacy, treaties and international institutions from the 'low politics' of legal reform, land expropriation and capitalist industrialization impoverishes our understanding of international society. An approach to this category that emphasizes the capitalist origins of the European standard of civilization, on the other hand, offers a perspective attentive to the changes at the level of civil society, and their interaction with international transformations. Keeping an eye on the relationship between these two distinct spheres, it has been argued, provides for a much richer historical and sociological understanding of the expansion of international society.

The revolt against the west: popular sovereignty and national liberation

The English school's concern with the historical evolution of international society did not stop with the universalization of this phenomenon at the turn of the century, but was extended into the post-war period. The disintegration of European empires in the aftermath of World War II and the accompanying creation of new states across the Third World posed important challenges to the notion of an international society. Did the emergence of new states undermine or reinforce the values and institutions of international society? Were the norms and values of international society actually encouraging claims to sovereignty and self-determination? What was the nature of sovereign statehood acquired by the ex-colonial peoples? These and other related questions have occupied much of the (mainly recent) literature on international society. In essence, the argument developed in this section is that, far from representing a 'revolt against the west', the Third World struggles for national liberation reflected the adoption of so-called 'western' values and practices – sovereignty, nationalism, mass political mobilization, democracy – precisely as a means of combating colonial oppression. The values and practices deployed by non-western civil society in the struggle for independence were similar to those adopted by their western counterparts in their own experience of state-formation. It is therefore fair to say that imperialist expansion created its own antithesis in the shape of nation-alist and socialist movements which identified the nation-state as the appropriate locus of their political aspirations. To be sure, the way in which such 'western' values and norms were applied was conditioned by the specific historical and cultural legacies of each colonial society. None the less, the fact remains that, rather than challenging the accepted norms of international society such as sovereign equality, national self-determination or international law, the Third World movements for national liberation actually endorsed these principles as they lent legitimacy to their political demands, both domestically and internationally.

The suggestion that national liberation should be understood as an outgrowth and not an obstacle in the expansion of international society runs contrary to the general position of those English school authors dealing with the issue. As will be indicated below, the rela-tionship between decolonization and international society is one of the more contentious areas within the work of the English school. At the one extreme, Robert H. Jackson claims that the end of empire repre-sented the shift to a 'new sovereignty game' which had substantially altered the nature of international society. James Mayall, on the other hand, accepts that Third World liberation might be interpreted as a realization of popular sovereignty which simultaneously challenged and reinforced the norms and institutions of international society. Operating in a middle ground between these two positions, Hedley

Bull offered equivocal responses to the question of how decolonization had affected international society: while in some instances his writings accept that the expansion of international society encouraged colonial peoples to achieve their own statehood, other passages insist on anti-colonialism as a 'revolt' against the western standard of civilization. Despite these contrasting views, the English school's approach to decolonization and its impact upon international society displays an important common denominator: all these authors fail to consider the grassroots pressures for decolonization. Typically, popular anti-colonial politics are ignored, deemed at best to be a marginal expression of dissatisfaction among westernized elites and, at worst, an entirely negligible factor in the emergence of new states. Thus the historiography underscoring much of the 'international society' approach to decolonization adopts the elitist, 'official mind' perspective which views the end of empire as the outcome of a planned strategy devised by prescient civil servants at Whitehall. This flawed history in turn leads to an understanding of post-colonial states as somehow distinct from their 'western' counterparts, either because, as Jackson would have it, they are 'quasi-states' or, as Bull suggests, because the norms and values that guide their behaviour are non-western. The paragraphs that follow aim to dispel the view of post-colonial states as being artificial entities conjured up in metropolitan capitals and propped up by colonial elites. Certainly many post-colonial *regimes* have proved to be undemocratic and illegitimate, but it does not follow from this that post-colonial *states* are in any sense less legitimate than other members of international society. In order to avoid this double misrepresentation of anti-colonial nationalism and its consequences for international society, it is necessary, I argue, to address the social roots of post-colonial states – that is, to consider the legitimation of newly independent states 'from below'.

Underlying the English school's understanding of post-colonial international society is the assumption that the end of empire marked a significant departure from the prevailing norms and values of international society. This understanding is premised on a view of decolonization that focuses almost exclusively on the legal-political features of this process and obscures their historical-sociological dimensions. Robert H. Jackson's influential argument on the 'negative' nature of post-colonial sovereignty, for example, relies very heavily on an account of decolonization as the product of an international moral victory by anti-colonial forces. According to Jackson,

> Independence became an unqualified right of all colonial peoples: self-determination. Colonialism like-wise became an absolute wrong: an

injury to the dignity and autonomy of those peoples and of course a
vehicle for their economic exploitation and political repression. This is a
noteworthy historical shift in moral reasoning because European overseas colonialism was originally and for a long time justified on legal
positivist and paternalist grounds.[56]

By way of explaining this momentous reversal in the international
legitimacy of colonialism, Jackson considers different routes to the end
of empire. For the author, some European empires faced anti-colonial
movements with 'positive' claims to national self-determination; in the
British colonies, however, a 'forceful and credible anti-colonial nationalism capable of inheriting sovereignty in rough conformity with
positive international law usually did not develop.'[57] In a move that
remains unexplained, Jackson takes the British experience of decolonization as being paradigmatic of the 'new sovereignty game' where
'numerous artificial ex-colonial entities are postulated, created and
protected' through the international acceptance of the right to self-
determination for colonial peoples.

While Jackson's work remains one of the most thorough examin-
ations of the impact of decolonization on international society, in
some respects it is unrepresentative of the broader consensus of English school authors on this theme. Both James Mayall and Hedley
Bull, for example, accept that the states emerging out of decolonization shared many of the key characteristics of their 'western' counterparts. Mayall is most forthright when he states categorically that
'Perhaps Asian and African societies have found some western ideas
indigestible, but the concept of the sovereign state is not one of them.
On the contrary it is the most successful western export to the rest of
the world.'[58] Bull, on the other hand, is more elusive: although he
consistently argues that the revolt against western *domination* did not
necessarily entail the revolt against western *values*, his writings on the
subject leave open the question whether since the 1960s and 1970s
the former was being conflated with the latter. In the Hagey lecture
on the concept of 'justice in international relations' Bull initially
concedes that 'Third World demands for just treatment seem entirely
compatible with the moral ideas that now prevail in the West; indeed
all of these demands take western moral premises as their point of
departure', only to insist later that 'we have to remember that
when these demands for justice were first put forward, the leaders of
Third World peoples spoke as supplicants in a world in which the
western powers were still in a dominant position ... the moral appeal
had to be cast in terms that would have most resonance in Western
societies'.[59]

Despite the important nuances in their understanding of decolonization, the work of these three English school authors displays two commonalities relevant to our argument. The first of these involves contrasting an ideal-type of Westphalian sovereign state (what Jackson unabashedly terms 'empirical statehood') with the quasi-states emerging out of decolonization. This allows the English school to consider post-colonial states as problematic for international society in so far as they fail to uphold domestic norms of governance and respect for basic rights such as life, property and the freedom of speech and association. Second, as was noted earlier, virtually nowhere in the English school's elaborations on decolonization is there a sustained consideration of the role played by collective action in this process. With the notable exception of Mayall's passing reference to popular sovereignty, the authors associated with this school seem uninterested in exploring the kind of socio-political dynamics that led to the campaigns for national self-determination in the first place. From the perspective of the English school, post-colonial sovereignty was above all the result of a recognition by the imperialist powers that colonial peoples might have a moral claim to national self-determination; independence therefore appears as something that was granted from above and not actually fought for politically from below. Both these assumptions are highly problematic historically and, furthermore, lead to thoroughly contestable readings of the status of international society as an analytical category in IR.

Let us first consider the distinction between positive and negative sovereignty which, according to Jackson, marks the break between the 'old' and the 'new' sovereignty games. There are two related objections here: one concerns the validity of this distinction; the other, the place of the distinction in Jackson's overall argument on quasi-states.

For Jackson, as we have seen, post-colonial states at the time of decolonization lacked the 'empirical sovereignty' of their European counterparts, as they were essentially products of colonial administration bereft of popular legitimacy and merely sovereign by virtue of a 'negative' international recognition. By contrast, the European states-system crafted at the Peace of Westphalia reflected both a legitimate overlap between states and the populations they ruled over, and the recourse to a 'positive' sovereignty capable of providing 'political goods for its citizens'.[60] Leaving aside for the moment the legitimacy and effectiveness of the methods deployed by European states securing such 'political goods', a brief survey of European history since 1648 would unmask Jackson's picture of 'empirical sovereignty' for the chimera that it is. Far from reflecting a clearly defined and continuous states-system, the 'old sovereignty' game in Europe has been characterized by the constant revision of territorial boundaries between states and the protracted social and political instability within states fuelled by wars, revolutions, annexations and struggles for national unification. To suggest that the European system of states can be held up as an ideal-type of how positive and negative sovereignty combine to produce the 'old sovereignty game' is to overlook how both these notions of sovereignty have been violated at regular intervals in the modern history of the continent. If the capacity of a state to 'provide political goods for its citizens'[61] is a crucial benchmark in the distinction between states and quasi-states, then European states like Spain, Greece, Germany or France to name but a few must have at different junctures during the past three centuries qualified as quasi-states.[62]

In fairness, Jackson does recognize that 'History offers many examples of large or strong states and small or weak states and indeed ramshackle or derelict states both inside Europe and outside.'[63] Hence, he is careful to emphasize that 'What has changed is not the empirical conditions of states but the international rules and institutions concerning those conditions.'[64] The point, however, is that both inside and outside Europe the claims to self-determination of the peoples living in these 'weak or ramshackle' states were premised not merely on lofty ethical principles, but on the very material shortcomings of the existing political and social arrangements. The benefit of hindsight might allow observers to debate whether the living conditions of ex-colonial peoples have improved or not after independence. But it would take a highly tendentious account of colonial history (and a large dose of imperialist nostalgia) to argue that at the time of independence the colonial powers were delivering 'positive' sovereignty to their subject populations, either in Africa or elsewhere. Jackson's elitist and legalistic view of international society 'from above' fails to consider why the rules and institutions that define the 'empirical condition of states' were questioned in the first place. For all his disclaimers to the contrary, Jackson's central argument on the 'new sovereignty game' ultimately hinges upon an idealized view of the 'classical' European system of 'positively' sovereign states, to be contrasted with an equally ephemeral post-colonial system of 'quasi-states'.

Recognizing that European state sovereignty has historically been subject to the same challenges as those faced by post-colonial 'quasi-states' undermines Jackson's radical contrast between the old and the new sovereignty games: historical evidence suggests that the sharp break posited by Jackson cannot be treated as an accurate rendition of the differences between two historical ideal-typical forms of sovereignty, but should rather be seen as a rhetorical exaggeration aimed at highlighting the shortcomings of contemporary post-colonial regimes. That Jackson's specific historical-geographical distinction is unsustainable, however, should not preclude identifying the varying expressions of state sovereignty across time and place. Clearly, the processes of post-colonial state-formation taking place in Africa during the 1960s and 1970s differed substantially from those experienced by European peoples during the preceding centuries. The challenge therefore lies in explaining why and how specific historical conjunctures give rise to diverse expressions of sovereignty. The argument of this book is that in order to address this challenge we need to pay attention to the expansion of international civil society. In the specific case of post-colonial states, the form taken by state sovereignty was heavily conditioned by the nature of the collective struggles for national liberation. In order to explain the claims to national self-determination of colonial peoples, it is necessary to investigate their forms of social and political organization and the processes which they engendered. In other words, it is essential to probe the dynamic inter-relationship between state and civil society within an international context.

Whereas the English school's account of decolonization focuses upon inter-state relations and their attendant international organisms, the approach adopted here emphasizes the role of modern social and political agency typical of civil society. Thus, contrary to the English school's juridical-diplomatic approach to the end of empire and Third World state-formation, the aim here is to highlight the place of modern social movements in the realization of national liberation. As an Africanist, Jackson chooses the experience of that continent to illustrate his theoretical claims about the nature of quasi-states and the 'new sovereignty game' for the whole of the post-colonial world. Although he recognizes that, even within Africa, many national liberation movements did actually meet the criteria necessary for the construction of 'positively' sovereign states, Jackson seems to draw his conclusions exclusively from those British colonies where national liberation movements appeared weakest. This in itself is patently inadequate. At the very least, one would expect Jackson to qualify his blanket denomination of post-colonial states as quasi-states, and contrast, say, the revolutionary road to independence in Algeria or Mozambique with the reformist routes taken by some of the British colonies he mentions. Yet, even if we accept Jackson's narrow focus on Britain's African colonies as being paradigmatic of weak and inefficient anti-colonialism yielding artificial and unstable quasi-states, empirical objections must again be raised. In comparative terms, the political parties and trade unions of Britain's African colonies may not have been as powerful and numerous as, say, their French or Portuguese counterparts, but they existed and played an important role in the end of empire. Successive generations of colonial historians have debated the impact of anti-colonial movements such as the Ghanaian Convention People's Party or the Nigerian Action Group in achieving independence for their countries. These historical disputes will undoubtedly continue unresolved, but they do at least acknowledge the relevance of collective action in the process of decolonization. IR scholars, and the English school in particular, on the other hand, have failed to account for the role of anti-colonial civil society in the construction of the post-colonial international order. This is not just a problem of historical insensitivity in IR but, more seriously, reflects the discipline's embedded disregard for the role of social and political agency in the construction and transformation of the international system. In the specific case of decolonization and its impact upon international society, it leads to a static and elitist account of struggles for national liberation and the post-colonial order it gave rise to, where the dynamics of international society remain restricted to the negotiation of moral and legal norms among statesmen in diverse international forums.

Conclusions: international civil society and international society

The basic aim of this chapter has been to outline the theoretical value of the term 'international civil society' for the study of international relations. I have chosen to do so through a critique of one of the defining categories of our discipline: international society. While accepting that the research agendas opened up by the study of international society still remain central to IR, the arguments presented in this chapter have suggested that the prevailing approach to international society – that associated with the English school – is unsatisfactory in two key respects. First, through its limited conception of 'society' as applied to international relations, the 'international society' approach is unable to accommodate broader social phenomena such as capitalist social relations or collective social and political agency into its account of the international system. Second, and following on from this, the interpretations of world politics offered by the 'international society' perspective tend to reify existing international norms, values and institutions in ways that obscure their socially and politically contested nature. In other words, contrary to some of their best intentions, many of the authors adopting the 'international society' school assume an elitist, statist and ultimately conservative view of international relations.

As I hope the preceding sections have demonstrated, some of the key components of international society – sovereign statehood, the standard of civilization, national self-determination – must be explained with reference to historical processes such as the global reproduction of capitalism and social forces like modern social movements. In order to identify and explain the origins and transformations of modern international society, it is imperative to look beyond the surface expressions of international intercourse among ruling classes and their attendant norms, values and institutions, and consider the social processes which engender these practices both domestically and internationally.

It was proposed that the conceptual tool employed in this endeavour should be that of international civil society. As applied thus far, international civil society refers to that domain of international relations where the modern social movements emerging out of the global expansion of capitalism pursue their political goals. These movements have from the outset been forged in constant interaction with the institutions of international society, and have in turn shaped the values, norms and institutions of this very society of states. Thus, as this chapter has sought to demonstrate, the development of sovereign statehood, the extension of a western 'standard of civilization' or the emergence of a post-colonial international society cannot be adequately explained without making reference to the social and political transformations taking place at the level of civil society. One important feature of the term 'international civil society', therefore, is that it allows students of international relations to investigate systematically the way in which the historical interaction between state and civil society has constructed modern international society.

A second significant benefit in considering international civil society when explaining the dynamics of international society relates to the political horizons it holds out. The incapacity of most 'international society' theorists to encompass collective social and political agency within their account of international relations severely limits the political potential of the concept. If, as the prevailing understanding presents it, international society is essentially a society of states sustained by a code of international conduct agreed upon by ruling elites, then the scope for radical social and political change at both the domestic and the international level is immediately circumscribed. From this perspective, change in international society only arises when government officials and international bureaucrats reach a new consensus on the norms and values that should guide their international behaviour. Thus, as we have seen, the end of empire is explained by authors such as Robert H. Jackson and Hedley Bull as the outcome of a reversal in the ethical assumptions among western elites on the right of colonial peoples to self-determination. Likewise, the appearance of racial equality as a principle of post-war international society is ascribed to 'the new dominance of two strongly anti-colonial great powers, the United States and the Soviet Union'.[65] On this account, momentous social and political transformations in world politics are attributed to the logic of statecraft as it is manifested in international fora like the United Nations or to the bilateral negotiations between diplomats. International political change is ultimately effected by states, and social forces beyond the state remain tangential to global transformations.

The concept of international civil society on the other hand aims deliberately to incorporate social forces outside the state into an account of international social and political change. It seeks not only to identify the way in which non-state actors have influenced the course of modern international society, but also to emphasize that international society itself has proved instrumental in forging many of these social movements which inhabit international civil society. What is at stake here, therefore, is not so much the sterile arguments within our discipline as to whether it is inter-state or transnational forces that best define the workings of the international system but, rather, how these two spheres of the international combine to produce a wider totality of international relations. The history of modern international society is the history of the interaction between state and civil societies within an international context. Once this premise is accepted, the potential of international social and political transformation is no longer limited to an international society of states, but comes to embrace collective social and political activity outside, though not necessarily against, the state. While it is unlikely that such social movements will in the future ignore the territorial state as the locus of their political aspirations, it would be equally short-sighted to reduce the possibilities of international political change exclusively to the realm of inter-state activity. In order to avoid the pitfalls of both unalloyed transnationalism and state-centric realism, it is, I have argued, necessary to complement the study of international society with the investigation of international civil society. This injunction is perhaps especially relevant when considering the current debates in IR and beyond on civil society and globalization – the subject matter of the next chapter.

5

The Promises of International Civil Society

Global Governance, Cosmopolitan Democracy and the End of Sovereignty?

The present chapter returns full circle to the starting point of this book by considering contemporary debates on international (or global) civil society and its political promises. For over a decade since the end of the Cold War, scholars, observers, activists and political practitioners have increasingly invoked the notion of 'civil society' in their discussion of global issues. Though characterized as much by disagreement and contention as by overlapping views, these discussions can be said to converge upon three associated dimensions of globalization: global civil society, global governance and cosmopolitan democracy. Students of globalization have generally included the transnational extension of activist networks as part of this process of 'space–time compression'. For their part, theorists preoccupied with the new forms of planetary political rule – or 'global governance' – underline the prominent role of civil society in the definition of this concept. Likewise, scholars concerned with the political challenges of globalization have issued path-breaking arguments for a cosmopolitan democracy rooted in a transnational civil society.

The preceding chapters in this study have already indicated how the notion of civil society should be at the core of such discussions, independently of whether it is explicitly invoked or not. After all, as we have seen thus far, the rise and international expansion of civil society is germane to the explanation of those very structures like capitalism and state sovereignty that arguably underpin phenomena such as globalization and global governance. But the fact that civil society figures so prominently in the recent literature on globalization, governance and cosmopolitanism provides all the more reason for critically engaging with these debates. The concern of this chapter, therefore, is the place of civil society in the processes associated with globalization and global governance, and indeed in the theoretical reflections on these processes. More specifically, the pages that follow aim to draw together the arguments on sovereignty, modern collective agency and the limits to international change made in preceding chapters, deploying them in the context of current debates on civil society and globalization. The central argument of this chapter is that, contrary to the claims of most globalization theorists, the concept of international (or global) civil society should not be exclusively or even principally associated with globalization and the accompanying notions of global governance and cosmopolitan democracy. This is so for at least three reasons.

First, international civil society must be disassociated from globalization because the former's existence long pre-dates the advent of the latter process. This claim represents more than a simple backdating of the historical emergence of international civil society, for it highlights the very modern properties of this category, thereby situating the relation between civil society and globalization in the broader context of the socio-historical epoch we have come to identify as 'modernity'. On this account, globalization represents the current phase of a wider historical process, one dimension of which was the expansion of international civil society since the late eighteenth century – a process which arguably set the terrain for contemporary 'global' civil society.

Second, international civil society should not be equated with a new, transnational domain of socio-political activity that acts as a democratic bulwark against the unaccountable institutions of global governance because, as will be suggested below, many agents of international civil society are themselves thoroughly unaccountable and undemocratic. Again, far from being a purely contingent circumstance, questions surrounding the political legitimacy of agents in international civil society are intimately connected to the territorial character of modern political rule. In so far as this is the case, it follows that democratic politics cannot so readily disown its historical connection with the institutions of state sovereignty. Put differently, undermining state sovereignty can be as detrimental to the objective of accountable, democratic politics as it is in some instances beneficial: many agents of international civil society, however, often fail to note that being 'non-governmental' does not mean being 'non-political' – that is, that their actions, however 'transnational', necessarily impinge on existing, territorially bounded 'communities of fate'. To that extent, and contrary to most discussions of civil society and globalization, there is nothing intrinsically progressive or democratic about international civil society.

Finally, and following from the latter point, the expansion of international civil society should not be seen as heralding the end of state sovereignty and the concomitant rise of institutions of global governance built in interaction with a rising global civil society. As has been suggested throughout this book, the agents of international civil society are necessarily implicated in the reproduction of the inter-state system and to that extent must still formulate their demands with reference to the sovereign state, regardless of whether these demands are actually executed domestically through the national state or internationally via the institutions of global governance. This is not to ignore the obvious interface between international civil society and the institutions of global governance – many social movements that operate within international civil society can and do engage with the institutions of global governance, and indeed influence the operation and policies of these institutions. Nor is it to underestimate how states have been forced to alter their structures and strategies to accommodate the challenges of globalization. It is, however, to insist that the interaction between social movements of civil society and the institutions of global governance is still mediated through the structure of state sovereignty in ways that preclude the facile domestic analogy between the state and civil society on the one hand, and 'global civil society' as a counterpart to international institutions of global governance on the other. The interesting question in this context, therefore, is not so much 'is state sovereignty disappearing in the face of globalization?', but rather 'how is the relation between state and civil society being reshaped internationally under the pressures of globalization?'

This three-pronged critique of contemporary discussions on global civil society and global governance will proceed as follows: the first section surveys some of the more influential contemporary formulations of the nexus between globalization and civil society. Thus, the work of Richard Falk on 'global civil society', that of Hardt and Negri on empire and the end of sovereignty and the writings of David Held on 'cosmopolitan democracy' will be taken as representative samples of how this juxtaposition is being theorized inside and outside the field of IR. A second part of the chapter develops the critical arguments summarized above, dealing in turn with the historical, sociological and political limitations to the prevailing conception of the relation between civil society and globalization. Without wishing to negate the historical particularity and the political significance of this relation, a case will be made for a more nuanced approach to the interaction between 'global non-state actors' and 'global governance'; one that places it within the broader historical process of the expansion of international civil society, and therefore recognizes the political limits to the idea of 'global civil society' as it is presently conceived. Finally, due consideration will be given to the real normative promises that, however qualified, the idea of international civil society holds out for activists engaged in the politics of a globalizing world. Here the claim is that, if international civil society is considered as a socio-historical domain intrinsic to the modern international system, a more sober, and therefore more effective, assessment of the potential of global transformative agency will make itself available.

Civil society and globalization

The idea of civil society has been invoked with reference to globalization in at least three different though plainly interrelated contexts. First, there are those studies that see the growing economic, technological and cultural integration of a globalizing world as spurring on greater co-operation among socio-political activists across the globe. From this perspective, globalization is a process that is unifying political actors both 'from above' and 'from below' and to that extent we can group authors who take this view under the rubric of 'grassroots globalization theorists'.

Tied to this view of globalization as a process that fosters global grassroots solidarity is a second view of globalization and civil society: one that sees activities of 'global' civil society as undermining traditional state sovereignty. On this account, the globalization of capitalist production and exchange (i.e. the globalization of civil society) has forced states to transfer their sovereign functions in the management and regulation of socio-economic affairs on to international institutions of 'global governance' – particularly the United Nations (UN) and its specialized agencies. This in turn has encouraged social movements within civil society to displace the locus of transformative politics from a purely national to a global plane, thereby further abetting the transformation of the modern state's policy structures in accordance with these new modes of globalized contestation. I shall label the diverse group of scholars attached to this viewpoint as the 'global governance theorists'.

Finally, whether they agree in the detail of the preceding formulations of globalization or not, political theorists such as David Held and Daniele Archibugi have accepted the existence of such a process as a starting point for rethinking the nature of democracy in a globalizing world, and more concretely, developing the conceptual and practical mechanisms for the establishment of a 'cosmopolitan democracy' or 'cosmopolitan governance'. These authors recognize that there are both barriers and opportunities for the extension of liberal democracy inherent in the process of globalization. But in so far as they generally welcome the erosion of the national state's sole prerogative over popular sovereignty, and advocate the increasing transfer of such sovereignty to various international multilateral bodies (principally the UN), these authors can aptly be classed as 'cosmopolitan democrats'.

It should be emphasized that this threefold classification of theorists serves a purely heuristic purpose. There is considerable overlap in the analytical interests of the various groupings, and their differentiation does not correspond to an agreement over the political or normative implications of juxtaposing globalization and civil society. With these caveats in mind, it is now possible to explore in greater detail these three different approaches to our subject matter.

Grassroots globalization

For many globalization theorists, the world-wide compression of time and space is a phenomenon that has engulfed all aspects of our social life, including political activism. On this view, the rise of specifically 'planetary' concerns such as ozone layer depletion or the international spread of AIDS/HIV has encouraged activists to organize and conceptualize their struggles on a global scale. Furthermore, such transnational grassroots activism is increasingly facilitated by the globalization of audio-visual media, the popularization of electronic mail and the Internet, greater international mobility (at least for those living in OECD countries) and indeed the increased familiarity with the globally dominant socio-cultural norms and values (such as 'human rights', 'democracy' or 'civil society') resulting from all these phenomena. The upshot of all this is clear for concerned scholars like Richard Falk:

> Such cumulative developments are facilitating the birth and growth of global civil society at this time. They carry the possibility of an exten-

sion of the movement for democratization beyond state/society relations to all arenas of power and authority, including international
institutions.... These expressions of globalization from below can be
contrasted with a geopolitical approach to geogovernance, and amount
to a multifaceted struggle to achieve a new equilibrium that reorients
market and state to an extent that is nurturing toward both nature and
its human inhabitants. Such reorientation embodies the spirit and
substance of humane governance.[1]

Falk is not alone in his sanguine appraisal of globalization 'from
above' encouraging a corresponding globalization 'from below'.[2]
We saw in chapter 1 how many IR scholars (those labelled there
as 'new transnationalists') have associated globalization with a
fresh wave of transnational activism which has signalled the rise of
global civil society. Similarly, most recent studies of globalization
seem to include a requisite section or chapter on global or transnational civil society as an expression of grassroots globalization
that bears the promise of democratization.[3] Some theorists go even
further in arguing that transnational social movement activity is politicizing previously unexplored spaces in the international system.
In his study of environmental movements and world politics, for
example, Paul Wapner suggests that, by refusing to limit their conception of political power to that exercised by sovereign authorities,
such movements are actively generating new political spaces beyond
the states-system: 'Activists pursue ... types of action that aim not
to establish governmental institutions nor to dismantle existing
ones but to enlist the governing capabilities of instruments available
below, above, and at the level of the state. These instruments are
part of global civil society, and by employing them activists engage
in world civic politics.'[4] Such a view has been echoed from different
disciplinary and methodological starting points by various other theorists (some discussed in chapter 1), and in many respects it could
be interpreted as a globalized rendition of the liberal 'republican'
understanding of civil society briefly examined in chapter 2. The
relevant conclusion for present purposes is that these accounts of
'grassroots globalization' not only recognize the extension of social
movement activity beyond state boundaries but, perhaps more importantly, see this as prising open previously sealed arenas in world
politics, thus gradually replacing the national state as the major
locus of political power. In this respect, 'grassroots globalization'
theorists pave the way for the discussion of civil society and the
international form of political rule that has come to be known as
'global governance'.

Civil society and global governance

For many observers, a key outcome of globalization is the gradual but irreversible erosion of the modern state as the sole depository of political legitimacy. This process is being accompanied by the rise of what Michael Hardt and Antonio Negri have recently called a new 'constitution of Empire'. Under this new global juridico-political arrangement,

> Government and Politics come to be completely integrated into the system of transnational command. Controls are articulated through a series of international bodies and functions, [while] the global People [*sic*] is represented more clearly and directly not by governmental bodies but by a variety of organizations that are at least relatively independent of nation-states and capital. These organizations are often understood as functioning as the structures of global civil society, channelling the needs and desires of the multitude into forms that can be represented within the functioning of the global power structures.[5]

Again, other theorists have put this same point in different terms, with Stephen Gill, for example, speaking of the 'new constitutionalism' of 'disciplinary liberalism' where 'neoliberalism is institutionalized at the macro-level of power in the quasi-legal restructuring of the state and international political forms.... This discourse of global economic governance is reflected in the conditionality policies of the Bretton Woods organizations, quasi-constitutional regional arrangements such as NAFTA or Maastricht, and the multilateral regulatory framework of the new World Trade Organization.'[6] Without wishing to paper over the often radical differences in interpretation, it can none the less be said that, for our purposes, the overarching concern of these scholars is 'global governance'. Moreover, because of the multiple meanings attached to 'global governance', it may be worth highlighting just two interrelated dimensions of this category: its association to state sovereignty and the place of civil society in its constitution.

Most approaches to the idea of global governance start from the premise that the processes of globalization unleashed after the crisis of the 1970s forced OECD states to transfer political responsibilities previously allocated to the national state on to international multilateral institutions. According to one recent study of globalization, 'there is little doubt that there has been a growing internationalization of political decision-making and of diverse aspects of global governance – that is there has been a marked extension of the infrastructures and institutions of global political networks, rule-making and activity.'[7] As we shall see below, one shortcoming of such a formulation is the absence of a clear historical demarcation of when global governance was set in motion. This is worth underlining because, in most accounts, the UN and its accompanying specialized agencies (including, of course, the Bretton Woods institutions) are generally identified as the main depositories of those sovereign responsibilities 'internationalized' by the national state. Thus, global governance has become closely associated with the rise of 'international regimes' on, say, the international drugs trade or human rights, monitored and regulated by the UN system. In so far as this represents the gradual hollowing out of state sovereignty it must also have, according to the structural view adopted in chapter 3, severe implications for the agents of civil society: for, if the modern state is devolving its legitimate monopoly over political rule on to multilateral institutions, where do social movements of civil society target their socio-political grievances?

The answer for most theorists of global governance lies in the development of a global civil society that interacts with the multilateral institutions of the UN. Such a response was especially clear in the Commission on Global Governance's influential report *Our Global Neighbourhood*: 'At the global level, governance has been viewed primarily as intergovernmental relationships, but it must now be understood as also involving non-governmental organizations (NGOs), citizen's movements, multinational corporations, and the global capital market.'[8] This answer has, however, been replicated in numerous academic studies, the most sophisticated of which is perhaps the collection edited by Leon Gordenker and Thomas G. Weiss on *NGOs, the United Nations and Global Governance*. In their introduction to this volume, the editors suggest:

> In their own ways, NGOs and intergovernmental organizations (IGOs) grope, sometimes co-operatively, sometimes competitively, sometimes in parallel towards a modicum of 'global governance'. We define global governance as efforts to bring a more orderly and reliable response to social and political issues that go beyond the capacities of states to address individually. Like the NGO universe, global governance implies an absence of central authority, and the need for collaboration or co-operation among governments and others who seek to encourage common practices and goals in addressing global issues.[9]

Global civil society therefore emerges from these readings as a domain that simultaneously reacts to the 'internationalization' of the state and encourages the latter process. On this interpretation, the agents of global civil society fulfil a functional or 'operational' role as 'grass-roots partners' of multilateral institutions in the administration of global governance. As such, they contribute to the shifting locus of sovereign power from the national state on to international organizations like the UN, thereby also 'politicizing', as we saw above, new arenas of 'world civic politics'. In short, for theorists of global governance the agents of civil society play a crucial role in defining the former category because, first, in adopting transnational socio-political causes (such as the defence of women's rights) they foster the establishment of multilateral regimes that can manage global governance, and, second, because they lend popular legitimacy to such regimes by representing a putative 'global *demos*', or at the very least acting on behalf of assorted INGOs and global social movements deemed to be representative of an equally imaginary 'global public opinion'.

Civil society and cosmopolitan democracy

While there is a perceptible, sometimes explicit, normative undercurrent to most of the analyses of civil society and global governance discussed above, the positive endorsement of globalization as a process that can potentially extend liberal democracy across the world must be reserved for the group of theorists classed earlier as 'cosmopolitan democrats'.[10] The most comprehensive and influential formulation of this promise behind globalization and its attendant institutions of global governance and global civil society is that found in David Held's proposals for 'cosmopolitan democracy'. The work of Held is predictably complex and multifaceted. Moreover, it is characterized in equal measure by analytical and prescriptive (and therefore sceptical and optimistic) assessments of the democratizing potential of globalization. There are, however, two basic claims in the cosmopolitan democratic agenda which are especially relevant to the present discussion of civil society and globalization.

The first is Held's insistence that the dominant understanding of international relations – what he terms the 'Westphalian model' of sovereign states – severely limits the realization of any democratic impulse that may lie behind civil society. For Held, the sovereign state continues to play a crucial role both in the analysis of international affairs and in the promotion and protection of democratic politics. Yet since the end of World War II it has been subjected to a series of pressures through the process of globalization which require thinking about democratic politics beyond the system of states: 'there cannot be an account of the democratic state any longer without an examination of the global system and there cannot be an examination of the global system without an account of the democratic state. The way forward is to transcend the endogenous and exogenous frameworks of the theoretical traditions which have informed hitherto the analysis of the modern polity and international relations.'[11] Moreover, 'Democratic institutions and practices have to be articulated with the complex arena of national and international politics, and the mutual interpenetration of the national and the international must be mapped.'[12] Thus, Held's initial premise in this context coincides with the theories of global governance considered above in that it identifies democratic power with institutions both within and beyond the sovereign state. From this perspective, the world-wide extension of liberal democracy must be interpreted in a cosmopolitan vein as emerging through globally constituted political institutions, or what Held terms 'a cosmopolitan authority system'.[13]

This association of cosmopolitan democracy and global governance leads to the second area where Held's analysis dovetails with our present concerns, and that is his emphasis on the role of civil society in sustaining any project for cosmopolitan democracy. Here, again, the objective is not somehow to subsume local, 'domestic' agents of civil society under an overarching global civil society but, rather, to transcend the 'inside/outside' dichotomy and channel the increasing interpenetration between discrete states and societies within an overlapping 'cosmopolitan legal framework'.[14] For Held, this new legal framework is to be built upon 'a network of regional and international agencies and assemblies that cut across spatially delimited locales'. Such a network in turn is sustained by a 'number of processes and forces, including: the development of transnational, grass-roots movements with clear regional or global objectives ... and the emergence and proliferation in the twentieth century of international institutions to coordinate transnational forces and problems, from the UN and its agencies to regional political networks and organizations.'[15] Indeed, in outlining the institutional architecture of cosmopolitan democracy, Held identifies the 'articulation of political institutions with the key groups, agencies, associations and organizations of economy and civil society, national and international' as one of the three basic requirements for such an experiment to become viable. Accordingly, he reserves a privileged role for global civil society in a proposed UN 'Second Chamber' of peoples.

Overall, therefore, it is clear that Held's proposal for a cosmopolitan democracy envisages a substantial role in the realization of such a project for the internationally organized agents of civil society. While accepting that other political actors and institutions – including the sovereign state – are essential in shaping the contours of a 'cosmopolitan authority system', Held sees transnational socio-political activism as one of the motors behind the democratic overhaul of the 'Westphalian model'. Furthermore, he assigns transnational social movements an important function as mediators between the institutions of cosmopolitan governance and the corresponding cosmopolitan *demos*. In all these respects, Held's work overlaps with much of the grassroots globalization and global governance literature examined above, and indeed imbues it with specific normative content.

Civil society and the limits of globalization

We have thus far seen how the idea and practice of civil society has been incorporated into recent discussions on globalization and its attendant notions of global governance and cosmopolitan democracy. Notwithstanding the differences in emphasis and divergent areas of focus, it can reasonably be said that each of the three theories agrees on two basic points about contemporary world politics. First, that socio-political activists are increasingly organizing transnationally, thereby shifting the sites of socio-political power and legitimacy above and beyond the sovereign state; and, second, that these shifts in the locales of power are largely positive developments in the extension of liberal democracy and the enforcement of transparency and accountability at the global level. When these claims are made, civil society is generally invoked in one form or another as a key component in the unfolding of these processes.

At one level, it would be churlish to reject these claims wholesale. Even the most sceptical of commentators have conceded that the last quarter of the twentieth century witnessed the transfer of sovereign authority from the national state on to international multilateral institutions – that is, that institutions of global governance have acquired increasing political power.[16] Moreover, it must be accepted that the exponential growth in the number of international non-governmental organizations (INGOs) since the 1970s has been matched by their increasing presence in and influence over diverse aspects of international relations.[17] To that extent, a broadly conceived notion of globalization has indeed produced new frameworks of international political rule known as 'global governance' and a fresh wave of transnational socio-political activism which might reasonably be described as constituting a 'global civil society'.

The assumption throughout this book has been that these changes are real and substantial, and that they must therefore be explained. The underlying argument, however, has been that in order to do so we must take a deeper historical and sociological understanding of both the modern states-system and international civil society. Reference to globalization, global governance and global civil society takes us part of the way, but not the full stretch: it may help to *describe* and narrow our focus on these new developments in world politics, but it will not adequately *explain* the phenomena in question. The idea of international civil society presented in this study, on the other hand, aims to offer an explanatory account of how modern social movements have organized internationally and thereby shaped the modern international system. On this understanding, globalization and its accompanying processes must be seen as part of the far-reaching structural transformations inaugurated by capitalist modernity. In particular, the interrelation between civil society and globalization should be analysed in the context of these changes which, as we have seen, ushered in transnational socio-political activity long before the advent of globalization. In sum, the debates over globalization, governance and civil society explored above are plainly relevant to the notion of international civil society presented in this study; but as the following sections will demonstrate, in their current formulation, these debates suffer from three major shortcomings which severely weaken their explanatory power and limit their political promise as purveyors of global democratic change.

Historical limitations: the legacy of internationalism

One of the major areas of dispute in the debates on globalization concerns the historical novelty of this process. For many, globalization represents an epochal break in modern world history, signalling in fact the transition to a post-modern global society where the accepted notions of sovereignty, politics, work, culture, time, space and so forth are rapidly being undermined and replaced by the logic of a post-Fordist, decentred and 'disorganized' capitalism. Other observers are more cautious in their assessment of the degree and scope of change, but even they recognize that the term 'globalization' aptly captures a sense of socio-historical movement and transformation which has affected most parts of the world since at least the end of World War II.

There is no space here to consider in detail the various arguments surrounding globalization and epochal change (although it is worth noting that they are often predicated on a progressivism and a technological determinism usually associated with a long-discarded 'vulgar' Marxism). It should, however, be clear from the argument presented thus far that I consider 'globalization' to be a temporal expression of, and not a qualitative alternative to, capitalism in the same way that the 'new imperialism' of the late nineteenth century or the first Cold War of the late 1940s and 1950s were also manifestations of particular 'moments' in the history of capitalism. In other words, globalization is recognized in this study as marking a distinct *phase* in the historical development of capitalism, and not as somehow representing a historical *departure* from the dominant system of capitalist social relations. This historical understanding of globalization has significant implications for the present discussion of international civil society in at least two key respects.

First, situating the process of globalization within the wider development of capitalist modernity helps to underline the fact that the trans-boundary, transnational or globalized socio-political activism so often and exclusively associated with globalization is by no means historically unprecedented. As this study has indicated throughout, modern social movements have organized across and sometimes above territorial political communities since at least the end of the eighteenth century. Indeed, it has further been argued that in some historical contexts (e.g. European national unifications of the nineteenth century) modern social movements have been instrumental in constituting new, integrated political communities out of previously fragmented entities. At the very least, therefore, discussion of the role of social movements and civil society in the processes of globalization should be mindful of the historical precedents to contemporary 'grassroots globalization'.

Once again, this reminder is not aimed at discrediting those studies that identify very real modifications in the form and content of transnational social movement activity over the past three or four decades. Nor is it to suggest that such activity can simply be read off as the natural outcome of centuries of accumulated social movement experience. It is, however, to insist that these changes must be analysed in the context of broader structural transformations of world politics since the seventeenth century, and that, moreover, an adequate explanation of how transnational social movements emerge in the first place, and what their impact on world politics might be, requires placing their activity within this longer historical time-frame.[18] To take but one example: it would be a very weak, almost disingenuous account of contemporary global feminist activism that did not consider the nine-teenth- and twentieth-century internationalist precedents to such activ-ity. For it is arguably the first and second generations of international women's organizations that set out the ideological principles and mobilizing frameworks which today make it possible for feminists across the world to pursue their global socio-economic and political objectives. Put bluntly, no amount of dedicated websites, conference networking or INGO umbrella groups can replace the legacy of 'clas-sical' feminist internationalism as the major factor in explaining the existence of global women's movements today. However, in over-emphasizing the latter, seemingly post-modern aspects of global social movement activity (feminist or otherwise), 'grassroots globalization' theorists tend to overlook the crucial legacy of more old-fashioned, quaintly modernist international social movements – an oversight which, as will be argued below, often carries significant political implications.

Second, identifying the temporal location of globalization is crucial in divesting notions of global or transnational civil society from any direct association with claims about the end of state sovereignty. As was shown earlier in the chapter, many analysts of globalization, especially those labelled here as 'grassroots globalization' and 'global governance' theorists, see in the consolidation of a global civil society the necessary erosion of state sovereignty. Yet it is, again, by looking back at the historical evolution of transnational socio-political activ-ism that it becomes apparent how deeply implicated modern social movements are in the reproduction of modern state sovereignty. If the theoretical arguments and historical illustrations of previous chapters are in any way compelling, it should be clear by now that we cannot simply equate transnational activism, be it in an age of globalization or otherwise, with the end of state sovereignty. In fairness, few global-ization theorists stake out their claims in such bold terms, but the underlying assumption in their discussions of global civil society is that the socio-political agents operating in this domain are contrib-uting to the irreversible replacement of the national state as the major locus of political authority. Most globalization theorists seem so engrossed with recent expressions of transnational activism that they forget how, historically, transnational socio-political activity has re-inforced state sovereignty as much as it has undermined it. There is therefore little reason to believe that, as one influential commentator has put it, 'the growth of global civil society has, in tandem with the spread of supraterritoriality more generally, shifted the framework of politics away from its previous core principle of sovereign state-hood.'[19] Once the emergence and development of international social movements is traced back to the past two centuries, the current fixation of globalization theorists with trans-boundary activism and its accompanying threat to territorial state sovereignty appears rather short-sighted. Indeed, recent studies on the historical evolution of 'governance' highlight the ways in which capitalist states have sought since the Industrial Revolution to co-ordinate and regulate the boundless dynamics of capital through liberal institutions of 'global governance'.[20] From the very outset of industrial capital's international diffusion, the ideas and institutions of what used to be called 'liberal internationalism' were fostering a global inter-state *and* inter-societal consensus over the norms, rules and values which should regulate the international economy (or what is today known as 'global governance').

Globalization, therefore, may be ushering in new combinations of relations between states and civil societies, but, in line with the arguments presented in chapter 3, there is little sign that these changes are in any way structural changes. In other words, it is quite possible, as this study has endeavoured to show, to acknowledge the increasing incidence of transnational socio-political activism in international relations while at the same time suggesting that state sovereignty is a major structural determinant in the dynamics of the international system. Viewing the agents of international civil society *historically*, it has been argued, contextualizes the current interaction between globalization and civil society in ways that both explain the existence of a so-called 'global civil society' and severely qualify any claims about its contribution to the erosion of state sovereignty.

Sociological limitations: the politics of accreditation

The previous paragraphs focused on one initial shortcoming of recent studies surrounding civil society and globalization, namely the historical myopia of much of this literature. Such historical insensitivity, it has been suggested, is of concern not only because it ignores the legacy of 'classical' internationalism in explaining the contemporary resurgence of transnational activism but, more seriously, because in so doing it underestimates the historically forged structural relations between the agents of civil society and the institutions of state sovereignty.

It will be argued in the present section that something similar happens with the sociological content of globalization theories of civil society. For, as we saw above, no matter what their angle on the issue, globalization theorists concerned with transnational civil society tend to make two highly contestable assumptions: first, that the latter domain somehow acts as a fairly homogeneous, non-hierarchical and disinterested counterpoint to the power-driven system of states; and, second, that global civil society is therefore representative of an otherwise marginalized 'global people's power' or a disenfranchised 'global citizenry' which stands outside the realm of inter-state relations. These two assumptions in turn generate inflated expectations about the possibilities of socio-political change through the participation of agents of civil society in the institutions of global governance. For, it will be argued, INGOs are far too heterogeneous, unrepresentative and functional in character to act as collective agents of global structural change – at best, they may be seen as *part* of a broader international civil society, but never as sole representatives of this sphere of international relations. The transformative and representative limits of a global civil society, thus understood, are especially visible when considering the role of NGOs and other 'grassroots groups' at international conferences and in their interaction with multilateral institutions. It is in this respect that 'the politics of accreditation' serves as a useful epithet with which to examine these limitations.

One index of the growing influence of civil society in international relations, it is often noted, is the increased participation of non-state actors in global governance. As we saw earlier in the chapter, global governance theorists such as Leon Gordenker and Thomas Weiss have spoken of the 'pluralization' of this phenomenon through the incorporation of NGOs and other non-state actors into the governance process: 'Constituent NGOs working in different sectors can interact in these bridging organizations that furnish what otherwise would be absent – a forum for discussion and cooperation. As a consequence, grassroots groups get a voice and attempt to influence policy-making.'[21] Similarly, in their recent study on the contestation of global governance by global social movements, Robert O'Brien, Jan Aart Scholte and Marc Williams have highlighted the development of a 'complex multilateralism' which, in response to such social movement pressure, 'has incrementally pluralized governing structures' so that 'MEIs [multilateral economic institutions] are moving beyond their interstate mandates to actively engage civil society actors in numerous countries.'[22]

The first thing to be said about these claims for the 'pluralization' of governance is that it is helpful, once again, to broach them within an appropriate historical context. As Gordenker and Weiss readily acknowledge, NGO participation in global governance can be stretched back to the founding of the International Labour Organization in 1919 and the establishment of the UN's Economic and Social Council (ECOSOC) in 1946 – both, incidentally, in response not so much to 'grassroots' activism but to the pressures emanating from a revolutionary *state*, the Soviet Union. It was the ECOSOC that laid down the terms of NGO accreditation at the UN which according to Peter Willetts '[determined] many of the main features of the system as it still operates today'.[23] The details of the UN Charter's Article 71 setting out the conditions for NGO consultative status need not detain us here.[24] For present purposes, it is enough simply to underline how the ECOSOC framework for NGO consultative status has been the mainstay of those recent UN world conferences on environment (Rio de Janeiro, 1992), human rights (Vienna, 1993) and women (Beijing, 1995) which have been so insistently portrayed as representative fora of global civil society. It is by focusing briefly on these conferences and their 'politics of accreditation' that a more sober perspective on the representative and transformative role of NGOs becomes apparent.

There is no doubt that the number and range of NGOs represented at UN world conferences has risen spectacularly since the Stockholm Conference on the Environment in 1972. Different studies cite hundreds of NGOs officially accredited and thousands unofficially represented at the various world conferences held since then, while the geographical and ideological scope of their representation has arguably also been extended. Moreover, regardless of their formal participation in official conference proceedings, the sheer number of NGOs attending such specialized conferences has made these events a focal point both for transnational 'networking' and in raising global awareness through media coverage. At one level, therefore, UN-sponsored world conferences have indeed occasioned the unique convergence of global agents of civil society.

Yet, on closer inspection, the form, content and eventual outcomes of such gatherings are so heavily circumscribed by the interests of states that it is difficult to see how the agents of global civil society can be said to be genuinely representative of an autonomous and undifferentiated 'global citizenry'. In this regard, the experience of world conferences during the 1990s suggests that, to adapt a phrase, 'global civil society is what states make of it'. In the first place, the geographical and political origins of NGOs has a considerable influence on whether they are granted consultative status or not by the UN. Thus, it is unsurprising that well-endowed INGOs such as Save the Children Fund, Amnesty International or Médicins sans Frontières, based in or originating from liberal OECD states, have generally secured an influential position at such meetings – especially at the crucial preparatory committee (PrepCom) stages – to the detriment of Third World NGOs with fewer material resources and more explicitly 'political' goals. One recent survey of three world conferences speaks of a *de facto* division of labour at the 1992 Rio Summit whereby

> The NGOs more interested in networking, or lacking official accredit-ation, took advantage of the fertile ground for NGO exchange provided by the [unofficial] forums. The strongest, most active, and most effective lobbying organizations came from the North, while the South, often represented by Latin American groups, spearheaded the NGO network-ing. In the words of one NGO newspaper writing in Rio, 'the Africans were watching, the Asians listening, the Latin Americans talking while the North Americans and Europeans were doing business'.[25]

Second, if national origin of NGOs plays an important role in limiting the geographical representation of global civil society at the special-ized conferences, the interests of the host state are even more pro-nounced. The administrative and logistical obstacles placed by the Chinese authorities on participants at the unofficial NGO forum during the 1995 Beijing Conference on Women attracted much atten-tion at the time.[26] But similar expressions of state interests influencing the composition of PrepComs and NGO groups accredited at the official conferences can be cited for almost every specialized confer-ence since the Tehran Conference on Human Rights of 1968. Once again, therefore, and despite their best intentions, NGOs and social movements attending these world conferences are necessarily party to the inter-state power politics that inform these meetings, as their very presence is generally conditional upon the approval of states. In the last instance, as Kal Raustiala has noted with reference to inter-national environmental regimes, 'NGO participation remains a privil-ege granted and mediated by states.'[27]

Finally, a cautionary note must be struck regarding the social representativeness of many NGOs and other groups accredited at world conferences. Article 71 of the UN Charter and its subsequent amendments set out fairly comprehensive principles for NGOs seeking consultative status, including accountability to members, administra-tive transparency, a broad geographical reach and an issue relevance to the UN's remit. Yet in practice, because of the inter-governmental and largely functional nature of ECOSOC, the type of NGO granted consultative status tends to be 'representative' in a very narrow sense. Thus, organizations such as the International Organization for Stand-ardization or Rotary International which in any other context would not usually be recognized as being socially 'representative' are currently accredited with Category I consultative status at ECOSOC. Although these and other NGOs accredited by the UN may indeed be worthy in an 'operational' or 'functional' sense, they can hardly be seen as representing the emerging 'people power' of a transformative global civil society. In the final analysis, NGOs are – as one would expect – only representative of their membership, and not of a global *demos* or the like, as some global governance theorists would make us believe. Furthermore, their legitimacy as representatives of 'grass-roots' interests is ultimately sanctioned through the 'politics of ac-creditation' by states and their attendant inter-governmental organizations.

All these reflections plainly aim to throw a more sceptical light on some of the overly rosy accounts of how INGOs are 'pluralizing' global governance. But it would of course be wrong to suggest that INGO participation in world conferences and other expressions of global governance is inconsequential to international relations. As was already noted, UN specialized conferences and INGO participation in ECOSOC at the very least provide a forum for transnational activist 'networking' and, perhaps more significantly, draw widespread media attention to the global agendas being addressed. In some instances, there is concrete evidence of NGO lobbying actually shaping the policy commitments arising out of these deliberations.[28] The point, therefore, is not to deny the impact of INGOs on global governance and the 'pluralization' of the latter (nor for that matter to place a blanket censure on all their actions) but rather to spell out the limits of such influence and the highly selective nature of such plurality.

So long as 'global civil society' is understood in a liberal sense as representing a sphere of grassroots consent and co-operation, there is little doubt that it features as a key component of global governance. Thus, on the prevailing liberal-internationalist understanding, global civil society is seen as a domain of consultation and co-operative participation. From such a perspective, socio-political change is neces-sarily limited by the existing international social structures, and the transcendence of such structures is acknowledged to lie beyond the purview of agents of civil society. As Lee-Ann Broadhead has pointed out,

> Through renewed faith in liberal ideology [proponents of global gov-ernance] would like to convince 'citizens of the world' that the end of the Cold War has miraculously left them with the power to influence decision-making, and that the likely result will be a more enlightened, peaceful and just international system. This power will be realized, however, only if these civil society organizations agree to work with

international organizations and within the established rule of law to achieve change.[29]

The fact that this consensual stance is not simply a matter of political choice or preference on the part of civil society agents, but rather a structural property of the current relation between global civil society and global governance, is especially apparent when we consider the role of social movements and INGOs in what O'Brien et al. have called a new 'complex' multilateralism.

In their comprehensive study of how the central multilateral economic institutions (MEIs) of global governance (World Bank, IMF and WTO) interact with critical global social movements (GSMs), O'Brien, Scholte and Williams highlight two telling features of this encounter. The first is that, though MEIs have during the 1990s been obliged to address the grievances of GSMs and under some circumstances incorporate them into their decision-making mechanisms, they have done so under terms which do not compromise the overall MEI policy objectives and which therefore clearly place GSMs in a subordinate position within this 'partnership'. In line with Lee-Ann Broadhead's argument cited above, MEIs will engage with GSMs so long as the latter accept their operational function as subordinate 'partners' in the administration of global governance. In other words, GSMs tend to act as global agents in 'commissioning consent'.

The second characteristic of the MEI–GSM encounter, according to O'Brian et al., is the deep political divisions among GSMs, generally resulting from their distinct geographical and social positions in the international system. Thus, empirical studies on the impact of global feminist, labour and environmental activism reveal how these agents of civil society are not, as many 'grassroots globalization' theorists often imply, united in a harmony of interests, but rather replicate the diverse social cleavages which characterize global capitalism. This may appear an obvious point to make, but, in the context of claims about an undifferentiated 'global civil society' representing a bulwark against an equally homogenized states-system, they bear repeating. More importantly, however, these two aspects of the 'contest over governance' underline the structural limits to international change under an international system governed by state sovereignty and capitalist social relations. As O'Brien, Scholte and Williams conclude, while a transformation in the nature of global governance may be taking place in response to GSM activity,

> To date the transformation has largely taken the form of institutional modification rather than substantive policy innovation. . . . In the short

run the MEI–GSM nexus is unlikely to transform either institutional functions or their inherent nature to any significant degree. In the longer run, there is the possibility of incremental change in the functioning ambit of these key institutions. Complex multilateralism has not challenged the fundamentals of existing world order, but it has incrementally pluralised governing structures.[30]

These conclusions are of course tentative, and should never foreclose future possibilities of change. In so far as incremental change and the 'pluralization' of governing structures bear some promise for the improvement of people's lives across the world, they are obviously worth struggling for. But such struggles must always be guided by an acute sense of the social structures that govern the international system and which therefore set limits to change through 'grassroots' participation in the institutions of global governance. This participation, as the various studies cited above show, is characterized more by the obstacles it places in the way of significant change than by the possibilities it opens up for the radical transformation of the international system.

Political limitations: democracy, legitimacy and communities of fate

The foregoing sociological discussion regarding the representative and transformative limits to the liberal conception of global civil society as a sphere of 'grassroots' non-governmental activity is closely linked to the issue of the democratic potential of international or global civil society. For the latter concept, and the social domain it refers to, is generally assumed to be impregnated with the prospect of global democratic change. This is usually suggested in either of two (by no means incompatible) ways. On the one hand, some of the global governance theories explored above establish a correlation between the 'pluralization' of global governance and notions traditionally associated with liberal democracy such as accountability, transparency, legitimacy, representation or consent. On this reading, the more global governance incorporates the agents of global civil society, the more democratic it becomes. A second approach – the major focus of this section – is that adopted by proponents of cosmopolitan democracy. Here, the role of transnational civil society and global governance in the promotion of liberal democracy is more complex, as, from this angle, cosmopolitan democracy is to be realized through the global articulation of myriad socio-political forces and centres of authority, not just those of global civil society.

Notwithstanding these differences, it will be argued that in both instances the association of democracy with the agents of transnational civil society is theoretically objectionable on two counts. First, because in questioning the legitimacy of the modern state as the main depository of political authority, these theories underestimate the need for democracy to be rooted in 'communities of fate': that is, 'a community that rightly governs itself and determines its future'.[31] Second, and following on from this, in separating out forms of political authority, like the sovereign state, from their broader position in the totality of socio-economic relations, such theories risk reifying civil society (be it local, regional or global) as the exclusive or principal sphere of democratic deliberation. However, as this book has stressed throughout, not only is it conceptually misleading to endorse such a rigid separation between state and civil society, but, furthermore, it is also politically disabling because the sovereign state still represents the sturdiest base on which to build a genuinely democratic polity. In substantiating these claims, the argument will deal first with the proposals for cosmopolitan democracy which, being the more challenging of the two approaches to democracy and global civil society, will hopefully make evident the shortcomings of the other, more simple equation of democratization with the 'pluralization' of global governance.

David Held has lucidly spelt out the predicament of contemporary democratic politics in the following terms:

> the problem, for defenders and critics alike of modern democratic systems, is that regional and global interconnectedness contests the traditional national resolutions of the key questions of democratic theory and practice. The very process of governance can escape the reach of the nation-state. National communities by no means exclusively make and determine decisions and policies themselves, and governments by no means determine what is appropriate exclusively for their own citizens.[32]

As Held rightly suggests, democracy in its various guises has been historically tied to the notion of popular sovereignty invested in territorially bounded national states. Under conditions of globalization, however, this prevailing conception of democratic politics is compromised by a number of juridico-political, socio-economic and cultural 'disjunctures' which according to the author means 'that the concept of legitimate political power or authority has to be separated from its exclusive traditional association with states and fixed national borders'.[33] In response to these changes, Held contends, democrats must embrace the possibilities opened up by the processes of globalization and develop novel forms of theorizing and implementing democracy via interlocking structures of local, national and global governance, i.e. through a 'cosmopolitan democratic law'. Civil society, conceived as a domain of socio-economic and political interests outside the direct control of the state, is considered as a major building block of such a project at all the levels of governance.

In several important respects, Held's analysis of the contemporary democratic predicament and the 'disjunctures' that characterize it is to be welcomed. For a start, his cosmopolitan imagination elegantly dispenses with the still pervasive notion that the modern state must be a *nation*-state if it is to be legitimate. As is well known, very few so-called 'nation-states' are ethnically homogeneous in ways that might justify this title, and most forms of nationality are artificially constructed by diverse administrative and ideological bodies of the state. There is, therefore, no a priori reason (contrary to what most nationalists contend) why the 'community of fate' that is the modern state should coincide with a particular national or ethnic group – modern states are *national* states by virtue of historical and geographical contingencies which in great measure only endure through the imposition of a national identity by the state. Moreover, Held's proposals for cosmopolitan governance should be valued for audaciously concretizing how such forms of governance might operate in reality – whatever other criticisms might be levelled at such proposals, they do at least display the empirical courage of their theoretical convictions.

There is, however, a central tension in Held's account of cosmopolitan democracy which is arguably irresolvable so long as the structural relations that underpin global capitalism are not fully recognized. And this determining contradiction is that between, on the one hand, the modern democratic struggle for collective autonomy and human self-realization in the context of a delimited political community and, on the other, the boundless quest for surplus-value which characterizes the global reproduction of capitalism. Held is, of course, keenly aware of this tension – it is in fact the key problematic underlying *Democracy and Global Order*, and indeed that of most recent political theory which engages with 'the international'. Yet in characteristically liberal fashion he reduces capitalist social relations to one of seven sites of power – that of 'production' or 'economics' – thereby foregoing the opportunity to associate the various disjunctures explored with the dynamics of a broader totality of *social* (not just 'productive' or 'economic') relations which characterize capitalism. In other words,

Held fails to establish the crucial link between the structural requirement for capitalism constantly to generate surplus-value and the
diverse socio-historical disjunctures which he rightly claims define
the contemporary democratic predicament. This in turn leads – cru-
cially – to a misplaced emphasis on the 'Westphalian model' of sovereignty as the major source of such a predicament, and not on the
broader system of surplus appropriation responsible for the disjunctures of globalization. Held, in short, falls into the trap of fetishizing
the political expressions of global capitalism by assuming that the
political forms of rule it throws up can be transformed in isolation
from the social relations that underpin this system.

Far from representing a minor (and predictable) theoretical quibble
between liberal and Marxist notions of 'production' or 'social relations', these considerations are germane to the present discussion in
that they underline how even projects for a cosmopolitan democracy
will be unable to overcome the 'disjunctures' generated by global
capitalism unless they address the structural basis of that mode of
production. To use Held's own terminology, in so far as global capitalism necessarily feeds off 'nautonomic' social relations,[34] the challenge
for any project of cosmopolitan *democracy* lies not so much in the re-
articulation of political community, but in the overhaul of the social
relations that generate such 'nautonomy' in the first place. In other
words, so long as it is *capitalist* social relations that are being regulated, no amount of global governance will do away with the 'nautonomic' relations that characterize the contemporary international
system. On the other hand, a democratic empowerment of the sovereign state can at least begin to redress the 'asymmetric production and
distribution of life-chances' under capitalism. For, whereas the autonomy and self-realization of the capitalist ruling class is secured when-
ever it is able to accrue surplus-value through the market, that of
exploited classes is much more dependent on the democratic rights
(both positive and negative) procured by the sovereign state. One of
the unique properties of capitalism is, as Justin Rosenberg has suggested, that 'It is now possible, in a way that would have been
unthinkable under feudalism, to command and exploit productive
labour (and natural resources) located under the jurisdiction of another state.'[35] In contrast, however, it is much harder for a citizen or
subject of one state to share in the rights and benefits of another
state.[36] In other words, the 'disjuncture' between political and
human emancipation which Marx once identified as being axiomatic
to civil society is replicated in the international domain with the
discrepancy between the freedom of capital to reproduce itself through
a borderless 'global economy', and the existence of discrete political

communities which set limits on the power of citizens to exercise democratic control of their 'life-chances' under that set of global social relations. This predicament is especially invidious when we consider how closely the 'life-chances' of those members of a particular political 'community of fate' are conditioned by the virtually footloose dynamics of global capital.

By arriving at these conclusions it is not being suggested that the dynamics of global capitalism cannot or indeed are not being regulated by institutions of global governance. They clearly are, and often to the benefit of exploited classes. Cosmopolitan democracy, however, cannot – as Held would no doubt readily agree – be reduced to a mere regulation or administration of the disjunctures thrown up by capitalist globalization. It must also, and fundamentally, entail the exercise of autonomy and self-realization through a legitimate political community. For Held, the sovereign 'Westphalian' state can no longer fulfil the exclusive role of legitimate political community, and in its stead democrats must now conceive of forms of cosmopolitan governance where 'People would come ... to enjoy multiple citizenship – political membership in diverse political communities which significantly affected them. They would be citizens of their own immediate political communities, and of the wider regional and global networks which impacted upon their lives.'[37] Attractive as this proposal is in theory, the claim made thus far is that it is unlikely to be realized under the existing system of social relations where the struggle for democratic rights of exploited classes is still principally mediated through the institutions of state sovereignty. Paradoxical as it may seem, the firmest guarantee against global extension of exploitation and alienation (or, to use Held's terms, the loss of self-determination and autonomy) lies in strengthening the democratic sovereign state. Naturally, this should not undermine the cosmopolitan ambition of eventually transcending the artificial division of humanity into distinct national states – cosmopolitanism has and should continue to be a fundamental democratic value. But, if the arguments explored above carry any weight, it would appear that a cosmopolitan democracy can only be realized once the class relations which define capitalism have been superseded, and that aspiration, it has been further argued, is best secured through internationalized struggles for the democratic sovereignty of states.

The foregoing disagreements with Held's formulation of cosmopolitan democracy essentially revolve around his understanding of capitalist social relations and the strategic place of the sovereign state in the pursuit of cosmopolitan democracy. In other key areas, however, the arguments presented in this book coincide and are therefore sympathetic with the broad objectives of cosmopolitan democracy. Much of this agreement rests on Held's nuanced view of civil society as a sphere of social life which not only produces hierarchical and antagonistic social relations, but also must consequently be balanced by the socio-economic and political intervention of the state if democracy is to be sustained. Translated on to the international sphere, what this amounts to is an equally cautious assessment of the democratic potential of global civil society.

The same can unfortunately not be said about other discussions of global civil society and democratization. As was noted in the earlier survey of globalization literature, many grassroots globalization and global governance theorists uncritically equate the global expansion of civil society and its attendant insertion into the processes of global governance with the improved prospects for democratization. Yet, as the discussion thus far has emphasized, there is nothing inherently democratic in the global reproduction of civil society, either within states or internationally through the institutions of global governance. As this study has argued throughout, the expansion of international civil society certainly opens up political spaces for democratic change, but such democratic openings must be seized and articulated by specific social movements – often against other agents of civil society – and their potential ultimately realized through the institutions of a specific form of political authority, usually the sovereign state. Two issues in particular should therefore be borne in mind when considering the relations between global civil society and democracy: the one relating to the legitimacy of agents of global civil society; the other to the anti-statist pitfalls attached to this latter category.

Central to any conception of democratic association worth its name is the collective deliberation over the affairs that impact upon the life-chances of its members, and the subsequent commitment to the legitimate use of authority in the implementation of such decisions that arise out of these deliberations. The notions of constituency, consent, legitimacy, constitutional procedure – in short, the idea of a democratic 'community of fate' explored above – are usually invoked in this context. The problem of contemporary democratic politics, as we also saw above, is that the 'fate' of particular communities is no longer (if it ever was) determined within the bounds of the prevailing form of political community – the national state. Furthermore, it is argued, the past decades have witnessed the rise of alternative political associations to that of the national state in the shape of, for example, the European Union, while global governance has given rise to institutions which might provide the embryonic structures for the growth of even more radically alternative modes of political community. It is in the context of these perceived changes that the assorted social movements, NGOs and advocacy groups usually encompassed under the concept of 'global civil society' are identified as the potential democratic representatives of these emerging forms of political association.

Independently of whether such transformations are illusory or not, the democratic claims in favour of global civil society immediately raise thorny questions about its agents: who are the constituents of global civil society? How has their mandate been legitimated? What is the remit of their representation? How can their actions be made accountable?

The sensible response to these questions is of course that there can be no single, general answer: the agents of global civil society claim to represent different (often incompatible) constituencies; their mandate is (as we saw above) either legitimated through the inter-state 'politics of accreditation' or simply self-arrogated by virtue of being present at specialized world conferences; their remit is determined by factors ranging from state sponsorship (in the case of GONGOs) to resolutions voted by a membership at annual conventions; while their accountability depends to a great extent on the internal arrangements of each organization and the willingness of other agents – be it 'public opinion', the media or indeed the fiscal authorities – to scrutinize civil society activism.

One thing, however, does transparently emerge from these interrogations, namely that it is precisely the absence of an overarching constitutional or procedural framework to guide the democratic deliberations of a putative global civil society that renders this domain unrepresentative in a political sense. However much individual INGOs and global social movements may have contributed to the extension of democratic politics across the world, they do not currently possess the requisite degree of legitimacy and accountability to be considered as democratic representatives in a globalized political community. It should hastily be added that INGOs and social movements do not generally claim such a status themselves, and that the preceding arguments are therefore targeted at theorists and practitioners that envisage such a role for INGOs and other agents of civil society in their proposals for global governance. This said, it is worth underlining once more how this 'democratic deficit' within global civil society further strengthens the case presented above in favour of the sovereign state's continuing potential as the site of democratic change. For, however imperfect and limited its powers over the political fate of its citizens, the democratic sovereign state and the agents of civil society that operate within it can at least rightfully claim to be democratically representative of their respective constituencies.

A second arena where the democratic credentials of global civil society must be closely scrutinized lies in the policy impact of INGO and other global social movement activity. For several years after the end of the Cold War, these agents of global civil society figured very prominently in the processes of 'democratization' and 'reconciliation' across Central America, southern Africa and South-East Asia. The mushrooming of NGOs and other 'advocacy groups' in these regions during the 1990s was enthusiastically embraced by many liberals across the world as heralding the consolidation of civil society in previously 'totalitarian' or 'authoritarian' revolutionary states. Other commentators and activists, however, soon became more circumspect about this particular reading of the international expansion of civil society. (It is said that in the early 1990s an article circulated in Central America entitled 'How to get rich quick in the 1990s: the rise of NGOs in Central America'.) Indeed it would be fair to say that ten years on, and with the inevitable benefit of hindsight, the balance has shifted toward a far more critical, even dismissive view of INGO activity in the promotion of democracy and other social goods. Thus James Petras, for example, summarized the view on NGOs of many on the left in the following fashion:

> In reality, non-governmental organizations are not non-governmental. They receive funds from overseas governments or work with private subcontractors of local governments. Frequently they openly collaborate with governmental agencies at home or overseas. This 'subcontracting' undermines professionals with fixed contracts, replacing them with contingent professionals. The NGOs cannot provide the long-term comprehensive programs that the state can furnish. Instead they provide limited services to narrow groups of communities. More importantly, their programs are not accountable to the local people but to overseas donors. In that sense NGOs undermine democracy and their elected officials to create dependence on non-elected, overseas officials and their locally anointed officials.[38]

Petras's criticisms are in some respects unwarranted and inconsistent: overseas governments are often more transparent and democratic in their role as donors than local (also often unelected) officials or agencies. Similarly, NGO programmes can hardly be said to be replacing the 'comprehensive programs that the state can furnish' in the many regions where the state and its programmes don't exist in the first place! Yet plainly his stance also reinforces some points on democracy and civil society made implicitly or explicitly throughout this chapter, three of which bear repeating.

First, the transnational activities of NGOs and other agents of global civil society must be analysed in the context of the broader dynamics of capitalist social relations. In this respect, they must be seen as fully fledged political actors that carry with them ideological biases and class interests which in turn affect (sometimes decisively) the socio-economic and political fate of particular states. In her excellent account of the international dimensions of civil society activism in Central America during the 1990s, Laura Macdonald documents how the diverse NGOs and social movements were heavily implicated in the tumultuous process of 'democratization' in that region, concluding that 'NGO behaviour is neither completely determined and impotent nor substantially autonomous – instead it is a contested political terrain where various actors (both national and international) vie for influence. The results of these contests will depend on the overall balance of forces within specific social formations.'[39] This view has increasingly become accepted within the specialized literature on civil society and democratization, particularly in the Third World.[40]

Second, and as a result of their involvement in the wider complex of socio-political relations, INGOs and other agents of global civil society are often purveyors of anti-democratic *laissez-faire* policies. For if by 'democracy' it is meant not only the protection of 'negative' civil liberties like the freedom of speech or the right to due process, but also the development of 'positive' rights to employment, housing, education, social security and so forth, then clearly the record of many agents of civil society is thoroughly undemocratic. Indeed several recent studies (both empirical and conceptual) have made a powerful case for equating the global extension of civil society with the forceful imposition of neo-liberal economic policies.[41] The institutions of global governance, therefore, have increasingly and unashamedly promoted this liberal vision of global civil society as a domain that can be utilized or, as we saw above, 'operationalized' in the project of universalizing capitalist rationalization and exploitation. In so far as the interventionist institutions of the state are seen to stand in the way of such universalization, global civil society becomes a useful tool of this anti-statist, *laissez-faire* and ultimately undemocratic project.

Finally, the political dangers of such anti-statist uses of global civil society lie, paradoxically, in their potential obliteration of that very civil society. For, as this book has consistently argued, one of the most damaging conceits of liberal views of civil society is the notion that this is a domain always and everywhere threatened by the power of the state. Yet, both empirically and conceptually, a thriving, democratic civil society (liberal or otherwise) requires the legitimate regulation through the authority of the state. Historically, civil society in all the dimensions examined in chapter 2 has emerged and developed under the aegis of a legitimate and extensive state. Clearly, this is not to say that strong and powerful states have always generated equally dynamic civil society; it is, however, to suggest that, where the structures of state authority are weak or non-existent, the prospects of modern civil society are very bleak indeed. To the extent that democratic politics – whatever their ideological hue – can only survive in the context of an enduring civil society (global or otherwise), the democratic agents of civil society have an interest in supporting a robust and operative state.

Conclusions: the promises of international civil society

The preceding pages have staked out the various limitations of different contemporary conceptions of the relation between globalization and civil society. It has been argued that current usages of the term 'global civil society' are unsatisfactory in three respects: they suffer from an ahistorical 'presentism' that overlooks the crucial explanatory legacy of internationalism and the deep implication of transnational social movements in the formation of the sovereign state; they uncritically embrace non-representative, functional and democratically unaccountable INGOs as agents of socio-political change within a putative global civil society; and, finally, they therefore invest inflated expectations in a liberal global civil society as an international force of democratic politics. Underlying these shortcomings, it has been suggested, is a generally unacknowledged liberal conception of sovereignty and the market (or the 'political' and the 'economic') which underestimates the structural relations between these two spheres and which consequently underplays the potentially progressive role of state sovereignty in democratically transforming the global capitalist system.

Most of this chapter has been taken up with critical surveys of other people's views on globalization and civil society. It is now necessary, therefore, to conclude with a positive statement of what the idea of international civil society presented in this study offers the contemporary analyst and activist. In particular, given the growing use of the concept in strategic discussions on how to effect global political change, it is important to identify the possibilities for radical socio-political transformation emanating from international civil society as it has been understood in this book.

International civil society was defined in chapter 2 as a realm of socio-political activity created domestically and internationally by the expansion of capitalist social relations, where modern social movements pursue their stated goals. Cast in this light, the various agencies associated with the rise of a global civil society – INGOs, transnational advocacy groups, global social movements and so forth – can readily be encompassed by the category 'international civil society'. In most respects, these forms of socio-political mobilization are not significantly distinct from their nineteenth- and twentieth-century predecessors, and in that sense they can, as chapter 3 suggested, be considered as the latest generation of internationalist organizations that have operated across established political borders. The crucial difference between the usage of civil society defended here and that proposed by the various globalization theorists discussed earlier, therefore, revolves not so much around what transnational agents are included within this domain, but rather around how they are related to other spheres of social life. On the definition offered here, international civil society is considered as an arena of antagonistic class relations where conflicting socio-economic interests and rival political programmes contend for power. This political competition between social movements unfolds in a context constrained by the structures of capitalism and state sovereignty, but it does so on an international plane that aims to cut across existing state boundaries. As such, international civil society is a political terrain which radical social movements must seek to understand and occupy for the purposes of genuine democratic transformation on a global scale. In particular, those socialists who still aim to transcend the existing capitalist system and undermine the power of its various political forms must recognize the importance of this contested realm of world politics. For, while the socialist tradition has from the very outset been premised on the theory and practice of working-class internationalism, it is not alone in this articulation of transnational or trans-boundary socio-political activity, and as such faces stiff competition from equally internationalist rivals. Socialists would therefore do well to appropriate international civil society both conceptually and politically as a domain which generates class struggles capable of being harnessed to the project of global socialist transformation. In sum, and in contrast to prevailing theories of global civil society examined above, the theory of international civil society presented here insists on the politically competitive and socially antagonistic nature of this domain, thereby reinforcing the claim that it is a sphere of the international system which progressive politics cannot afford to ignore or disdain.

Assuming that this latter point is accepted, the question still remains as to whether the forms of mobilization pioneered and developed by 'classical' internationalism are of any political relevance today. In other words, have the processes of globalization rendered working-class, feminist or Third World internationalism obsolete? The answer intimated throughout this book and this chapter in particular has been a fairly emphatic 'no'. So long as globalization is considered as an expression of capitalism and not an alternative to it, the structure of social relations that underpin this system – whether globalized or not – in essence remain the same as those that informed, say, 'new' capitalist imperialism of the late nineteenth century. This is not to say that the way in which the structural relations between the state and civil society have played themselves out have remained unaltered by processes associated with globalization. Clearly, the transfer of political authority to multilateral agencies which was examined above under the rubric of global governance has shifted various political expressions of class struggle – for example, over minimum wages, industrial policy or equal opportunities – on to the international sphere. But it should once again be noted that in most instances such transfers in regulatory authority are not historically unprecedented and, more importantly, that they still remain the essential prerogative of the sovereign state and the social forces that operate within its boundaries. Contrary to some readings of this phenomenon (especially those emanating from the left), global governance mostly serves to resolve domestic class struggles through a recourse to international norms, which are in turn legitimated by nationally based class forces. To take two examples: Mexico's adoption of neoliberal policies during the 1980s and 1990s and its later accession to the North American Free Trade Association (NAFTA) should be read as an expression of the domestic class interests represented by the then President Salinas de Gortari. In so far as the multilateral institutions of global governance were involved in these policies, they did so as instruments of the Mexican ruling class and not vice versa; there may, to be sure, have been a harmony of interests between Washington and Mexico City, but the political and socio-economic benefits to be made out of Mexico's endorsement of the so-called 'Washington consensus' were largely accrued by the Mexican ruling class, and not by economists at the Bretton Woods institutions.[42]

Likewise, the critical intervention of the OECD and the ILO in favour of the opposition (South) Korean Confederation of Trade Unions during the winter strikes of 1996–7 underlines how the institutions of global governance can also serve to legitimate working-class victories domestically. In sum, globalization may have changed some of the *forms* of state–civil society relations by, for example, shifting the sites of decision-making and regulation on to international multilateral bodies; but it has not decisively altered the *content* of the structural relations that underpin capitalism as a system which differentiates a private sphere of surplus production and extraction called the market (or civil society) from a public domain of sovereign juridico-political authority (the state). To the extent that this structural separation, and the exploitative relations that underpin it, continue to determine class politics across the world, any radical transformation of the international system will have to be premised on the increased politicization of civil society on an international scale. And it is the practices and principles associated with internationalism in general, and socialist internationalism in particular, which arguably continue to furnish the most robust legacy in the pursuit of this objective. For, as this book has endeavoured to show, the history of the modern world has in large measure been shaped by similar internationalist activism within the distinctive sphere of international civil society.

Conclusions

The Uses of International Civil Society

This book has aimed to offer a novel interpretation of the 'international civil society' by focusing on two basic dimensions of this concept. In the first instance, the objective has been to situate the historical and socio-logical study of non-state actors in international relations at the centre of the analytical concerns of International Relations (IR) as a discipline. Though drawing generously from the successive waves of transnationalist literature in IR, this study has sought to go beyond these approaches, highlighting their theoretical and historical shortcomings and arguing that a more rigorous investigation of the relations between states and civil societies under the rubric of 'international civil society' can render the central arguments of transnationalism more forceful. More specifically, the claim has been that the term 'international civil society' should be associated not only with the agents that operate outside the immediate control of the state, but also with those social forces that have shaped the international society of states. It is for this reason that a special emphasis has been placed upon the *interaction* between the agents of civil society and those of the state, rather than on their mutual exclusiveness and opposition. From this perspective, the expansion of international civil society is seen as a process that re-inforced the institutions and boundaries of the modern sovereign state as much as it helped to undermine them.

This first major concern of the book therefore speaks to those IR theorists interested in the origin and evolution of international society, and to the role of non-state actors in this process. To this extent, the preceding chapters represent an engagement with the more orthodox preoccupations of our discipline – those dealing with international society, sovereignty, nationalism and international institutions. Throughout this study, however, a further important issue has been at stake, namely the normative or political implications of using the term 'international civil society'. By investigating the relations of modern social movements across different frontiers, I have sought to uncover the existence of an international relations 'from below'. Such activity has been interpreted as part of the experience of internationalism over the last two centuries: that is, the conscious attempt by a mobilized constituency to transcend national, ethnic and religious barriers in the pursuit of specific political goals. A second underlying objective of this book, therefore, has been to explore the expansion of international civil society as a starting point for the imagination of new modes of political agency; to draw from the historical experience of social movements that have operated socially and politically across national, ethnic and religious boundaries in order to inform an internationalist politics for the present and future. This concluding part to the book is perhaps the best place to make more explicit the normative and political content of international civil society. For international civil society represents a social and political space that progressive movements must appropriate and defend if the emancipatory aspirations of modernity are to be realized, however imperfectly. Before elaborating this claim, however, it is necessary to offer a restatement of the basic features of international civil society as it has been defined in this study. Special emphasis is again placed upon the complex interface between the agents of civil society and the institutions of the state within an international context. Here, the paradoxical nature of the relationship between state and non-state actors will be explored with particular reference to the tensions between nationalism and internationalism in the expansion of international civil society.

The meanings of international civil society

Throughout this study, the idea of international civil society has been defined with regard to three of its basic components. At the most elementary level, international civil society describes that arena of world politics where modern social movements pursue their political goals. It was argued in chapter 2 that specifically modern attributes can be identified in the modes of political engagement characteristic of civil society. Moreover, the argument was made that such modern forms of political agency have from their inception been conditioned by international factors. In other words, it was suggested that modern social movements which have for the past three centuries been the mainspring of civil society should be viewed as international phenomena and not, as is traditionally done, within an exclusively national context.

A full explanation for the emergence and development of these modern movements, however, requires making reference to the socio-economic and political forces unleashed by the global reproduction of capitalism. Thus, international civil society has also been treated throughout this book as an arena permeated by capitalist social relations that generate antagonistic class interests. It is through the international articulation of these antagonisms, I have argued, that modern forms of social and political agency take shape.

Lastly, the preceding chapters have insisted that the term 'international civil society' does not assume the existence of a world community of non-state actors seeking to undermine the international system of states. To be sure, the constituent agents of international civil society often represent a threat to state sovereignty in so far as they, by definition, operate across existing national and more occasionally ethnic and religious boundaries. Yet such transgressions are neither constant nor unidirectional: as was argued in chapter 3 and illustrated in chapter 4, the social movements that inhabit international civil society are as likely to reinforce the existing boundaries of the sovereign state as they are to undermine them. Indeed, the experience of non-state actors with regard to experiments in global governance analysed in chapter 5 exemplified how international social movements must engage and thereby legitimize the existing structures of state sovereignty, while all the time mobilizing their diverse transnational resources to undermine such forms of national sovereignty. In short, much of this book has endeavoured to show that the study of international civil society is closely tied to the examination of the origins and development of the international society of states. From this perspective, international civil society is not a category associated exclusively with the study of non-state actors, but rather with the historical interaction between states and civil societies under the conditions of capitalist modernity.

These, in sum, have been the basic features of international civil society as it has been understood in these pages. There is, however, one very specific aspect of the concept which merits closer attention in these closing paragraphs of the study, namely the relationship between international civil society and nationalism. Chapter 3 briefly mooted this question, but it was in chapter 4 that this relationship was more deeply considered with reference to the idea of international society. It was argued there that the norms, values and institutions of international society helped to reinforce the political goals of nationalist movements of the Third World and that the latter in turn contributed toward the legitimization of post-war international society. As in the rest of the book, the emphasis of that chapter was upon the mutual interdependence of these two spheres of social action, rather than upon their radical opposition. This overlap, however, raises some interesting contradictions in the definition of international civil society as it has been employed in this study. If social movements participating in international civil society choose to focus specifically upon a particular national struggle, do they thereby cease to be part of this domain of international politics? Once state sovereignty has been achieved, are the bonds with international civil society severed? What are the consequences for international civil society of social movements becoming the backbone of one-party states? These and other questions point to the seemingly irremovable tension between the universal pretensions of a concept like international civil society and its concrete manifestations in particularist movements – for example, nationalist parties.

The way out of this impasse lies in recognizing that the universal can find expression in the concrete. In more specific terms, there is no necessary incongruity in positing an international civil society that encompasses nationalist as well as internationalist social movements. All of these, I have argued, were moulded by the international dimensions of civil society outlined in the second chapter of this book. Consider, for instance, the case of Maghrebi nationalism. The origins and development of North African nationalism were inextricably tied to an ideological, institutional and historical interaction with the outside world. The Neo-Destour, Istiqlal and North African Star parties and their predecessors derived much of their programme from a combination of European liberalism, Mashreqi Islamic reformism and Arab and Turkish nationalism. They borrowed the organizational structure and the modes of political protest from their European and Third World counterparts, and put to good strategic use the impact of world-historical events such as the outbreak of the two World Wars or the creation of international organizations like the UN and the Arab League. To this extent, it is thoroughly misleading to interpret the rise of Maghrebi nationalism as a purely autochthonous phenomenon (as much nationalist historiography would have us believe) or to see it as being at odds with the expansion of international civil society. On the contrary, explaining the nature of North African nationalism (or any other form of nationalism for that matter) requires investigating the international reproduction of ideas and practices characteristic of modern civil society. In this respect, studying the expansion of international civil society provides fertile ground for the consideration of the international genesis of nationalism – one of the major forces shaping the contemporary international system.

From a historical perspective, then, the concept of international civil society can readily incorporate agents of civil society with a narrower political agenda like that of nationalist movements. Far from undermining this arena of world politics, nationalist social movements have historically been the product of those international forces that I have identified with the expansion of international civil society. The more pressing question now becomes how such a historical experience can become integrated into a *conceptual* model that adequately accounts for the interaction of centrifugal and centripetal forces such as nationalist and internationalist social and political movements. In other words, how can the category of international civil society simultaneously accommodate social movements that seek to go beyond the sovereign state with those that aim to establish bounded national states?

One answer to this paradox offered in this study has been to distinguish between the form and the content of those social movements that operate within international civil society. On this account, the expansion of international civil society is premised not on the homogenization of political programmes, but on the adoption of certain comparable modes of political engagement. What upholds the existence of international civil society is not an abstract universal harmony of interests but an identifiable commonality in the mechanisms of social and political protest – what I have referred to as modern social and political agency. Thus, international civil society aspires to become a category capable of recognizing the dynamics of modern social and political agency in international relations, without thereby positing some necessary unity between the movements that are its protagonists. In fact, this study has sought to underline that international civil society is a domain of conflict and contradiction as much as it is an arena of co-operation and solidarity. While the normative impulse of this category plainly seeks to identify an international social and political space that may foster transnational alliances, there is – it should be stressed again – no requirement that such a communion of interests emerge out of the expansion of international civil society.

A second response to the question of how international civil society can coexist with state sovereignty focuses upon the contribution of modern social movements toward the construction of a modern states-system. Here the argument is that the origin and development of state sovereignty is intimately related to the expansion of international civil society. As chapter 4 sought to illustrate, the notion of popular sovereignty and the political struggles it inspired made the territorial state a privileged site of modern social and political activity. If it is accepted that all forms of political engagement require the delimitation of a particular community (what in chapter 5 was termed a 'community of fate') where conflicting interests are played out, then the national state should be seen as the dominant political community during the modern epoch. The social agents characteristic of civil society were instrumental in lending legitimacy to the legal and political institutions of the modern national state, by both contesting and affirming the validity of territorially bounded political entities. It therefore follows that the reproduction of modern social and political agency throughout time and place is an international phenomenon simply by virtue of the fact that it reinforced the status of the modern territorial state as the highest source of political sovereignty.

Although the notion of international civil society may indeed be able to explain the historical configuration of the present international society of states, the processes attached to globalization have in the past decades challenged the conceptual reach of this category. As we saw in chapter 5, numerous contemporary theorists have addressed the interrelation between civil society and globalization, suggesting that this conjunction is producing new, 'post-Westphalian' forms of political rule which in turn have generated innovative, de-territorialized modes of socio-economic and political protest encompassed under the term 'global civil society'. For many, these novel forms of political engagement bear encouraging prospects for an increased democratic contestation of the institutions of global governance; so much so that, for some of these observers, global civil society can potentially develop as a representative domain of the 'global *demos*' or 'global grassroots interests'.

While agreeing that a broadly conceived process of globalization and the attendant institutions of global governance have indeed altered important dimensions of international relations, the argument of chapter 5 was that such changes are constrained by the dual structures of the international system examined in chapter 3. The capacity of a so-called 'global civil society' to effect substantive socio-economic and political change on a global scale was especially challenged on two basic counts. On a conceptual front, it was suggested that experiments in cosmopolitan democracy cannot by themselves remove the 'disjuncture' between the footloose dynamic of the capitalist market and the 'nautonomic' relations it engenders on the one hand, and the capacity of democratic political communities (states) to exercise reasonable control over these dynamics and redress their accompanying loss of autonomy and self-determination on the other. It was thus argued that addressing this particular discrepancy between private market forces and public political power requires an increasing politicization of civil society – a task which, it was suggested, can best be accomplished through the internationalized struggle for the democratic sovereignty of states. At an empirical level, the prevailing contrast between a de-territorialized, 'post-Westphalian' form of sovereignty and the traditional notion of territorial state sovereignty was also contested, by suggesting that the institutions of global governance are themselves predicated on the willing transfer of political authority on the part of states. In other words, it was suggested that, far from undermining the power of the sovereign state, globalization and global governance should be seen as the displacement of power to international multilateral institutions by states themselves, generally as a means of resolving (however temporarily) their own domestic class conflicts. On this reading, globalization has altered some of the *forms* of exercising political authority by transferring sovereign power on to international multilateral institutions, but it has not substantially changed the *content* of the relations that underpin such forms of rule: global institutions govern *on behalf* of states, and not vice versa. Accordingly, it has been argued throughout this book that the traditional, territorial sovereign state remains, however paradoxically, the major locus for effecting radical global socio-economic and political change.

The uses of international civil society

The ultimate test of the validity of any concept in the social sciences lies in its capacity to explain and to transform our collective social and political lives. The term 'civil society' has in recent years been subject to uses and abuses that have, on these terms, rendered this classical concept of western political thought invalid for contemporary purposes. Civil society has been burdened with so many meanings and has has such high political expectations attached to it that it has paradoxically become an increasingly shallow concept capable of explaining very little and transforming even less. This tendency to underestimate the very specific and often politically radical nature of civil society both in theory and in practice has been a feature of IR theory, as we saw in chapter 1. The present study has evidently participated in this retrieval of civil society and its application within the domain of IR. Yet it has also aimed to restore some of the historical and sociological complexity of the category, often in critical dialogue with those IR theorists who employ the term. What will have hopefully emerged out of this process is a conception of international relations that gives collective social and political agency a central explanatory role in IR. I have argued that modern social movements have been shaped by international phenomena from their inception and that they represent a key explanatory component of the past and present structure of international society. Thus, one measure of the concept's utility for IR and the social sciences more broadly lies in its success in inspiring further studies into the processes that instigated the rise of modern social and political agency across the globe.

It has, however, also been suggested that a proper historical and sociological investigation of this experience can serve present and future struggles for the construction of political solidarities across national, ethnic and religious boundaries. The tallest order for international civil society, therefore, rests upon its capacity to inform the future internationalist politics. This study will have hopefully illustrated the historical and conceptual reality of an international social and political space where progressive agents can operate. As we have seen, this arena of international civil society is open to contestation by divergent and often distinctly unpalatable political projects. But the fact that the concept of international civil society can be appropriated by oppressive political movements should not blind us to its historical and sociological reality.

The expansion of capitalism has generated variegated social formations – albeit articulated by the overarching logic of capitalist production and exchange – which in turn yield myriad social forces. Political identities forged around notions of nationalism, ethnicity, race or religious affiliation have often found expression within the ambit of international civil society. None the less, rather than writing off such movements as atavistic remnants of a parochial past, it is crucial to explain – and confront – these phenomena precisely with reference to the complex reproduction of global capitalism. At the same time, however, socialists and other progressive movements must counter these social forces in world politics by retracing and revising their own powerful tradition of internationalist thought and action that has sought to organize politically around universalist principles that transcend nationality, ethnicity or creed. I have argued that the idea of international civil society can serve to accomplish these two inter-related objectives. Conceptualizing the complex and contradictory nature of the expansion of international civil society could represent the first step in the identification of the social and political sources of this new socialist internationalism.

Notes

CHAPTER 1   INTRODUCTION

1 J. Burton, *World Society* (London: Macmillan, 1972); J. Rosenau, *Linkage Politics: Essays on the Convergence of National and International Systems* (New York: Free Press, 1969); E. L. Morse, *Modernization and the Transformation of International Relations* (New York: Free Press, 1976); R. W. Mansbach, Y. H. Ferguson and D. E. Lampert, *The Web of World Politics: Nonstate Actors in the Global System* (Englewood Cliffs, NJ: Prentice-Hall, 1976); E.-O. Czempiel (ed.), *Die anachronistische Souveränität* (Köln-Opladen: Westdeutscher Verlag, 1969). For a good overview of the literature falling under the category of 'transnationalism' see Michael Clarke, 'Transnationalism', in Steve Smith (ed.), *International Relations: British and American Perspectives* (Oxford: Basil Blackwell, 1985), pp. 146–70.
2 R. Keohane and J. Nye (eds), *Transnational Relations and World Politics* (Cambridge, MA, and London: Harvard University Press, 1970), p. x.
3 See, respectively, R. Aron, *Peace and War: A Theory of International Relations* (Weidenfeld & Nicolson, 1966), and A. Wolfers (ed.), *Discord and Collaboration* (Baltimore, MD: Johns Hopkins University Press, 1962).
4 Keohane and Nye, *Transnational Relations*, p. 398.
5 James N. Rosenau, 'International studies in a transnational world', *Millennium: Journal of International Studies*, 5, 1 (Spring 1976), pp. 1–20, p. 8.
6 Ibid., p. 9.
7 Keohane and Nye, *Transnational Relations*, p. 389. See also Ekkehart Krippendorff, 'The dominance of American approaches in International

Relations', *Millennium: Journal of International Studies*, 16, 2 (Summer 1987), pp. 207–14.

8 Keohane and Nye, *Transnational Relations*, p. 379.

9 D. Easton, *A Framework for Political Analysis* (Englewood Cliffs, NJ: Prentice-Hall, 1965), and R. A. Dahl, *Modern Political Analysis* (Englewood Cliffs, NJ: Prentice-Hall, 1963).

10 Michael Clarke, 'Transnationalism', p. 146.

11 Keohane and Nye, *Transnational Relations*, p. 386.

12 Fred Northedge, 'Transnationalism: the American illusion', *Millennium: Journal of International Studies*, 5, 1 (Spring 1976), pp. 21–7, p. 25.

13 This is the view adopted and put to good use in T. Risse-Kappen (ed.), *Bringing Transnational Relations Back In: Non-State Actors, Domestic Structures and International Institutions* (Cambridge: Cambridge University Press, 1995). See also R. A. Higgott, G. R. D. Underhill and A. Bieler (eds), *Non-State Actors and Authority in the Global System* (London and New York: Routledge, 1999).

14 See, respectively, R. D. Lipschutz, 'Reconstructing world politics: the emergence of global civil society', *Millennium: Journal of International Studies*, 21, 3 (Winter 1992), pp. 389–420; M. J. Peterson, 'Transnational activity, international society and world politics', *Millennium: Journal of International Studies*, 21, 3 (Winter 1992), pp. 371–88; M. Shaw, 'Global society and global responsibility: the theoretical, historical and political limits of "international society"', *Millennium: Journal of International Studies*, 21, 3 (Winter 1992), pp. 421–34.

15 R. B. J. Walker, 'Social movements/world politics', *Millennium: Journal of International Studies*, 23, 3 (Winter 1994), pp. 669–700, p. 699. M. Hardt, 'The withering of civil society', *Social Text*, 14, 4 (Winter 1995), pp. 27–44.

16 See, respectively, R. D. Lipschutz (with J. Mayer), *Global Civil Society and Global Environmental Governance: the Politics of Nature From Place to Planet* (Albany, NY: State University of New York Press, 1996), and M. Shaw, *Civil Society and Media in Global Crises: Representing Distant Violence* (London: Pinter, 1996).

17 Lipschutz, 'Reconstructing', p. 392.

18 Shaw, 'Global society', p. 431.

19 M. Shaw, 'Civil society and global politics: beyond a social movements approach', *Millennium: Journal of International Studies*, 23, 3 (Winter 1994), pp. 647–67, p. 651.

20 Peterson, 'Transnational activity', p. 387.

21 Walker, 'Social movements/world politics', p. 695.

22 Hardt, 'The withering of civil society', p. 36.

23 Ibid., p. 36.

24 Stephen Gill, 'Structural change and global political economy: globalizing elites and the emerging world order', in Y. Sakamoto (ed.), *Global Transformation: Challenges to the State System* (Tokyo: United Nations University Press, 1994), p. 173.

25 K. van der Pijl, *The Making of an Atlantic Ruling Class* (London: Verso, 1983).

26 R. D. Germain and Michael Kenny, 'Engaging Gramsci: International Relations theory and the new Gramscians', *Review of International Studies*, 24, 1 (January 1998), pp. 2–21, p. 17.

27 For a lucid defence of this paradox, see E. P. Thompson, 'Eighteenth-century English society: class struggle without class?', *Social History*, 3, 2 (May 1978), pp. 133–63. See also E. Meiksins Wood, *Democracy Against Capitalism: Renewing Historical Materialism* (Cambridge: Cambridge University Press, 1995), ch. 2.

28 P. Abrams, *Historical Sociology* (Shepton Mallet: Open Books, 1982), p. 2.

29 Ibid., p. 2.

30 E. Gellner, *Contemporary Thought and Politics*, edited with a preface by I. C. Jarvie and J. Agassi (London and Boston: Routledge & Kegan Paul, 1974), pp. 116, 122.

31 G. A. Cohen, *Karl Marx's Theory of History: A Defence* (Oxford: Clarendon, 1978).

32 A. Wendt, 'The agent–structure problem in International Relations theory', *International Organization*, 41, 3 (Summer 1987), pp. 335–70.

33 Ibid., p. 348.

34 Ibid., p. 339.

35 Ibid., p. 365.

36 D. Sayer, 'Reinventing the wheel: Anthony Giddens, Karl Marx and social change', in J. Clark, C. Modgil and S. Modgil (eds), *Anthony Giddens: Consensus and Controversy* (London, New York and Philadelphia: Falmer Press, 1990), pp. 235–50.

37 Wendt himself concedes as much when making reference to Thrift's classification of Philip Abrams, Roy Bhaskar, Pierre Bourdieu and Derek Layder as 'structurationists' (albeit often despite themselves).

38 See R. Bernstein, *Praxis and Action* (London: Duckworth, 1972). For a discussion within the context of IR see Christian Heine and Benno Teschke, 'Sleeping Beauty and the dialectical awakening: on the potential of dialectic for International Relations', *Millennium: Journal of International Studies*, 25, 2 (Summer 1996), pp. 399–423.

39 Sayer, 'Reinventing the wheel', p. 236.

CHAPTER 2   CIVIL SOCIETY

1 I refer to three contemporary approaches to the idea of 'civil society' which have proved especially influential: J. Habermas, *The Structural Transformation of the Public Sphere: An Inquiry into a Category of Bourgeois Society* (Cambridge: Polity, 1992); E. Gellner, *The Conditions of Liberty: Civil Society and its Rivals* (Oxford: Oxford University Press, 1994); A. Arato and J. Cohen, *Civil Society and Political Theory* (Cambridge, MA: MIT Press, 1992). Two excellent collections of essays on the subject are J. Keane (ed.), *The State and Civil Society: New European Perspectives* (London: Verso, 1988), and J. Hall (ed.), *Civil Society:*

Theory, History, Comparison (Cambridge: Polity, 1995). See also V. Pérez-Díaz, *La esfera pública y la sociedad civil* (Madrid: Taurus Ciencias Sociales, 1997).

2   See R. Williams, *Keywords: A Vocabulary of Culture and Society* (London: Fontana Press, 1976), p. 293, and D. Frisby and D. Sayer, *Society* (New York: Ellis Horwood, 1986), p. 17. An interesting account of the concept's origins in the Spanish language can be found in P. Álvarez de Miranda, *Palabras e ideas: El léxicon de la Ilustración temprana en España, 1680–1760* (Madrid: Anejos del Boletín de la Real Academica Española LI, 1992), ch. 6.

3   K. Tester, *Civil Society* (London and New York: Routledge, 1992), p. 6. This point is also made by M. B. Becker, who suggests that during the seventeenth and eighteenth centuries, 'For the first time in the history of the West the word *society* defined an entity both distant and abstract.' *The Emergence of Civil Society in the Eighteenth Century: A Privileged Moment in the History of England, Scotland and France* (Bloomington and Indianapolis, IN: Indiana University Press, 1994), p. 2.

4   T. Hobbes, *Leviathan*, edited with an introduction by C. B. Macpherson (Harmondsworth: Penguin, 1968), p. 82.

5   Ibid., p. 186.

6   C. B. Macpherson, *The Political Theory of Possessive Individualism: From Hobbes to Locke* (Oxford and New York: Oxford University Press, 1990), p. 25.

7   Hobbes, *Leviathan*, p. 226.

8   Ibid., p. 228.

9   M. Riedel, 'Gesellschaft, bürgerliche', in O. Brunner, W. Conze and R. Koselleck (eds), *Geschichtliche Grundbegriffe: Historisches Lexikon zur politisch-sozialen Sprache in Deutschland* (Stuttgart: Ernst Klett Verlag, 1975), pp. 736–7 (italics added). (Thanks to Benno Teschke for help in the translation from the German original.)

10 J. Locke, *Two Treatises on Government*, edited with an introduction and notes by P. Laslett (Cambridge: Cambridge University Press, 1988), p. 271.

11 Ibid., p. 282.

12 Ibid., p. 325; italics in the original.

13 J.-J. Rousseau, *The Social Contract and the Discourses*, translation and introduction by G. D. H. Cole (London, Melbourne and Toronto: Everyman's Library, 1979), p. 44.

14 Ibid., p. 45.

15 Ibid., p. 83.

16 Ibid., p. 89.

17 Ibid., p. 177.

18 Tester, *Civil Society*, p. 40.

19 Rousseau, *The Social Contract and the Discourses*, p. 76.

20 Macpherson, *The Political Philosophy of Possessive Individualism*, p. 243.

21 N. Wood, *John Locke and Agrarian Capitalism* (Berkeley, Los Angeles, CA, and London: University of California Press, 1984), p. 113.

22 This is what Charles Taylor denominates the 'L-stream' within civil society. He uses this shorthand term with reference to a picture of civil society first represented in John Locke: 'a picture of society as an "economy", that is, as a whole of interrelated acts of production, exchange and consumption which has its own internal dynamic, its own autonomous laws.' C. Taylor, 'Modes of civil society', *Public Culture*, 3, 1 (Fall 1990), pp. 95–118, p. 107.

23 See, for example, T. Hutchison, *Before Adam Smith: The Emergence of Political Economy, 1662–1776* (Oxford: Basil Blackwell, 1988), and J. O. Appleby, *Economic Thought and Ideology in Seventeenth-Century England* (Princeton, NJ: Princeton University Press, 1978).

24 N. Wood, *Foundations of Political Economy: Some Early Tudor Views on State and Society* (Berkeley, Los Angeles, CA, and London: University of California Press, 1994). See also N. Wood and E. Meiksins Wood, *A Trumpet of Sedition: Political Theory and the Rise of Capitalism, 1509–1688* (London: Pluto Press, 1997).

25 Ibid., p. 36.

26 Appleby, *Economic Thought and Ideology*, p. 41.

27 This is an interpretation favoured by José Manuel Naredo in his otherwise excellent introduction to economic thought, *La economía en evolución: historia y perspectivas de las categorías básicas del pensamiento económico* (Madrid: Siglo XXI, 1987).

28 Ibid., ch. 3.

29 R. L. Meek examines what he labels as the 'four-stages theory' in *Social Science and the Ignoble Savage* (Cambridge: Cambridge University Press, 1976). He deals with Ferguson and Smith in ibid., ch. 4.

30 A. Ferguson, *An Essay on the History of Civil Society*, ed. F. Oz-Salzberger (Cambridge: Cambridge University Press, 1996), p. 7.

31 Ibid., p. 81.

32 Ibid.

33 Ibid., p. 172.

34 Ibid., p. 173.

35 The debt owed by Hegel and Marx to Ferguson and other eighteenth-century theorists is stressed by John Keane in his outstanding survey, 'Despotism and democracy: the origins and development of the distinction between civil society and the state 1750–1850', in Keane (ed.), *The State and Civil Society*, pp. 35–71.

36 K. Marx, extract from *Critique of Hegel's Philosophy of Right*, in D. Sayer, *Readings From Karl Marx* (London and New York: Routledge, 1989), p. 121.

37 Ibid., p. 121; italics in the original.

38 J. L. Cohen, *Class and Civil Society: The Limits of Marxian Critical Theory* (Amherst, MA: University of Massachusetts Press, 1982), p. 57.

39 From K. Marx, *The German Ideology*, cited in Sayer, *Readings From Karl Marx*, pp. 114–15.

40 Ibid., p. 25.

41 From *A Critique of Hegel's Philosophy of Right*, cited in Sayer, *Readings From Karl Marx*, p. 120.

42 Ibid., p. 116; italics in the original.
43 Arato and Cohen, *Civil Society and Political Theory*, p. 91.
44 Keane, 'Despotism and democracy', p. 54.
45 G. W. F. Hegel, *Elements of the Philosophy of Right*, ed. A. W. Wood, tr. H. B. Nisbet (Cambridge: Cambridge University Press, 1995), §230, pp. 259–60; italics in the original.
46 Ibid., §302, p. 342.
47 C. Taylor, *Hegel* (Cambridge: Cambridge University Press, 1975), p. 431.
48 Hegel, *Elements of the Philosophy of Right*, §253, p. 271.
49 Keane, 'Despotism and democracy', p. 53.
50 J. C. Alexander (ed.), *Real Civil Societies: Dilemmas of Institutionalization* (London and Thousand Oaks, CA: Sage Publications, 1998), p. 7.
51 Ibid., p. 10.
52 Antony Black makes an original and forceful case for the existence of 'civil society' in medieval Europe in his *Guilds and Civil Society in European Political Thought from the Twelfth Century to the Present* (London: Methuen, 1984). Yet Black's notion of 'civil society' is at once excessively broad and too narrow. By defining civil society as 'freedom of ... the person from violence' (p. 32), Black renders this concept too general and almost transhistorical, missing out the qualitative transformation in the notions of 'freedom', 'property', 'equality' and 'exchange' which accompanied the birth and spread of capitalism. Simultaneously, however, in focusing more narrowly on the urban socio-economic life of medieval Europe, Black fails to address the *un*freedom which governed feudal social relations outside towns in that continent, in some regions until well into the early modern period. As the author himself concedes, 'One of the earliest statements of urban political thought started with the definition of the *specific character of cities*, which emphasized security of person from arbitrary violence. ... The town rescues men from seigneurial oppression' (pp. 38–9; italics added). Even within medieval towns and communes, however, the 'freedom' and 'exchange' of civil society was heavily regulated through corporatist institutions such as guilds or liveries in ways that preclude an immediate comparison with the 'double freedom' of the capitalist market and its accompanying modes of protest. As Steven Epstein suggests in his *Wage Labour and Guilds in Medieval Europe* (Chapel Hill, NC, and London: University of North Carolina Press, 1991): 'Guilds were not likely to figure in any revolt against masters of any kind. ... Even where some form of guild-dominated city government exercised real authority, the interests of the master and the diversity of guilds represented in government worked against any swift and effective action ... the guilds, communes, monarchies and estates did not exist to foster the hopes of journeymen and apprentices. Workers sometimes joined together to promote their own self-interest, but these shadowy organizations only appear in the records of efforts to deny their petitions or to suppress their associations' (pp. 255–6).
53 Arato and Cohen, *Civil Society and Political Theory*, p. ix.
54 Alexander (ed.), *Real Civil Societies*, p. 6.

55 Habermas, *Structural Transformation*, p. 74.
56 Habermas refers to these three 'institutional criteria' as 'the parity of "common humanity"'; 'the problematization of [socio-political] areas that had until then not been questioned [the domain of "common concern"]'; and the notion of 'the public as in principle being inclusive'. Ibid., pp. 36–7.
57 An excellent collection of critical essays can be found in C. Calhoun (ed.), *Habermas and the Public Sphere* (Cambridge, MA: MIT Press, 1993).
58 'Our investigation is limited to the structure and function of the liberal model of bourgeois public sphere....Thus it refers to a historical constellation that attained dominance and leaves aside the plebeian public sphere as a variant that in a sense was suppressed in the historical process.' Habermas, *Structural Transformation*, p. xviii.
59 G. Eley, 'Nations, publics and political cultures', in Calhoun (ed.), *Habermas and the Public Sphere*, p. 326.
60 G. Lottes, *Politische Aufklärung und plebejisches Publikum: zur Theorie und Praxis des englischen Radikalismus in späten 18 Jahrhundert* (Munich and Vienna: Oldenbourg Verlag, 1979).
61 J. Brewer, *Party Ideology and Popular Politics at the Accession of George III* (Cambridge: Cambridge University Press, 1976), p. 6.
62 E. P. Thompson, *The Making of the English Working Class* (London: Penguin, 1980), p. 20.
63 E. P. Thompson, 'Patrician society, plebeian culture', *Journal of Social History*, 2, 7 (Winter 1974), pp. 382–405, p. 396.
64 Eley, 'Nations, publics and political cultures', p. 326.
65 I have examined this process in an unpublished paper on 'The expansion of civil society to the Maghreb', where a case is made for the emergence of a public sphere in that region at the turn of the century, principally sustained by three sets of movements: liberal-reformist educational circles, Islamic reformist associations inspired by the *salafiyya* trend, and working-class organizations. For a fascinating account of a similar process in Indochina see Hue-Tam Ho Tai, *Radicalism and the Origins of the Vietnamese Revolution* (Cambridge and London: Harvard University Press, 1992).
66 Habermas, *Structural Transformation*, p. 74.
67 E. Meiksins Wood, *The Pristine Culture of Capitalism: A Historical Essay on Old Regimes and Modern States* (London and New York: Verso, 1991), p. 1.
68 Ibid., p. 78.
69 J. Rosenberg, *The Empire of Civil Society: A Critique of the Realist Theory of International Relations* (London: Verso, 1994), p. 123.
70 See B. Teschke, *The Making of the Westphalian System of States: Property Relations, Geopolitics and the Myth of 1648* (London: Verso, 2001), for a cogent discussion and an alternative formulation of the origins of modern sovereignty.
71 P. Anderson, *Lineages of the Absolutist State* (London: Verso, 1974), p. 19.
72 E. R. Wolf, *Europe and the People without History* (Berkeley, CA: University of California Press, 1982), ch. 10. I have tried to address the

implications of this 'differentiated' mode of production for international-ist political strategies in A. Colás, 'Exploitation and solidarity: putting the political back into IPE', in M.-A. Tétreault et al. (eds), *New Odysseys in International Political Economy* (London and New York: Routledge, 2001).

73 Cited in D. Mack Smith, *Mazzini* (New Haven and London: Yale University Press, 1994), p. 52.

74 See, for example, L. Hirszowicz, *The Third Reich and the Arab East* (London: Routledge & Kegan Paul, 1966), and S. Wild, 'National Socialism in the Arab Near East between 1933 and 1939', *Die Welt des Islams*, 25 (1985), pp. 126–73.

75 See the useful summary provided by D. Stienstra, *Women's Movements and International Organization* (London: Macmillan Press, 1994), chs 3 and 4.

76 This summary is drawn from Fred Halliday's essay on internationalism, 'Three concepts of internationalism', *International Affairs*, 64, 2 (1988), pp. 187–97.

77 Useful accounts of this experience in working-class internationalism can be found in M. Foreman, *Nationalism and the International Labor Movement: the Idea of the Nation in Socialist and Anarchist Theory* (Pennsylvania, PA: Pennsylvania University Press, 1998); M. Ishay, *Internationalism and its Betrayal* (Minneapolis, MT: Minnesota University Press, 1995); M. van der Linden and F. van Holtoon (eds), *Internationalism in the Labour Movement* (Leiden: E. J. Brill, 1988); and S. Milner, *The Dilemmas of Internationalism: French Syndicalism and the International Labour Movement, 1900–1914* (New York: Berg, 1990). I have analysed the experience of socialist internationalism as a form of cosmopolitanism in 'Putting cosmopolitanism into practice: the case of socialist internationalism', *Millennium: Journal of International Studies*, 23, 3 (1994), pp. 513–34.

78 P. Ghils, 'International civil society: international non-governmental organizations in the international system', *International Social Science Journal*, 44, 133 (August 1990), pp. 417–29, p. 429.

79 R. D. Lipschutz, 'Reconstructing world politics: the emergence of global civil society', *Millennium: Journal of International Studies*, 21, 3 (1992), pp. 389–420, p. 391.

80 M. Shaw, 'Civil society and global politics: beyond a social movements approach', *Millennium: Journal of International Studies*, 23, 3 (1994), pp. 647–67, p. 655.

81 Lipschutz, 'Reconstructing world politics', p. 391.

82 R. B. J. Walker, 'Social movements/world politics', *Millennium: Journal of International Studies*, 23, 3 (1994), pp. 669–700, p. 699.

83 Ibid., p. 685.

84 For a survey of struggles for liberal democracy that incorporates a notion of international civil society, see D. Held (ed.), *Prospects for Democracy: North, South, East, West* (Cambridge: Polity, 1993).

85 M. Hoffman, 'Agency, identity and intervention', in I. Forbes and M. Hoffman, *Political Theory, International Relations and the Ethics of Intervention* (London: Macmillan Press, 1993), pp. 194–211, p. 203.

CHAPTER 3   AGENCIES AND STRUCTURES IN IR

1 J. Foweraker, *Theorizing Social Movements* (London and Boulder, CO: Pluto Press, 1995), p. 4.
2 P. Anderson, 'Agency', in *Arguments within English Marxism* (London: New Left Books, 1978), p. 20.
3 Eric Hobsbawm, for example, contrasts 'pre-political' and 'archaic' social movements with modern ones in his *Primitive Rebels: Studies in Archaic Forms of Social Movement in the 19th and 20th Centuries* (Manchester: Manchester University Press, 1959). George Rudé also distinguishes between the pre-industrial and industrial 'crowd' in his *The Crowd in History: A Study of Popular Disturbances in France and England, 1730–1848* (New York and London: John Wiley, 1964).
4 Ibid., p. 20.
5 For a good account of Luther King and the US civil rights movement see A. Fairclough, *To Redeem the Soul of America: The Southern Christian Leadership Conference and Martin Luther King Jr* (Athens, GA, and London: University of Georgia Press, 1987).
6 David Zaret, 'Petitions and the "invention" of public opinion in the English Revolution', *American Journal of Sociology*, 101, 6 (May 1996), pp. 1497–555, p. 1498.
7 Hobsbawm, *Primitive Rebels*, p. 3.
8 A. Gramsci, *Selections from the Prison Notebooks*, ed. Q. Hoare and G. Nowell-Smith (London: Lawrence & Wishart, 1972), p. 276.
9 For two illuminating discussions of the modernity of Islamism see: E. Abrahamian, *Khomeinism* (London: IB Tauris, 1990), and A. Al-Azmeh, *Islam and Modernities* (London: Verso, 1993). See also F. Halliday, *Nation and Religion in the Middle East* (London: Saqi Books, 2000).
10 As presented in Max Weber, 'Science as vocation'; repr. in H. H. Gerth and C. Wright Mills (eds), *From Max Weber: Essays in Sociology* (London: Routledge, 1991).
11 R. Koselleck, *Futures Past: on the Semantics of Historical Time* (Cambridge, MA: MIT Press, 1985).
12 This point is made in the opening lines of E. P. Thompson's *The Making of the English Working Class* (London: Victor Gollancz, 1963). Referring to the first of the 'leading rules' of the London Corresponding Society, which claims 'That the numbers of our Members be unlimited', Thompson says: 'Today we might pass over such a rule as commonplace: and yet it is one of the hinges upon which history turns. It signified the end to any notion of exclusiveness, of politics as the preserve of any hereditary élite or property rule. . . . To throw open the doors to propaganda and agitation in this "unlimited" way implied a new notion of democracy, which cast aside ancient inhibitions and trusted to self-activating and self-organising processes among the common people' (p. 22).

13 Civil society is, like most other classical keywords of political theory, a gendered concept. Yet the fact that it has been invoked by some contemporary feminists and, more importantly, that feminist critiques emerged precisely from social movements which operate within civil society suggest that the category can be useful to those engaged in feminist politics.

14 L. A. Tilly and C. Tilly (eds), *Class Conflict and Collective Action* (London and Beverly Hills, CA: Sage Publications, 1981), p. 21.

15 See the illuminating essay by Craig Calhoun, ' "New social movements" of the early nineteenth century', *Social Science History*, 17, 3 (Fall 1993), pp. 387–425, and the useful discussion of new social movement theory in F. Jamison and R. Eyerman, *Social Movements: A Cognitive Approach* (Cambridge: Polity, 1990).

16 Indeed, as the discussion of the two historical expressions of early civil society in chapter 2 suggested, that the history of the international system can be read as a competition since the mid-seventeenth century between alternative forms of modernity – what Kees van der Pijl has called the 'process of uneven expansion of the Lockean heartlands, challenged by successive generations of Hobbesian contender states'. K. van der Pijl, *Transnational Classes and International Relations* (London and New York: Routledge, 1998), p. 83. In this respect also, the early historical experience of modern social movements clearly overlaps with that of the modern states-system.

17 That the French Revolution and its political agents were not in the main bourgeois does not preclude defining it as a bourgeois revolution. As van der Pijl indicates, 'the bourgeois revolution was never the revolution of the bourgeoisie. It was made by revolutionaries clearing the way for bourgeois order.' Ibid., p. 78. For a detailed historical discussion of this notion of bourgeois revolutions without a bourgeoisie see, *inter alia*, D. Blackbourn and G. Eley, *The Peculiarities of German History* (Oxford: Oxford University Press, 1984); C. Lucas, 'Nobles, bourgeois and the origins of the French Revolution', *Past and Present*, 60 (August 1973), pp. 84–126; and C. Mooers, *The Making of Bourgeois Europe: Absolutism, Revolution and the Rise of Capitalism in England, France and Germany* (London and New York: Verso, 1991).

18 See, *inter alia*, R. Cohen and S. M. Rai (eds), *Global Social Movements* (London and New Brunswick, NJ: The Athlone Press, 2000); D. Della Porta, H. P. Kriesi and D. Rucht (eds), *Social Movements in a Globalizing World* (New York: St Martin's Press, 1999); J. Smith et al. (eds), *Transnational Social Movements and Global Politics* (Syracuse, NY: Syracuse University Press, 1997); P. Waterman, *Globalization, Social Movements and the New Internationalisms* (London and Washington: Mansell, 1998).

19 See, for example, A. Touraine et al., *Le Pays contre l'Etat: luttes occitanes* (Paris: Editions du Seuil, 1981), and the recent special issue of *Ethnic and Racial Studies*, 'Hindutva movements in the west: resurgent Hinduism and the politics of the diaspora', 23, 3 (May 2000), ed. Parita Muckta and Chetan Bhatt.

20 The African National Congress (ANC), for example, has historically drawn its support from a wider network of national liberation and progressive movements, and to this day it continues to play a significant solidary role within that ambit of world politics described in this book as international civil society.

21 S. Tarrow, *Power in Movement: Social Movements and Contentious Politics* (Cambridge: Cambridge University Press, 1998), p. 182.

22 Ibid., p. 192.

23 Smith et al. (eds), *Transnational Social Movements*.

24 Ibid., p. 68.

25 T. Risse-Kappen, *Bringing Transnational Relations Back In: Non-State Actors, Domestic Structures and International Institutions* (Cambridge: Cambridge University Press, 1995), 'Introduction', p. 15.

26 See G. Devin, *L'Internationale socialiste: histoire et sociologie du socialisme international, 1945–1990* (Paris: Presses de la Fondation Nationale des Sciences Politiques, 1993). On the role of European social democrats in the Spanish transition to democracy see C. T. Powell, 'La dimensión exterior de la transición española', *Afers Internacionals*, 26 (1994), pp. 37–64.

27 For a thoughtful recent overview of this form of social activity see T. Morris-Suzuki, 'For and against NGOs', *New Left Review* (March–April 2000), pp. 61–85.

28 See, for example, R. R. Palmer, *The Age of the Democratic Revolutions*, 2 vols (Princeton, NJ: Princeton University Press, 1959).

29 F. S. L. Lyons, *Internationalism in Europe 1815–1914* (Leiden: A. W. Sythoff, 1963).

30 L. S. Snyder, *Macro-Nationalisms: A History of the Pan-Movements* (Westport, CT, and London: Greenwood Press, 1984). For specific studies of the extra-European internationalisms mentioned see J. M. Landau, *The Politics of Pan-Islam: Ideology and Organisation* (Oxford: Clarendon Press, 1990); R. Schulze, *Islamischer Internationalismus im 20. Jahrhundert: Untersuchungen zur Geschichte der Islamischen Weltliga* (Leiden: E. J. Brill, 1990); R. P. Mitchell, *The Society of Muslim Brothers* (Oxford: Oxford University Press, 1969); P. Gilroy, *The Black Atlantic: Modernity and Double Consciousness* (London and New York: Verso, 1993); W. James, *Holding Aloft the Banner of Ethiopia: Caribbean Radicalism in Early Twentieth-Century America* (London and New York: Verso, 1998); W. F. Santiago-Valles, 'The Caribbean intellectual tradition that produced James and Rodney', *Race and Class*, 42, 2 (October–December 2000), pp. 47–66; R. J. Alexander, *Aprismo: The Ideas and Doctrines of Victor Raúl de la Haya* (Kent, OH: Kent State University Press, 1973).

31 See M. Williams and L. Ford, 'The World Trade Organization, social movements and global environmental management', in C. Rootes (ed.), *Environmental Movements: Local, National and Global* (London: Frank Cass, 1999), pp. 268–89, for a study of the PGA and other 'rejectionist' global social movements.

32 A. Melucci, *Challenging Codes: Collective Action in the Information Age* (Cambridge: Cambridge University Press, 1996), p. 102.

33 Williams and Ford, 'The World Trade Organization, social movements and global environmental management', p. 282. See also G. Esteva and M. S. Prakash, *Grassroots Post-Modernism: Remaking the Soil of Cultures* (London and New York: Zed Books, 1998).

34 It should be stressed, however, that the historical dynamics of international relations are of course the product of this interaction and tension between the forces of change and continuity.

35 'Although the word has become a term of art in some quarters, its reference is quite straightforward. A problematic is a rudimentary organisation of a field of phenomena which yields problems for investigation .... In other words, one's problematic is the sense of significance and coherence one brings to the world in general in order to make sense of the particular.' Abrams, *Historical Sociology*, p. xv.

36 Much of the following discussion is indebted to Andrew Sayer's excellent account of the agent–structure problem generally, and the philosophically 'realist' approach to this problem in particular, in his *Method in Social Science: A Realist Approach*, 2nd edn (London and New York: Routledge, 1994).

37 This proposition has been defended in a number of forms and from varying methodological perspectives within IR. For a comprehensive overview of the 'democratic peace' literature see S. Chan, 'In search of democratic peace: problems and promise', *Mershon International Studies Review*, 41, 1 (May 1997), pp. 59–91. Two influential formulations are: M. W. Doyle, 'Kant, liberal legacies, and foreign affairs' (2 parts), *Philosophy and Public Affairs*, 12, 1 and 2 (1983), pp. 205–353, and B. M. Russett, *Grasping the Democratic Peace: Principles for a Post-Cold War World* (Cambridge, MA: Harvard University Press, 1993).

38 I am grateful to Branwen Gruffydd Jones for this example, and for clarifying some issues surrounding 'critical realism'.

39 Moreover, they are social, not natural structures, i.e. they cannot exist without human interaction. While the relation between social and natural structures is of course central to the explanation of all human societies, the present discussion focuses exclusively, for heuristic purposes, on *social* structures.

40 Two classic statements on the historical specificity of the modern international system can be found in J. G. Ruggie, 'Territoriality and beyond: problematizing modernity in International Relations', *International Organization*, 47, 1 (Winter 1993), pp. 139–74, and J. Rosenberg, *The Empire of Civil Society: A Critique of the Realist Theory of International Relations* (London: Verso, 1994).

  Recently, a sophisticated case has been made for the argument that the globalizing tendencies of capitalism are gradually eroding the territorial form of sovereignty and giving way to a transnational state in the shape, for example, of the institutions of global governance. See, for example, W. I. Robinson and J. Harris, 'Towards a global ruling class? Globalization and the transnationalist capitalist class', *Science and Society*, 64, 1 (Spring 2000), pp. 11–54. See also M. Hardt and A. Negri, *Empire* (Cambridge,

MA: Harvard University Press, 2000), and S. Gill, 'Market civilization and global disciplinary neoliberalism', *Millennium: Journal of International Studies*, 25, 3 (Winter 1995), pp. 399–423, both discussed in chapter 5.

It is of course the case that the internal relation between capitalism and the *territorial* sovereign state is, strictly speaking, historically contingent, i.e. the separation between the 'political' and the 'economic' could plausibly take a different, non-territorial form without thereby violating the structural nature of such a relation. As we shall see in chapter 5, however, this proposition remains hypothetical in the strong sense of the term: the available evidence suggests that, though the *potential* of global governance to structure international relations might be said to exist, it has not yet been realized. On the other hand, a strong empirical case can be made for the argument that in most parts of the world the territorial sovereign state has not acquired the degree of legitimacy and stability historically required for successful capitalist development. To that extent, the encouragement and consolidation of traditional, territorial state-building, particularly in so-called 'emerging markets', remains one of the major objectives of the capitalist classes – be they transnational or otherwise. Clearly, this is one instance where structural explanations cannot be detached from their application to, or 'testability' in, the concrete social world.

41 Recent 'structurationist' approaches to the structure–agent problematic in IR include P. G. Cerny, *The Changing Architecture of States: Structure, Agency and the Future of the State* (London and New York: Sage, 1990); J. A. Scholte, *International Relations of Social Change* (Buckingham: Open University Press, 1993); and A. Wendt, *Social Theory of International Politics* (Cambridge: Cambridge University Press, 1999). See also M. Hollis and S. Smith, 'Two stories about structure and agency', *Review of International Studies*, 20, 3 (1994), pp. 241–51; the accompanying exchange with Vivienne Jabri and Stephen Chan in the same journal *Review of International Studies*, 22, 1 (1996), pp. 107–16; and a useful overview of the terms of this debate in IR by C. Wight, 'They shoot dead horses don't they? Locating agency in the agent–structure problematique', *European Journal of International Relations*, 5, 1 (March 1999), pp. 109–42.

42 R. Bhaskar, *Reclaiming Reality: A Critical Introduction to Contemporary Philosophy*, 2nd edn (London and New York: Verso, 1993), p. 80.

43 Sayer, *Method in Social Science*, p. 92.

44 Jeffrey Isaac also makes the point forcefully: 'Individuals certainly possess idiosyncratic powers. But what makes these socially significant is the way they are implicated in more enduring relationships. It makes perfect sense to claim that "David Rockefeller is a powerful man." But a social theory of power must explain what kinds of social relations exist and how power is distributed by these relations, such that it is possible for David Rockefeller to have the power that he has. To do this is not to deny that it is *he* who possesses this power, nor to deny those personal attributes determining the particular manner in which he exercises it. It is simply to insist that

the power individuals possess has social conditions of existence, and that these conditions should be the primary focus of theoretical analysis.' J. C. Isaac, *Power and Marxist Theory: A Realist View* (London and Ithaca, NY: Cornell University Press, 1989), p. 81. It should furthermore be stressed that we are dealing here with social-scientific *explanation*, not moral *evaluation*. Clearly, ascribing structural constraint to human action does not exonerate individuals or collectivities for the responsibility over those actions. Explaining the transatlantic slave trade with reference to the structures of mercantile capitalism does not preclude condemning the traders and masters responsible for the reproduction of slavery.

45 E. H. Carr, *What Is History?*, 2nd edn (Harmondsworth: Penguin, 1987), p. 91.

46 John Tosh's excellent introduction to method in history puts the point thus: 'To convey the immediacy of lived experience calls for intricate narrative and evocative description of several different levels. To approximate to an adequate explanation of past events, on the other hand, requires analytical complexity. Causation in particular is always multiple and many-layered, due to the manner in which different areas of human experience constantly obtrude on one another. *At the very least, some distinction needs to be made between background causes and direct causes: the former operate over the long term and place the event in question on the agenda of history, so to speak; the latter put the outcome into effect, often in a distinctive shape which no one could have foreseen.*' J. Tosh, *The Pursuit of History*, 2nd edn (London: Longman, 1983), p. 116; italics added.

47 Jeffrey Isaac once more puts this point well with the example of the role of Lenin's return to Russia as a catalyst for the Bolshevik Revolution: 'The Revolution of October 1917, for example, was a complex of events, of which Lenin's return to Petrograd by way of Finland Station was crucial. An account of the Revolution that left out the story of such events and processes would be hopelessly inadequate.... In this sense historical analysis must be narrative and concrete. If we are to understand the Revolution, however, we must also understand how Lenin's return (along with other occurrences, of course) could have precipitated the revolutionary upheaval. In order to do this, we must undertake an analysis of the structures and contradictions of Russian society, the international system and the balance of forces, the effects of World War I on these, and more. To analyze all this is not simply to analyze the choices of individuals and groups; it is also to analyze the enduring relationships that characterized Russian society and the way they were instantiated in the Revolution as the medium of the revolutionary process and as the transformed product of the Revolution.

'It should be clear that on the view suggested here there are different levels of analysis and abstraction which must be combined in order to understand the concrete social world, and that these levels of analysis are not reducible to one another.' Isaac, *Power and Marxist Theory*, p. 61.

48 F. Halliday, *Revolution and World Politics: The Rise and Fall of the Sixth Great Power* (London: Macmillan, 1999), p. 315.

49 See R. Saull, *Rethinking Theory and History in the Cold War: the State, Military Power and Social Revolution* (London: Frank Cass, 2001).

50 D. Armstrong, *Revolution and World Order: the Revolutionary State in International Society* (Oxford: Clarendon, 1993).

51 Gareth Evans and Kelvin Rowley present a compelling account of this tension between socialist nationalism and internationalism in their *Red Brotherhood at War: Vietnam, Cambodia and Laos since 1975*, 2nd edn (London: Verso, 1990): 'The weaknesses of socialist internationalism are particularly evident in dealing with the Communist revolutions in Asia where...the forces of state-building and mass nationalism are central aspects of the drive to modernity. The Third Indochina War was a product of these forces. Stripped to its essential, it is a story whose ingredients are familiar from other parts of the world that have undergone the experience of modernization' (p. 301).

52 Scholte, *International Relations of Social Change*, p. 130.

53 Ibid., p. 111.

54 Ibid., p. 67.

55 Ibid., p. 52.

56 Rosenberg, *The Empire of Civil Society*, p. 123.

57 H. Smith, 'The silence of the academics: international social theory, historical materialism and political values', *Review of International Studies*, 22, 2 (April 1996), pp. 191–212, p. 209. This point is echoed by Yohan Ariffin in his review of *The Empire of Civil Society* in 'The return of Marx to International Relations theory', *Economy and Society*, 25, 1 (February 1996), pp. 128–33: 'Something overall is missing in Rosenberg's sociological account. He complains rightly about realism's total disregard of "social relations between people", but his own account...eschews the problem of the actor or the agent of IR. If, one can agree with him, the realist "state-as-actor" model should be abandoned, "who" then is the subject of contemporary IR theory? Surely a Marxian perspective would opt for categories such as class, class fraction...social formation...social forces' (p. 132).

CHAPTER 4   INTERNATIONAL SOCIETY FROM BELOW

1 For the disputes over the existence or otherwise of the English school see R. E. Jones, 'The English school of International Relations: a case for closure', *Review of International Studies*, 7, 1 (1981), pp. 185–206; S. Grader, 'The English school of International Relations: evidence and evaluation', *Review of International Studies*, 14, 1 (1988), pp. 29–44; and P. Wilson, 'The English school of International Relations: a reply to Sheila Grader', *Review of International Studies*, 15, 1 (1989), pp. 101–29. Two recent helpful overviews of the English school and international society are: O. Waever, 'International society', *Cooperation and Conflict*, 27, 1 (1992), pp. 97–128; and T. Dunne, 'International society: theoretical

promises unfulfilled', *Cooperation and Conflict*, 30, 1 (1995), pp. 125–54. See also R. Fawn and J. Larkins, *International Society after the Cold War* (London: Macmillan Press in association with Millennium, 1996), for further elaborations and reworkings of the concept.

2 H. Bull, *The Anarchical Society: A Study of Order in World Politics*, 2nd edn (London and Basingstoke: Macmillan, 1995), p. 13.

3 A. James, *Sovereign Statehood: the Basis of International Society* (London: Allen & Unwin, 1986).

4 R. H. Jackson, *Quasi-States: Sovereignty, International Relations and the Third World* (Cambridge: Cambridge University Press, 1990).

5 J. Mayall, *Nationalism and International Society* (Cambridge: Cambridge University Press, 1990).

6 D. Armstrong, *Revolution and World Order: the Revolutionary State in International Society* (Oxford: Clarendon, 1993).

7 M. Wight, *Systems of States* (Leicester: Leicester University Press, 1977), p. 110.

8 Ibid., p. 113.

9 A. Watson, *The Evolution of International Society: A Comparative Historical Analysis* (London: Routledge, 1992).

10 H. Bull and A. Watson, *The Expansion of International Society* (Oxford: Oxford University Press, 1984).

11 Ibid., pp. 120–2.

12 G. W. Gong, *The Standard of 'Civilization' and International Society* (Oxford: Clarendon, 1984).

13 Ibid., p. 14.

14 Ibid., p. 21.

15 F. Halliday, 'International society as homogeneity: Burke, Marx, Fukuyama', *Millennium: Journal of International Studies*, 21, 3 (1992), pp. 435–61, p. 435.

16 See 'The Third World', in J. D. B. Miller and R. J. Vincent, *Order and Violence: Hedley Bull and International Relations* (Oxford: Clarendon Press, 1990), for a discussion of Bull's writings on the revolt against the west.

17 H. Bull, 'The revolt against the west', in Bull and Watson (eds), *The Expansion*, pp. 218–28.

18 Armstrong, *Revolution and World Order*, p. 167.

19 Jackson, *Quasi-States*, p. 34.

20 Ibid., p. 192.

21 Mayall, *Nationalism and International Society*, p. 145.

22 In D. Deudney, 'Binding sovereigns: authorities, structures, and geopolitics in the Philadelphian systems', in T. J. Biersteker and C. Weber (eds), *State Sovereignty as Social Construct* (Cambridge: Cambridge University Press, 1996), pp. 190–249.

23 I use this term in the sense employed by Wayne Te Brake in his *Shaping History: Ordinary People in European Politics 1500–1700* (Berkeley, CA: University of California Press, 1998). There, Te Brake suggests, 'What makes "ordinary" people ordinary in this strictly political sense is their

status as political subjects. Thus in situations in which power is concentrated in very few hands, it is quite possible that people who in a social, economic, or cultural sense could hardly be described as ordinary are nevertheless usefully seen as "ordinary" political subjects. By extension, what makes "popular" politics popular is its position relative to the domain of rulers and the politics of the official "elite" ' (pp. 6–7). As was suggested in chapter 2, the complex patterns of socio-political differentiation and stratification in medieval and early modern European society precludes specifying a single class (e.g. peasantry, burghers, journeymen) as the agents of popular protest; hence the resort to the more general (and ultimately unsatisfactory) terms such as 'populace', 'plebeian', 'subjects', 'mean sorts' or simply 'ordinary people'. For an excellent account of the uses and abuses of the idea of 'menu peuple' and 'sans-culottes' during the French Revolution see R. B. Rose, *The Making of the Sans-Culotte: Democratic Ideas and Institutions in Paris, 1789–92* (Manchester: Manchester University Press, 1983), ch. 1.

24 For two good historical-sociological accounts of how these antagonisms relate to the advent of modern sovereignty see Te Brake, *Shaping History*, and P. Zagorin, *Rebels and Rulers 1500–1660*, 2 vols (Cambridge: Cambridge University Press, 1982). See also P. Blickle (ed.), *Resistance, Representation and Community* (Oxford: Clarendon Press, 1997).

25 For good or ill, it was in these parts of the world where the sovereign form of state that now dominates the world was first established, and from where it expanded. Needless to say, this does not preclude recognizing, as this chapter will hopefully demonstrate, that modern sovereignty was given a significant local inflection through the influence of specific historical legacies and particular cultural norms.

26 There is no logical contradiction in positing an epochal rupture between medieval and modern geo-political systems while also recognizing that many of the characteristic features of modern state sovereignty can be found in late medieval forms of rule. Thus, for example, diplomatic emissaries, political/military alliances between territorial communities, taxation by a centralized bureaucracy or the idea of distinct nations were all familiar features of medieval and Renaissance Europe. What made these expressions of medieval 'sovereignty' distinctively modern was that by the seventeenth century they were generalized as the exclusive prerogative of unitary, depersonalized, territorial states. In Garret Mattingly's characteristically understated formulation, 'During the transition from medieval to modern times, in diplomacy as in some other fields, formal institutions changed less than might have been expected. It was the objects of policy and the vision of society which changed.' G. Mattingly, *Renaissance Diplomacy*, 2nd edn (Harmondsworth: Penguin, 1965), p. 15. See also M. S. Anderson, *The Origins of the Modern European State System 1494–1618* (London and New York: Longman, 1989); P. Anderson, *Passages from Antiquity to Feudalism* (London: New Left Books, 1974); M. van Creveld, *The Rise and Decline of the State* (Cambridge: Cambridge University Press, 1999), ch. 2; H. Schulze, *States, Nations and*

Nationalism: From the Middle Ages to the Present, tr. W. E. Yuill (Oxford: Blackwell, 1994), ch. 1; G. Poggi, *The Development of the Modern State: A Sociological Introduction* (Stanford, CA: Stanford University Press, 1978); Q. Skinner, *The Foundations of Modern Political Thought*, 2 vols (Cambridge: Cambridge University Press, 1978); J. Strayer, *On the Medieval Origins of the Modern State* (New Jersey, NJ: Princeton University Press, 1970).

27 E. M. Wood, *The Pristine Culture of Capitalism: A Historical Essay on Old Regimes and Modern States* (London and New York: Verso, 1991), p. 59.

28 R. Bendix, *Kings or People: Power and the Mandate to Rule* (Berkeley, Los Angeles, CA, and London: University of California Press, 1978), pp. 7–8.

29 R. Koselleck, *Critique and Crisis: the Pathogenesis of Modern Society* (Leamington Spa: Berg, 1987).

30 A. J. Mayer, *The Persistence of the Old Regime: Europe to the Great War* (London: Croom Helm, 1981). This represents a counterpart from the perspective of state development to the point made in chapter 3 about the persistence of pre-modern 'archaic' social movements under modern social formations.

31 Wight, *Systems of States*, pp. 151–2.

32 The past two decades have witnessed the publication of numerous outstanding, historically informed accounts of the rise of modern state sovereignty. All of the following texts acknowledge to different degrees the premodern antecedents to modern state sovereignty while at the same time demonstrating conclusively the historical specificity of the modern states-system. See, *inter alia*, L. Holzgrefe, 'The origins of modern International Relations theory', *Review of International Studies*, 15, 1 (1989), pp. 11–26; Friedrich Kratochwil, 'Of systems, boundaries and territory: an inquiry into the formation of the state system', *World Politics*, 39, 1 (1986), pp. 27–52; J. Rosenberg, *The Empire of Civil Society: A Critique of the Realist Theory of International Relations* (London: Verso, 1994); J. G. Ruggie, 'Continuity and transformation in the world polity: toward a neo-realist synthesis', in R. Keohane (ed.), *Neorealism and its Critics* (New York: Columbia University Press, 1986), pp. 131–57, and 'Territoriality and beyond: problematizing modernity in International Relations', *International Organization*, 47, 1 (Winter 1993), pp. 139–74; H. Spruyt, *The Sovereign State and its Competitors* (New Jersey, NJ: Princeton University Press, 1994); B. Teschke, 'Geopolitical relations in the European Middle Ages: history and theory', *International Organization*, 52, 2 (Spring 1998), pp. 325–58.

33 In the field of IR, Markus Fischer has made the neo-realist case for the perennial logic of 'international' anarchy with reference to the Middle Ages in his 'Feudal Europe, 800–1300: communal discourse and conflictual practices', *International Organization*, 46, 2 (Spring 1992), pp. 462–6. See the critique by R. B. Hall and F. V. Kratochwil, 'Medieval tales: neorealist "science" and the abuse of history', and Fischer's response, 'On context, facts and norms: response to Hall and Kratochwil', both in *International Organization*, 47, 3 (Spring 1993), pp. 479–500. See also

Teschke, 'Geopolitical relations'. Outside IR, numerous scholars have used the notions of 'state' and 'sovereignty' with reference to medieval Europe. See M. Bloch, *Feudal Society*, tr. L. A. Manyon, Vol. 2, 2nd edn (London: Routledge & Kegan Paul, 1962), part 7; S. Reynolds, *Kingdoms and Communities in Western Europe, 900–1300*, 2nd edn (Oxford: Clarendon Press, 1997); M. Wilks, *The Problem of Sovereignty in the Later Middle Ages* (Cambridge: Cambridge University Press, 1963). On the history of the concept of 'sovereignty' see J. Bartelson, *A Genealogy of Sovereignty* (Cambridge: Cambridge University Press, 1995); G. Mairet, *Le Principe de souveraineté: histoire et fondaments du pouvoir moderne* (Paris: Gallimard, 1997); and H. Shinoda, *Re-Examining Sovereignty: From Classical Theory to the Global Age* (London: Macmillan, 2000).

34 Ibid., p. 130.

35 B. Manning, *Aristocrats, Plebeians and Revolution in England, 1640–1660* (London and East Haven, CT: Pluto Press, 1996), p. 103. See also N. Wood and E. Meiksins Wood, *A Trumpet of Sedition: Political Theory and the Rise of Capitalism, 1509–1688* (London: Pluto Press, 1997).

36 Zagorin, *Rebels and Rulers*, Vol. 2, p. 164.

37 According to Nannerl O. Keohane: 'The use of these ancient phrases – *le bien commun, le salut du publique* – in this context indicates that the Ormists were aware that they were rejecting the politics of *raison d'état* for a very different vision, the vision of an assembled community of men pursuing the common good together. They had the grandiose thoughts of extending this vision to other parts of France, liberating other Frenchmen as they themselves were freed from tyranny and oppression.' N. O. Keohane, *Philosophy and the State in France: The Renaissance to the Enlightenment* (Princeton, NJ: Princeton University Press, 1980), p. 219. For an extensive study of the way the French public – both ruling and subordinate classes – linked the revolutionary upheavals in England to the French Fronde see P. A. Knachel, *England and the Fronde: the Impact of the English Civil War and Revolution on France* (Ithaca, NY: Cornell University Press, 1967).

38 See G. B. Nash, *The Urban Crucible: Social Change, Political Consciousness and the Origins of the American Revolution* (Cambridge, MA, and London: Harvard University Press, 1979).

39 Ibid., p. 86. See also M. Warner, *The Letters of the Republic: Publication and the Public Sphere in Eighteenth-Century America* (Cambridge, MA, and London: Harvard University Press, 1990).

40 Ibid., p. 384.

41 L. Hunt, *Politics, Culture and Class in the French Revolution* (Berkeley, Los Angeles, CA, and London: University of California Press, 1984), p. 2.

42 K. Marx, *Critique of the Gotha Programme*, in D. Fernbach (ed.), *The First International and After, Political Writings*, Vol. 3 (Aylesbury: Penguin Books in association with New Left Review, 1974), p. 350.

43 Two good historical discussions of this interaction can be found in J. J. Schwarzmantel, *Socialism and the Idea of the Nation* (New York:

Harvester Wheatsheaf, 1991), and E. Nimni, *Marxism and Nationalism: Theoretical Origins of a Political Crisis* (London: Pluto Press, 1991). See also E. Benner, *Really Existing Nationalisms: A Post-Communist View from Marx and Engels* (Oxford: Oxford University Press, 1995).

44 See F. Braudel, *A History of Civilisations*, tr. R. Mayne (London: Allen Lane/Penguin Press, 1994), ch. 1; E. de Dampierre, 'Note sur "culture" et "civilisation"', *Studies in Comparative Culture and Society*, 3 (1961), pp. 328–40; N. Elias, *The Civilizing Process: The History of Manners*, tr. E. Jephcott, Vol. 1 (Oxford and Cambridge, MA: Blackwell, 1982), part 2. For the historical evolution of this term, see R. Williams, *Keywords: A Vocabulary of Culture and Society* (London: Fontana, 1976). For the contemporaneous (generally hostile) reception of the word into the Spanish lexicon see P. Álvarez de Miranda, *Palabras e ideas: el léxicon de la Ilustración temprana en España, 1680–1760* (Madrid: Anejos del Boletín de la Real Academia Española LI, 1992), ch. 7.

45 G. C. Caffenztis, 'On the Scottish origin of "civilization"', in S. Federici (ed.), *Enduring Western Civilization: The Construction of the Concept of Western Civilization and Its 'Others'* (Westport, CT: Praeger, 1995), pp. 13–36, p. 14.

46 A welcome antidote to the facile assumption that the contrast between modern notions of 'civilization' and 'barbarism' is a purely ethnocentric construct can be found in Roger Bartra, *Wild Men in the Looking Glass: the Mythic Origins of European Otherness*, tr. C. T. Berrisford (Ann Arbor, MI: University of Michigan Press, 1994). For Bartra, 'the wild man and the European are one and the same, and the notion of barbarism was applied to non-European peoples as the transposition of a perfectly structured myth with a character that can only be understood within the context of Western cultural evolution' (p. 4). See also the illuminating study by R. P. Harrison, *Forests: The Shadow of Civilization* (Chicago: University of Chicago Press, 1992), where the relation between the outlawed world of the forest and the 'civilized' urban world *within* so-called 'western' societies is explored. Reading this cultural history of the forest in conjunction with the social history of the outlaws and bandits of modern Europe reveals some striking connections between the 'western' imagination of those that lie outside (*foris*) the pale of civilization and the law, and the ongoing processes of 'primitive' or 'original' accumulation in that part of the world.

47 Marx: 'the historical movement which changes the producers into wage-workers appears, on the one hand, as their emancipation from serfdom and from the fetters of the guilds.... But on the other hand, these new freedmen became sellers of themselves only after they had been robbed of all their own means of production, and all the guarantees of existence afforded by the old feudal arrangements. And the history of this, their expropriation, is written in the annals of mankind in letters of blood and fire.' K. Marx, *Capital*, Vol. I (Harmondsworth: Penguin, 1977), p. 713.

48 The contempt with which the British ruling classes held the country's 'lower orders' and 'labouring poor' during the eighteenth century and

beyond is well documented in the collective work of Douglas Hay et al., *Albion's Fatal Tree: Crime and Society in Eighteenth-Century England* (London: Penguin, 1975). Two further relevant studies emerged from that volume: P. Linebaugh, *The London Hanged: Crime and Civil Society in the Eighteenth Century* (London: Allen Lane, 1991), and E. P. Thompson, *Whigs and Hunters: The Origin of the Black Act* (Harmondsworth: Penguin, 1975). The cultural attitudes of this ruling class toward the urban and rural poor (the emphasis on their 'idleness', 'rudeness', 'slothfulness', 'lasciviousness', 'seditious' nature, and so forth) and the practices used to discipline and punish them into wage labour are, once again, strikingly reminiscent of the racist regimes that sustained European imperialism during that same period. Compare the above, for example, with the accounts of 'primitive' or 'original' accumulation in J.-M. Penvenne, *African Workers and Colonial Racism: Mozambican Strategies and Struggles in Lourenço Marques 1877–1962* (London: James Currey, 1995), and R. M. A. van Zwanenberg, *Colonial Capitalism and Labour in Kenya 1919–1939* (Kampala, Nairobi and Dar es Salaam: East African Literature Bureau, 1975). See also R. Miles, 'The civilization and racialization of the interior', in his *Racism after 'Race Relations'* (London and New York: Routledge, 1993), and the chapter on 'White Negroes' in J. Nederveen Pieterse, *White on Black: Images of Africans in European Popular Culture* (New Jersey, NJ: Princeton University Press, 1992).

49 Jörg Fisch, 'Law as a means and as an ends: some remarks on the function of European and non-European law in the process of European expansion', in W. J. Mommsen and J. A. de Moor (eds), *European Expansion and Law: The Encounter of European and Indigenous Law in 19th and 20th Century Africa and Asia* (Providence, RI, and Oxford: Berg Publishers, 1992), pp. 15–39, p. 21.

50 This is one of the main arguments developed by Halliday in 'International society as homogeneity'.

51 E. H. Norman, *Japan's Emergence as a Modern State: Political and Economic Problems of the Meiji Period* (Westport, CT: Greenwood Press, 1940), p. 101.

52 R. Kasaba, *The Ottoman Empire and the World Economy: the Nineteenth Century* (Albany, NY: State University of New York, 1988), p. 33.

53 Ibid., p. 33.

54 C. Keyder, *State and Class in Turkey: A Study in Capitalist Development* (London and New York: Verso, 1987), p. 28.

55 In their respective contributions to Bull and Watson, *The Expansion of International Society*.

56 Jackson, *Quasi-States*, p. 85.

57 Ibid., p. 83.

58 Mayall, *Nationalism and International Society*, p. 111.

59 H. Bull, *Justice in International Relations: the Hagey Lectures* reprinted in K. Alderson and A. Hurrell (eds) *Hedley Bull on International Society* (Basingstoke: Macmillan, 2000) pp. 206–45; 212–13.

60 Jackson, *Quasi-States*, p. 29.

61 Ibid., p. 29.
62 This argument is thoroughly explored in S. Halperin, *In the Mirror of the Third World: Capitalist Development in Modern Europe* (Ithaca, NY: Cornell University Press, 1997).
63 Jackson, *Quasi-States*, p. 22.
64 Ibid., p. 23.
65 R. J. Vincent, 'Racial equality', in Bull and Watson, *The Expansion of International Society*, p. 252.

CHAPTER 5   THE PROMISES OF INTERNATIONAL CIVIL SOCIETY

1 R. Falk, *On Humane Governance: Toward a New Global Politics* (Cambridge: Polity, 1995), p. 35. See also, by the same author, *Predatory Globalization: A Critique* (Cambridge: Polity, 1999) and 'The world order between inter-state law and the law of humanity: the role of civil society institutions', in D. Archibugi and D. Held (eds), *Cosmopolitan Democracy: An Agenda for a New World Order* (Cambridge: Polity, 1995).
2 See also R. Barnet, *Global Dreams: Imperial Corporations* (New York: Simon & Schuster, 1994); P. Ekins, *A New World Order: Grassroots Movements for Global Change* (London: Routledge, 1992).
3 See, for example, J. A. Scholte, 'Global civil society', in N. Woods (ed.), *The Political Economy of Globalisation* (Basingstoke: Macmillan, 2000).
4 P. Wapner, *Environmental Activism and World Civic Politics* (Albany, NY: State University of New York Press, 1996), p. 19.
5 M. Hardt and A. Negri, *Empire* (Cambridge, MA: Harvard University Press, 2000), p. 311.
6 S. Gill, 'Market civilization and global disciplinary neoliberalism', *Millennium: Journal of International Studies*, 25, 3 (Winter 1995), pp. 399–423.
7 D. Held et al., *Global Transformations: Politics, Economics and Culture* (Cambridge: Polity, 1999), p. 58.
8 Commission on Global Governance, *Our Global Neighbourhood* (Oxford: Oxford University Press, 1995), pp. 2–3.
9 L. Gordenker and T. G. Weiss (eds), *NGOs, the United Nations and Global Governance* (Boulder, CO: Lynne Rienner, 1996), p. 17.
10 Representative texts include: Archibugi and Held (eds), *Cosmopolitan Democracy*; D. Archibugi, D. Held and M. Köhler (eds), *Re-Imagining Political Community: Studies in Cosmopolitan Democracy* (Cambridge: Polity, 1998); and D. Held, *Democracy and the Global Order: From the Modern State to Cosmopolitan Governance* (Cambridge: Polity, 1995). A version of this approach in Spanish can be found in G. Jáuregui, *La democracia planetaria* (Oviedo: Ediciones Nobel, 2000).
11 Held, *Democracy and the Global Order*, p. 27.
12 Ibid., p. 22.
13 Ibid., p. 234.

14 Ibid., p. 234.

15 Ibid., p. 237.

16 See, *inter alia*, P. Hirst and G. Thompson, *Globalization in Question* (Cambridge: Polity, 1995), esp. ch. 8. H. Magdoff and P. M. Sweezy, 'Globalization – to what end?', parts 1 and 2, *Monthly Review*, 43, 9 and 10 (February and March 1992), pp. 1–18 and 1–19, respectively.

17 For the statistical breakdown see Held et al., *Global Transformations*; Gordenker and Weiss (eds), *NGOs, the United Nations and Global Governance*; P. J. Spiro, 'New global communities: nongovernmental organizations in international decision-making institutions', *The Washington Quarterly*, 18, 1 (Winter 1995), pp. 45–56; and P. Willetts (ed.), *'The Conscience of the World': The Influence of Non-Governmental Organisations in the UN System* (London: Hurst & Co, 1996).

18 A representative example of an emphatically 'presentist' account of global civil society can be found in C. Warkentin and K. Mingst, 'International institutions, the state and global civil society in the age of the world wide web', *Global Governance*, 6, 2 (April–June 2000), pp. 237–57.

19 Scholte, 'Global civil society', p. 188.

20 Craig N. Murphy has presented the most comprehensive version of this argument in his *International Organization and Industrial Change: Global Governance since 1850* (Cambridge: Polity, 1994). For an equally historically informed account of the evolution of governance see Christian Reus-Smit, 'Changing patterns of governance: from absolutism to global multilateralism', in A. J. Paolini, A. P. Jarvis and C. Reus-Smit (eds), *Between Sovereignty and Global Governance: The United Nations, the State and Civil Society* (Basingstoke: Macmillan Press, 1998), pp. 3–28.

21 Gordenker and Weiss (eds), *NGOs, the United Nations and Global Governance*, p. 27.

22 R. O'Brien, J. A. Scholte and M. Williams, *Contesting Governance: Multilateralism and Global Social Movements* (Cambridge: Cambridge University Press, 2000), pp. 2–3. See also J. A. Fox and L. D. Brown (eds), *The Struggle for Accountability: The World Bank, NGOs and Grassroots Movements* (Cambridge, MA: MIT Press, 1998), and P. J. Nelson, *The World Bank and Non-Governmental Organizations: The Limits of Apolitical Development* (London: Macmillan, 1995).

23 Willetts (ed.), *'The Conscience of the World'*, p. 33.

24 For detailed discussions of these principles see Gordenker and Weiss (eds), *NGOs, the United Nations and Global Governance*; D. Otto, 'Nongovernmental organizations in the United Nations: the emerging role of international civil society', *Human Rights Quarterly*, 18, 1 (1996), pp. 107–41; and Willetts (ed.), *'The Conscience of the World'*. For an update on the changes in the 'politics of accreditation' see P. Willetts, 'From "consultative arrangements" to "partnership": the changing status of NGOs in diplomacy at the UN', *Global Governance*, 6, 2 (April–June 2000), pp. 191–212.

25 A. M. Clarke, E. J. Friedman and K. Hochstetler, 'The sovereign limits of global civil society: a comparison of NGO participation in UN world

conferences on the environment, human rights and women', *World Politics*, 51, 4 (October 1998), pp. 1–35, p. 12.

26 Ibid., p. 18.

27 K. Raustiala, 'States, NGOs and international environmental institutions', *International Studies Quarterly*, 41, 4 (December 1997), pp. 719–40, p. 724. Or, as Clarke, Friedman and Hochstetler conclude, 'State sovereignty sets the limits of global civil society': 'The sovereign limits of global civil society', p. 35.

28 See, for example, the essays contained in Fox and Brown (eds), *The Struggle for Accountability*, and the analysis of P. J. Nelson, 'Internationalizing economic and environmental policy: transnational NGO networks and the World Bank's expanding influence', *Millennium: Journal of International Studies*, 25, 3 (Winter 1996), pp. 605–33.

29 L.-A. Broadhead, 'Commissioning consent: globalization and global governance', *International Journal*, 51, 4 (Autumn 1996), pp. 652–68, p. 660.

30 O'Brien, Scholte and Williams, *Contesting Governance*, p. 3.

31 D. Held, 'Cosmopolitan democracy and the global order: reflections on the 200th anniversary of Kant's "Perpetual Peace"', *Alternatives*, 20, 4 (October–November 1995), pp. 415–29, p. 418.

32 Held, *Democracy and the Global Order*, p. 16.

33 Ibid., p. 22.

34 See Held, 'the asymmetrical production and distribution of life-chances which limit and erode the possibilities of political participation'. Ibid., p. 171.

35 J. Rosenberg, *The Empire of Civil Society: A Critique of the Realist Theory of International Relations* (London: Verso, 1994), p. 129.

36 The obvious and important exception to this is, of course, the European Union. Impressive as the advance in Union-wide citizenship rights has been, however, such rights still lag far behind the right of European capital to exploit the single market created by the Union. Even more seriously, the rights and benefits secured by the European Union are exclusive to citizens of member states.

37 Held, *Democracy and the Global Order*, p. 233.

38 J. Petras, 'Imperialism and NGOs in Latin America', *Monthly Review*, 49, 7 (December 1997), pp. 10–27, p. 13; italics in the original.

39 L. Macdonald, *Supporting Civil Society: The Political Role of Non-Governmental Organizations in Central America* (New York: Macmillan, 1995), p. 153.

40 See, for example, S. Carapico, *Civil Society in Yemen: A Political Economy of Activism in Modern Arabia* (Cambridge: Cambridge University Press, 1998), and G. Clark, *The Politics of NGOs in South-East Asia: Participation and Protest in the Philippines* (London and New York: Routledge, 1998).

41 See, for example, T. Young, ' "A project to be realized": global liberalism and contemporary Africa', *Millennium: Journal of International Studies*, 24, 3 (Winter 1995), pp. 527–46.

42 See the interesting study of this period by S. Soederberg, 'State, crisis, and capital accumulation in Mexico', *Historical Materialism: Research in Critical Marxist Theory* (forthcoming 2001).

References

Abrahamian, E. 1990: *Khomeinism*. London: IB Tauris.

Abrams, P. 1982: *Historical Sociology*. Shepton Mallet: Open Books.

Al-Azmeh, A. 1993: *Islam and Modernities*. London: Verso.

Alexander, J. C. (ed.) 1998: *Real Civil Societies: Dilemmas of Institutionalization*. London and Thousand Oaks, CA: Sage Publications.

Alexander, R. J. 1973: *Aprismo: The Ideas and Doctrines of Victor Raúl de la Haya*. Kent, OH: Kent State University Press.

Anderson, B. 1983: *Imagined Communities: Reflections on the Origin and Spread of Nationalism*. London: Verso.

Anderson, M. S. 1989: *The Origins of the Modern European State System 1494–1618*. London and New York: Longman.

Anderson, P. 1974: *Lineages of the Absolutist State*. London: New Left Books.

—— 1974: *Passages from Antiquity to Feudalism*. London: New Left Books.

—— 1978: *Arguments within English Marxism*. London: Verso.

—— 1992: *English Questions*. London: Verso.

Appleby, J. O. 1978: *Economic Thought and Ideology in Seventeenth-Century England*. Princeton, NJ: Princeton University Press.

Arato, A., and Cohen, J. 1992: *Civil Society and Political Theory*. Cambridge, MA: MIT Press.

Ariffin, Y. 1996: The return of Marx to International Relations theory. *Economy and Society*, 25 (1): 128–33.

Armstrong, D. 1993: *Revolution and World Order: The Revolutionary State in International Society*. Oxford: Clarendon.

Aron, R. 1966: *Peace and War: A Theory of International Relations*. London: Weidenfeld & Nicolson.

Barnet, R. 1994: *Global Dreams: Imperial Corporations*. New York: Simon & Schuster.

Bartra, R. 1994: *Wild Men in the Looking Glass: the Mythic Origins of European Otherness*, tr. C. T. Berrisford. Ann Arbor, MI: University of Michigan Press.

Bartelson, J. 1995: *A Genealogy of Sovereignty*. Cambridge: Cambridge University Press.

Becker, M. B. 1994: *The Emergence of Civil Society in the Eighteenth Century: A Privileged Moment in the History of England, Scotland and France*. Bloomington and Indianapolis, IN: Indiana University Press.

Bendix, R. 1978: *Kings or People: Power and the Mandate to Rule*. Berkeley, Los Angeles, CA, and London: University of California Press.

Bhaskar, R. 1993: *Reclaiming Reality: A Critical Introduction to Contemporary Philosophy*. 2nd edn. London and New York: Verso.

Blackbourn, D., and Eley, G. 1984: *The Peculiarities of German History: Bourgeois Society and Politics in Nineteenth-Century Germany*. Oxford and New York: Oxford University Press.

Blickle, P. (ed.) 1997: *Resistance, Representation and Community*. Oxford: Clarendon Press.

Braudel, F. 1996: *A History of Civilisations*, tr. R. Mayne. London: Allen Lane/Penguin Press.

Broadhead, L.-A. 1996: Commissioning consent: globalization and global governance. *International Journal*, 51 (4): 652–68.

Bull, H. 1976: International studies in a transnational world. *Millennium: Journal of International Studies*, 5 (1): 1–20.

—— 1984: *Justice in International Relations: The Hagey Lectures*, reprinted in K. Alderson and A. Hurrell (eds) *Hedley Bull on International Society* (Basingstoke: Macmillan, 2000) pp. 206–45; 212–13.

—— 1995: *The Anarchical Society: A Study of Order in World Politics*. 2nd edn. London and Basingstoke: Macmillan.

Bull, H., and Watson, A. (eds) 1984: *The Expansion of International Society*. Oxford: Oxford University Press.

Burton, J. 1972: *World Society*. London: Macmillan.

Caffenztis, G. C. 1995: On the Scottish origin of 'civilization'. In S. Federici (ed.), *Enduring Western Civilization: The Construction of the Concept of Western Civilization and Its 'Others'*. Westport, CT: Praeger, 13–36.

Calhoun, C. 1993: 'New social movements' of the early nineteenth century. *Social Science History*, 17 (3): 387–425.

Carapico, S. 1998: *Civil Society in Yemen: A Political Economy of Activism in Modern Arabia*. Cambridge: Cambridge University Press.

Carr, E. H. 1987: *What Is History?* 2nd edn. Harmondsworth: Penguin, 1987.

Cerny, P. G. 1990: *The Changing Architecture of States: Structure, Agency and the Future of the State*. London and New York: Sage.

Chan, S. 1997: In search of democratic peace: problems and promise. *Mershon International Studies Review*, 41 (1): 59–91.

Clark, G. 1998: *The Politics of NGOs in South-East Asia: Participation and Protest in the Philippines*. London and New York: Routledge.

Clarke, A. M., Friedman, E. J., and Hochstetler, K. 1998: The sovereign limits of global civil society: a comparison of NGO participation in UN world conferences on the environment, human rights and women. *World Politics*, 51 (4): 1–35.

Clarke, M. 1985: Transnationalism. In S. Smith (ed.), *International Relations: British and American Perspectives*. Oxford: Basil Blackwell.

Cohen, J. L. 1982: *Class and Civil Society: The Limits of Marxian Critical Theory*. Amherst, MA: University of Massachusetts Press.

Cohen, R., and Rai, S. M. (eds) 2000: *Global Social Movements*. London and New Brunswick, NJ: The Athlone Press.

Colás, A. 1994: Putting cosmopolitanism into practice: the case of socialist internationalism. *Millennium: Journal of International Studies*, 23 (3): 513–34.

Commission on Global Governance 1995: *Our Global Neighbourhood*. Oxford: Oxford University Press.

Czempiel, E.-O. (ed.) 1969: *Die anachronistische Souveränität*. Köln-Opladen: Westdeutscher Verlag.

Dampierre, E. de 1961: Note sur 'culture' et 'civilisation'. *Studies in Comparative Culture and Society*, 3: 328–40.

Della Porta, D., Kriesi, H. P., and Rucht, D. (eds) 1999: *Social Movements in a Globalizing World*. New York: St Martin's Press.

Deudney, D. 1996: Binding sovereigns: authorities, structures, and geopolitics in the Philadelphian systems. In T. J. Biersteker and C. Weber (eds), *State Sovereignty as Social Construct*. Cambridge: Cambridge University Press, 190–249.

Devin, G. 1993: *L'Internationale socialiste: histoire et sociologie du socialisme international, 1945–1990*. Paris: Presses de la Fondation Nationale des Sciences Politiques.

Doyle, M. W. 1983: Kant, liberal legacies, and foreign affairs (2 parts). *Philosophy and Public Affairs*, 12 (1 and 2): 205–353.

Dunne, T. 1995: International society: theoretical promises unfulfilled. *Co-operation and Conflict*, 30 (1): 125–54.

Ekins, P. 1992: *A New World Order: Grassroots Movements for Global Change*. London: Routledge.

Elias, N. 1982: *The Civilizing Process: The History of Manners*. Vol. 1, tr. E. Jephcott. Oxford and Cambridge, MA: Blackwell.

Esteva, G., and Prakash, M. S. 1998: *Grassroots Post-Modernism: Remaking the Soil of Cultures*. London and New York: Zed Books.

Evans, G., and Rowley, K. 1990: *Red Brotherhood at War: Vietnam, Cambodia and Laos since 1975*. 2nd edn. London: Verso.

Fairclough, A. 1987: *To Redeem the Soul of America: The Southern Christian Leadership Conference and Martin Luther King Jr*. Athens, GA, and London: University of Georgia Press.

Falk, R. 1995: *On Humane Governance: Toward a New Global Politics*. Cambridge: Polity.

—— 1995: The world order between inter-state law and the law of humanity: the role of civil society institutions. In D. Archibugi and D. Held (eds),

Cosmopolitan Democracy: An Agenda for a New World Order. Cambridge: Polity.

—— 1999: *Predatory Globalization: A Critique.* Cambridge: Polity.

Ferguson, A. 1996: *An Essay on the History of Civil Society*, ed. F. Oz-Salzberger. Cambridge: Cambridge University Press.

Fisch, J. 1992: Law as a means and as an ends: some remarks on the function of European and non-European law in the process of European expansion. In W. J. Mommsen and J. A. de Moor (eds), *European Expansion and Law: The Encounter of European and Indigenous Law in 19th and 20th century Africa and Asia.* Providence, RI, and Oxford: Berg Publishers, 15–39.

Fischer, M. 1992: Feudal Europe, 800–1300: communal discourse and conflictual practices. *International Organization*, 46 (2): 462–6.

Foweraker, J. 1995: *Theorizing Social Movements.* London and Boulder, CO: Pluto Press.

Fox, J. A., and Brown, L. D. (eds) 1998: *The Struggle for Accountability: The World Bank, NGOs and Grassroots Movements.* Cambridge, MA: MIT Press.

Frisby, D., and Sayer, D. 1986: *Society.* New York: Ellis Horwood.

Gellner, E. 1974: *Contemporary Thought and Politics*, ed. with a preface by I. C. Jarvie and J. Agassi. London and Boston: Routledge & Kegan Paul.

—— 1994: *The Conditions of Liberty: Civil Society and its Rivals.* Oxford: Oxford University Press.

Germain, R. D., and Kenny, M. 1998: Engaging Gramsci: International Relations theory and the new Gramscians. *Review of International Studies*, 24 (1): 2–21.

Gerth, H. H., and Wright Mills, C. (eds) 1991: *From Max Weber: Essays in Sociology.* London: Routledge.

Ghils, P. 1992: International civil society: international non-governmental organisations in the international system. *International Social Science Journal*, 44 (133): 417–29.

Gill, S. 1994: Structural change and global political economy: globalizing elites and the emerging world order. In Y. Sakamoto (ed.), *Global transformation: Challenges to the State System.* Tokyo: United Nations University Press, 169–99.

—— 1995: Market civilization and global disciplinary neoliberalism. *Millennium: Journal of International Studies*, 25 (3): 399–423.

Gilroy, P. 1993: *The Black Atlantic: Modernity and Double Consciousness.* London and New York: Verso.

Gong, G. W. 1984: *The Standard of 'Civilization' and International Society.* Oxford: Clarendon Press.

Gordenker, L., and Weiss, T. G. (eds) 1996: *NGOs, the United Nations and Global Governance.* Boulder, CO: Lynne Rienner.

Grader, S. 1988: The English school of international relations: evidence and evaluation. *Review of International Studies*, 14 (1): 29–44.

Gramsci, A. 1972: *Selections from the Prison Notebooks*, ed. Q. Hoare and G. Nowell-Smith. London: Lawrence & Wishart.

Grosser, A. 1980: *The Western Alliance: European–American Relations since 1945*, tr. M. Shaw. New York: Seabury Press.

Habermas, J. 1992: *The Structural Transformation of the Public Sphere: An Inquiry into a Category of Bourgeois Society.* Cambridge: Polity.

Hall, J. (ed.) 1995: *Civil Society: Theory, History, Comparison.* Cambridge: Polity.

Halliday, F. 1988: Three concepts of internationalism. *International Affairs*, 64 (2): 123–42.

—— 1992: International society as homogeneity: Burke, Marx, Fukuyama. *Millennium: Journal of International Studies*, 21 (3): 435–61.

—— 1999: *Revolution and World Politics: The Rise and Fall of the Sixth Great Power.* London: Macmillan.

—— 2000: *Nation and Religion in the Middle East.* London: Saqi Books.

Halperin, S. 1997: *In the Mirror of the Third World: Capitalist Development in Modern Europe.* Ithaca, NY: Cornell University Press.

Hardt, M. 1995: The withering of civil society. *Social Text*, 14 (4): 27–44.

Hardt, M., and Negri, A. 2000: *Empire.* Cambridge, MA: Harvard University Press.

Harrison, R. P. 1992: *Forests: The Shadow of Civilization.* Chicago, ILL: University of Chicago Press.

Hay, D., Linebaugh, P., Ryle, J. G., Thompson, E. P., and Winslow, C. 1975: *Albion's Fatal Tree: Crime and Society in Eighteenth-Century England.* London: Penguin.

Hegel, G. W. F. 1995: *Elements of the Philosophy of Right*, ed. A. W. Wood, tr. H. B. Nisbet. Cambridge: Cambridge University Press.

Heine, C., and Teschke, B. 1996: Sleeping Beauty and the dialectical awakening: on the potential of dialectic for international relations. *Millennium: Journal of International Studies*, 25 (2): 399–423.

Held, D. (ed.) 1993: *Prospects for Democracy: North, South, East, West.* Cambridge: Polity.

Held, D. 1995: Cosmopolitan democracy and the global order: reflections on the 200th anniversary of Kant's 'Perpetual Peace'. *Alternatives*, 20 (4): 415–29.

—— 1995: *Democracy and the Global Order: From the Modern State to Cosmopolitan Governance.* Cambridge: Polity.

Held, D., McGrew, A. G., Goldblatt, D., and Perraton, J. 1999: *Global Transformations: Politics, Economics and Culture.* Cambridge: Polity.

Held, D., and Köhler, M. (eds) 1998: *Re-Imagining Political Community: Studies in Cosmopolitan Democracy.* Cambridge: Polity.

Hirst, P., and Thompson, G. 1995: *Globalization in Question.* Cambridge: Polity.

Hirszowicz, L. 1966: *The Third Reich and the Arab East.* London: Routledge & Kegan Paul.

Hobbes, T. 1968: *Leviathan*, ed. with an introduction by C. B. Macpherson. Harmondsworth: Penguin.

Hobsbawm, E. 1959: *Primitive Rebels: Studies in Archaic Forms of Social Movement in the 19th and 20th Centuries.* Manchester: Manchester University Press.

Hoffman, M. 1993: Agency, identity and intervention. In I. Forbes and M. Hoffman (eds), *Political Theory, International Relations and the Ethics of Intervention*. London: Macmillan Press, 194–210.

Hollis, M., and Smith, S. 1994: Two stories about structure and agency. *Review of International Studies*, 20 (3): 241–51.

Holzgrefe, L. 1989: The origins of modern International Relations theory. *Review of International Studies*, 15 (1): 11–26.

Hunt, L. 1984: *Politics, Culture and Class in the French Revolution*. Berkeley, Los Angeles, CA, and London: University of California Press.

Hutchison, T. 1988: *Before Adam Smith: The Emergence of Political Economy, 1662–1776*. Oxford: Basil Blackwell.

Isaac, J. C. 1989: *Power and Marxist Theory: A Realist View*. London and Ithaca, NY: Cornell University Press.

Jackson, R. H. 1990: *Quasi-States: Sovereignty, International Relations and the Third World*. Cambridge: Cambridge University Press.

James, A. 1986: *Sovereign Statehood: The Basis of International Society*. London: Allen & Unwin.

James, W. 1998: *Holding Aloft the Banner of Ethiopia: Caribbean Radicalism in Early Twentieth-Century America*. London and New York: Verso.

Jamison, F., and Eyerman, R. 1990: *Social Movements: A Cognitive Approach*. Cambridge: Polity.

Jáuregui, G. 2000: *La democracia planetaria*. Oviedo: Ediciones Nobel.

Jones, R. E. 1981: The English school of International Relations: a case for closure. *Review of International Studies*, (7) 1: 185–206.

Keane, J. (ed.) 1988: *The State and Civil Society: New European Perspectives*. London: Verso.

Keohane, N. O. 1980: *Philosophy and the State in France: The Renaissance to the Enlightenment*. Princeton, NJ: Princeton University Press.

Keohane, R. and Nye, J. (eds) 1970: *Transnational Relations and World Politics*. Cambridge, MA, and London: Harvard University Press.

Keyder, C. 1987: *State and Class in Turkey: A Study in Capitalist Development*. London and New York: Verso.

Knachel, P. A. 1967: *England and the Fronde: The Impact of the English Civil War and Revolution on France*. Ithaca, NY: Cornell University Press.

Koselleck, R. 1985: *Futures Past: On the Semantics of Historical Time*. Cambridge, MA: MIT Press.

—— 1987: *Critique and Crisis: the Pathogenesis of Modern Society*. Leamington Spa: Berg.

Kratochwil, F. 1986: Of systems, boundaries and territory: an inquiry into the formation of the state system. *World Politics*, 39 (1): 27–52.

Landau, J. M. 1990: *The Politics of Pan-Islam: Ideology and Organisation*. Oxford: Clarendon Press.

Linebaugh, P. 1991: *The London Hanged: Crime and Civil Society in the Eighteenth Century*. London: Allen Lane.

Lipschutz, R. D. 1992: Reconstructing world politics: the emergence of global civil society. *Millennium: Journal of International Studies*, 21 (3): 389–420.

Locke, J. 1988: *Two Treatises on Government*, ed. with introduction and notes by P. Laslett. Cambridge: Cambridge University Press.

Lucas, C. 1973: Nobles, bourgeois and the origins of the French revolution. *Past and Present*, 60: 84–126.

Lyons, F. S. L. 1963: *Internationalism in Europe 1815–1914*. Leiden: A. W. Sythoff.

Macdonald, L. 1995: *Supporting Civil Society: The Political Role of Non-Governmental Organizations in Central America*. New York: Macmillan.

Mack Smith, D. 1994: *Mazzini*. New Haven and London: Yale University Press.

Macpherson, C. B. 1990: *The Political Theory of Possessive Individualism: From Hobbes to Locke*. Oxford and New York: Oxford University Press.

McShane, D. 1992: *International Labour and the Origins of the Cold War*. Oxford: Clarendon Press.

Magdoff, H., and Sweezy, P. M. 1992: Globalization – to what end? *Monthly Review* part 1, 43 (9): 1–18; part 2, 43 (10): 1–19.

Mairet, G. 1997: *Le Principe de souveraineté: histoire et fondaments du pouvoir moderne*. Paris: Gallimard.

Manning, B. 1996: *Aristocrats, Plebeians and Revolution in England, 1640–1660*. London and East Haven, CT: Pluto Press.

Mansbach, R. W., Ferguson, Y. H., and Lampert, D. E. 1976: *The Web of World Politics: Nonstate Actors in the Global System*. Englewood Cliffs, NJ: Prentice-Hall.

Marx, K. 1974: *Critique of the Gotha Programme*. In D. Fernbach (ed.), *The First International and After, Political Writings*, Vol. 3. Aylesbury: Penguin Books in association with New Left Review, 339–59.

—— 1977: *Capital*, Vol. 1. Harmondsworth: Penguin.

Marx, K., and Engels, F. 1988: *The Communist Manifesto*. New York: Norton.

Mattingly, G. 1965: *Renaissance Diplomacy*. 2nd edn. Harmondsworth: Penguin.

Mayall, J. 1990: *Nationalism and International Society*. Cambridge: Cambridge University Press.

Mayer, A. J. 1981: *The Persistence of the Old Regime: Europe to the Great War*. London: Croom Helm.

Meek, R. L. 1976: *Social Science and the Ignoble Savage*. Cambridge: Cambridge University Press.

Meiksins Wood, E. 1991: *The Pristine Culture of Capitalism: A Historical Essay on Old Regimes and Modern States*. London and New York: Verso.

Melucci, A. 1996: *Challenging Codes: Collective Action in the Information Age*. Cambridge: Cambridge University Press.

Miles, R. 1993: *Racism after 'Race Relations'*. London and New York: Routledge.

Miller, J. D. B., and Vincent, R. J. 1990: *Order and Violence: Hedley Bull and International Relations*. Oxford: Clarendon Press.

Mitchell, R. P. 1969: *The Society of Muslim Brothers*. Oxford: Oxford University Press.

Mooers, C. 1991: *The Making of Bourgeois Europe: Absolutism, Revolution and the Rise of Capitalism in England, France and Germany*. London and New York: Verso.

Morris-Suzuki, T. 2000: For and against NGOs. *New Left Review*, 2: 61–85.

Morse, E. L. 1976: *Modernization and the Transformation of International Relations*. New York: Free Press.

Mukta, P., and Bhatt, C. (eds) 2000: Hindutva movements in the west: resurgent Hinduism and the politics of the diaspora. *Ethnic and Racial Studies*, 23 (3): 401–621.

Murphy, C. N. 1994: *International Organization and Industrial Change: Global Governance since 1850*. Cambridge: Polity.

Naredo, J. M. 1987: *La economía en evolución: historia y perspectivas de las categorías básicas del pensamiento económico*. Madrid: Siglo XXI.

Nash, G. B. 1979: *The Urban Crucible: Social Change, Political Consciousness and the Origins of the American Revolution*. Cambridge, MA, and London: Harvard University Press.

Nederveen Pieterse, J. 1989: *Empire and Emancipation*. London: Pluto Press.

Nelson, P. J. 1995: *The World Bank and Non-Governmental Organizations: The Limits of Apolitical Development*. London: Macmillan.

—— 1996: Internationalizing economic and environmental policy: transnational NGO networks and the World Bank's expanding influence. *Millennium: Journal of International Studies*, 25 (3): 605–33.

Norman, E. H. 1940: *Japan's Emergence as a Modern State: Political and Economic Problems of the Meiji Period*. Westport, CT: Greenwood Press.

Northedge, F. S. 1976: Transnationalism: the American illusion. *Millennium: Journal of International Studies*, 5 (1): 21–7.

O'Brien, R., Scholte, J. A., and Williams, M. 2000: *Contesting Governance: Multilateralism and Global Social Movements*. Cambridge: Cambridge University Press.

Otto, D. 1996: Nongovernmental organizations in the United Nations: the emerging role of international civil society. *Human Rights Quarterly*, 18 (1): 107–41.

Palmer, R. R. 1959: *The Age of the Democratic Revolutions*. 2 vols. Princeton, NJ: Princeton University Press.

Pérez-Díaz, V. 1997: *La esfera pública y la sociedad civil*. Madrid: Taurus Ciencias Sociales.

Peterson, M. J. 1992: Transnational activity, international society and world politics. *Millennium: Journal of International Studies*, 21 (3): 371–88.

Petras, J. 1997: Imperialism and NGOs in Latin America. *Monthly Review*, 49 (7): 10–27.

Pijl, K. van der 1983: *The Making of an Atlantic Ruling Class*. London: Verso.

—— 1998: *Transnational Classes and International Relations*. London and New York: Routledge.

Powell, C. T. 1994: La dimensión exterior de la transición española. *Afers Internacionals*, 26: 37–64.

Raustiala, K. 1997: States, NGOs and international environmental institutions. *International Studies Quarterly*, 41 (4): 719–40.

Reus-Smit, C. 1998: Changing patterns of governance: from absolutism to global multilateralism. In A. J. Paolini, A. P. Jarvis and C. Reus-Smit (eds), *Between Sovereignty and Global Governance: The United Nations, the State and Civil Society*. Basingstoke: Macmillan Press, 3–28.

Riedel, M. 1975: Gesellschaft, bürgerliche. In O. Brunner, W. Conze and R. Koselleck (eds), *Geschichtliche Grundbegriffe: Historisches Lexikon zur politisch-sozialen Sprache in Deutschland*. Stuttgart: Ernst Klett Verlag, 736–7.

Risse-Kappen, T. 1995: *Bringing Transnational Relations Back In: Non-State Actors, Domestic Structures and International Institutions*. Cambridge: Cambridge University Press.

Rose, R. B. 1983: *The Making of the Sans-Culotte: Democratic Ideas and Institutions in Paris, 1789–92*. Manchester: Manchester University Press.

Rosenau, J. 1969: *Linkage Politics: Essays on the Convergence of National and International Systems*. New York: Free Press.

Rosenberg, J. 1994: *The Empire of Civil Society: A Critique of the Realist Theory of International Relations*. London: Verso.

Rousseau, J.-J. 1979: *The Social Contract and the Discourses*, tr. with introduction by G. D. H. Cole. London, Melbourne and Toronto: Everyman's Library.

Rudé, G. 1964: *The Crowd in History: A Study of Popular Disturbances in France and England, 1730–1848*. New York and London: John Wiley.

Ruggie, J. G. 1986: Continuity and transformation in the world polity: toward a neo-realist synthesis. In R. Keohane (ed.), *Neorealism and its Critics*. New York: Columbia University Press, 131–57.

—— 1993: Territoriality and beyond: problematizing modernity in International Relations. *International Organization*, 47 (1): 139–74.

Russett, B. M. 1993: *Grasping the Democratic Peace: Principles for a Post-Cold War World*. Cambridge, MA: Harvard University Press.

Santiago-Valles, W. F. 2000: The Caribbean intellectual tradition that produced James and Rodney. *Race and Class*, 42 (2): 47–66.

Saull, R. 2001: *Rethinking Theory and History in the Cold War: the State, Military Power and Social Revolution*. London: Frank Cass.

Sayer, A. 1994: *Method in Social Science: A Realist Approach*. 2nd edn. London and New York: Routledge.

Sayer, D. 1989: *Readings From Karl Marx*. London and New York: Routledge.

—— 1990: Reinventing the wheel: Anthony Giddens, Karl Marx and social change. In J. Clark, C. Modgil and S. Modgil (eds), *Anthony Giddens: Consensus and Controversy*. London, New York and Philadelphia: Falmer Press, 235–50.

Scholte, J. A. 1993: *International Relations of Social Change*. Buckingham: Open University Press.

—— 2000: Global civil society. In N. Woods (ed.), *The Political Economy of Globalisation*. Basingstoke: Macmillan, 173–201.

Schulze, R. 1990: *Islamischer Internationalismus im 20. Jahrhundert: Untersuchungen zur Geschichte der Islamischen Weltliga*. Leiden, New York, Copenhagen, Köln: E. J. Brill.

Shaw, M. 1992: Global society and global responsibility: the theoretical, historical and political limits of 'international society'. *Millennium: Journal of International Studies*, 21 (3): 421–34.

—— 1994: Civil society and global politics: beyond a social movements approach. *Millennium: Journal of International Studies*, 23 (3): 647–67.

Shinoda, H. 2000: *Re-Examining Sovereignty: From Classical Theory to the Global Age*. London: Macmillan.

Smith, H. 1996: The silence of the academics: international social theory, historical materialism and political values. *Review of International Studies*, 22 (2): 191–212.

Smith, J., Chatfield, C., and Pagnucco, R. (eds) 1997: *Transnational Social Movements and Global Politics*. Syracuse, NY: Syracuse University Press.

Snyder, L. S. 1984: *Macro-Nationalisms: A History of the Pan-Movements*. Westport, CT, and London: Greenwood Press.

Soederberg, S. 2001: State, crisis, and capital accumulation in Mexico. *Historical Materialism: Research in Critical Marxist Theory*. Issue 9, 2002.

Spiro, P. J. 1995: New global communities: nongovernmental organizations in international decision-making institutions. *The Washington Quarterly*, 18 (1): 45–56.

Spruyt, H. 1994: *The Sovereign State and its Competitors*. New Jersey, NJ: Princeton University Press.

Stienstra, D. 1994: *Women's Movements and International Organization*. London: Macmillan Press.

Tarrow, S. 1994: *Power in Movement: Social Movements, Collective Action and Politics*. Cambridge: Cambridge University Press.

Taylor, C. 1975: *Hegel*. Cambridge: Cambridge University Press.

—— 1992: Modes of civil society. *Public Culture*, 3 (1): 95–118.

Te Brake, W. 1998: *Shaping History: Ordinary People in European Politics 1500–1700*. Berkeley, CA: University of California Press.

Teschke, B. 1998: Geopolitical relations in the European Middle Ages: history and theory. *International Organization*, 52 (2): 325–58.

—— 2001: *The Making of the Westphalian System of States: Property Relations, Geopolitics and the Myth of 1648*. London: Verso.

Tester, K. 1992: *Civil Society*. London and New York: Routledge.

Thompson, E. P. 1963: *The Making of the English Working Class*. London: Victor Gollancz.

—— 1975: *Whigs and Hunters: The Origin of the Black Act*. Harmondsworth: Penguin.

Tilly, L. A., and Tilly, C. (eds) 1981: *Class Conflict and Collective Action*. London and Beverly Hills, CA: Sage Publications.

Tosh, J. 1983: *The Pursuit of History*. 2nd edn. London: Longman.

Touraine, A., Wievorka, M., and Hegedus, Z. 1981: *Le Pays contre l'Etat: luttes occitanes*. Paris: Editions du Seuil.

Waever, O. 1992: International society. *Cooperation and Conflict*, 27 (1): 97–128.

Walker, R. B. J. 1994: Social movements/world politics. *Millennium: Journal of International Studies*, 23 (3): 669–700.

Wapner, P. 1996: *Environmental Activism and World Civic Politics*. Albany, NY: State University of New York Press, 1996.

Warkentin, C., and Mingst, K. 2000: International institutions, the state and global civil society in the age of the world wide web. *Global Governance*, 6 (2): 237–57.

Waterman, P. 1998: *Globalization, Social Movements and the New Internationalisms*. London and Washington: Mansell.

Watson, A. 1992: *The Evolution of International Society: A Comparative Historical Analysis*. London: Routledge.

Wendt, A. 1987: The agent–structure problem in International Relations theory. *International Organization*, 41 (3): 335–70.

—— 1999: *Social Theory of International Politics*. Cambridge: Cambridge University Press.

Wight, C. 1999: They shoot dead horses don't they? Locating agency in the agent–structure problematique. *European Journal of International Relations*, 5 (1): 109–42.

Wight, M. 1977: *Systems of States*. Leicester: Leicester University Press.

Willetts, P. 2000: From 'consultative arrangements' to 'partnership': the changing status of NGOs in diplomacy at the UN. *Global Governance*, 6 (2): 191–212.

Willetts, P. (ed.) 1996: *'The Conscience of the World': The Influence of Non-Governmental Organisations in the UN System*. London: Hurst & Co.

Williams, M., and Ford, L. 1999: The World Trade Organization, social movements and global environmental management. In C. Rootes (ed.), *Environmental Movements: Local, National and Global*. London: Frank Cass, 268–89.

Williams, R. 1976: *Keywords: A Vocabulary of Culture and Society*. London: Fontana Press.

Wild, S. 1985: National Socialism in the Arab Near East between 1933 and 1939. *Die Welt des Islams*, 25: 126–73.

Wilson, P. 1989: The English school of International Relations: a reply to Sheila Grader. *Review of International Studies*, 15 (1): 101–29.

Wolf, E. R. 1982: *Europe and the People without History*. Berkeley, LA: University of California Press.

Wolfers, A. (ed.) 1962: *Discord and Collaboration*. Baltimore, MD: Johns Hopkins University Press.

Wood, N. 1984: *John Locke and Agrarian Capitalism*. Berkeley, Los Angeles, CA, and London: University of California Press.

—— 1994: *Foundations of Political Economy: Some Early Tudor Views on State and Society*. Berkeley, Los Angeles, CA, and London: University of California Press.

Wood, N., and Meiksins Wood, E. 1997: *A Trumpet of Sedition: Political Theory and the Rise of Capitalism, 1509–1688*. London: Pluto Press.

Young, T. 1995: 'A project to be realized': global liberalism and contemporary Africa. *Millennium: Journal of International Studies*, 24 (3): 527–46.

Zagorin, P. 1982: *Rebels and Rulers 1500–1660*. 2 vols. Cambridge: Cambridge University Press.

Zaret, D. 1996: Petitions and the 'invention' of public opinion in the English Revolution. *American Journal of Sociology*, 101 (6): 1497–555.

Index